The Uniqueness of
JESUS CHRIST
THE SAVIOUR

The Revd Dr Gabriel J. Anan, PhD

Ordering Information:

Prime Seven Media
518 Landmann St.
Tomah City, WI 54660

Printed in the United States of America

(The special note: The author of this book sincerely gives thanks to all the ancient, medieval and contemporary historians. As the experts in your special fields in history, your contribution in this book is vastly appreciated, since the proceeds from the sale of this book for the charity).

CONTENTS

Also by the Author 1

Statement of Faith by the Author 2

Dedication 4

Acknowledgements 6

Preface 7

Introduction 10

PART ONE

The Uniqueness of Jesus Christ

Chapter 1: How Unique is Jesus Christ? 41

PART TWO

The True Identity of Jesus Christ

Chapter 2: Who is true Jesus? 83

PART THREE

The Rejection of Jesus Christ by the Jews

Chapter 3: Why do most Jews reject Jesus as their
Messiah? 101

PART FOUR

Importance of Effective Prayer

Chapter 4: The Purpose of Praying to Christ 139

PART FIVE

Faith in Jesus Christ for Salvation

Chapter 5: Did Jesus Create Everything, Including
The World? 179

PART SIX

Jesus Christ as Son of Man

Chapter 6: Is Jesus the Son of man? 201

CONCLUSION PART

The Second Coming of Jesus Christ the Saviour

Chapter 7: Jesus was misunderstood 249

Bibliography 286
A Note on the Author 291

ALSO BY THE AUTHOR

The Organic Church: A Practical Approach to Managing Change (2011).

The Illusive World of Love: Demystifying the Mindset of True Love (2015).

The Truth About Material Wealth: Is it God's Blessing in Disguise? (2015).

Discerning the Prophetic Message: Knowing the Truth (2016)

Baptism: Is the Avowal for Born Again Christian (2017)

The Creator God Blessed the Seventh Day: Keep it Holy (2018)

DYNAMISM OF SUCCESS: Revealing the Managing Strategies for Individuals and Organisations in the World of Uncertainty and Change (2018)

THE EFFECT OF ABSENT PROPHET FOR HAM DESCENDANTS: Ham - Japhet - Shem (2021)

Does the Creator of the World Answer Prayer? If so How? (2023)

Who's the True Creator of the World? (2023)

STATEMENT OF FAITH
BY THE AUTHOR

In the European Union, the title of *doctor* refers primarily to holders of post- graduate research *doctorates*, such as the *PhD*. With this regards, my attention was drawn to a personal issue regarding ambiguity of professional status in the UK due to the fact that unlike the UK, many European languages have the appropriate term for a medical practitioner. For example the term *Arzt* is in German, *iatros* in Greece, *Lääkäri* in Finnish, *Läkare* in Swedish and others; but in the UK, the term used for a medical practitioner is *doctor (Dr)*, same as the *doctor (Dr)* for the *PhD* holders. For this reason, I was compelled to declare publicly my status as a philosophy *doctor (Dr)*, and not a medical +*doctor (Dr)*, thus necessitated the use of appropriate title the *PhD* after my name on all my books.

It's undeniably fact that a *medical practitioner (or doctor)* in the UK, is a profession well known to many people, especially families and their children for health issues. In this respect, it's necessary to make a clear distinction between the two professions to show mostly parents and their children to know me as *philosophy doctor (PhD)* and not a *medical doctor*. Otherwise, they might be under the assumption that I could be a *medical doctor* who might be able to provide them with medical assistance for their health, especially in the case of emergency. Therefore, making such a distinction of the two professions clarifies any ambiguity or wrong perceptions people might have, especially parents with their children and young people.

The Revd Dr Gabriel J Anan

DEDICATION

*In the loving memory of my late parents especially my mother (Mansah), whose foreknowledge about me to be a priest, shaped my being and illuminated my heart to respond positively to the call of the Living God for the Ministry. I grew up in a Catholic family, both my parents were Catholics. In the pursuance of my faith I joined the Church of England. In the process I was trained and ordained priest. Encouraged to continue searching for the divine truth from the Scriptures led me to have written eight books. My greatest revelation came when I was deeply entrenched preparing a sermon for the Church of England parish church of St George and St Ethelbert, East Ham London for the 24th December 2017. The information l I gathered from my family and friends and the records of Christian History opened a new understanding from what I thought I knew. I also found that most of these New Bibles have removed some of verses and words on the deity of our Lord Jesus Christ from the KING JAMES Version, the most important one is in **Matthew 17:21** for **fasting** and **prayer** recommended by our Lord Jes us Christ Himself, the New Bibles include: NIV, NASV. It has also been compounded by the fact that some of the, The Ten Commandments of God have also been changed or even removed. This is to fulfil the prophecy of Daniel Chapters 2 and 7 about the Four Empires and what the **<u>Beast</u>** would do at the end time by changing God's law of the Seventh-Day Sabbath to replace it with the man-made sun-god Sunday Sabbath and other* *rules before the second coming of the Saviour as indicated fully in the book. I thank the Lord for revealing my salvation as He did to the Apostles in Luke 24:45 to open their minds to understand the Scriptures. The living God is worthy of praise, and I thank the Lord Jesus Christ on behalf of my parents and to forgive their lack of knowledge about changes made by the **Catholicism** the **Beast,** may they rest in His perfect peace.*

The Revd Dr Gabriel J. Anan

ACKNOWLEDGEMENTS

I am indebted for the advice of a number of people both men and women: who are experts in their fields of expertise. They contributed massively to the areas of most needed knowledge during my dialogue with them, with the view to gathering the necessary information for this book. Their willingness to speak out candidly and intellectually resulted in the collection of crucial materials without which this book would not have been in print. I am grateful to my publishers who found the manuscript useful for publication. I am also grateful for my family whose patience allowed me to get on with my loneliness as I continued to compose the message being received and digested for use. I thank my friends and readers of my previous books and the vicar, Revd Canon David Haokip at the Parish of St Georges and St Ethelbert to whom I have worked very closely for a number of years and all the staff of the Church for their morale support.

The Revd Dr Gabriel J Anan

PREFACE

Since human beings are in constant search for quick answers or solutions to many issues they face in this world, the book assesses the importance of prayer in the life of believers. Aside from that, the text of the book also highlights the important events and activities in the Bible where prayers on various issues have occurred including miracles, healings, raising up the dead and many more.

Further, the text is the investigation of historical backgrounds and the records of Christian history for the enrichment of the Christendom. It thus began by looking at the overall Four Empires of Daniel's Prophecies in Chapters 2 and 7 in the King James Bible (KJV) which is the authoritative Word of God. The Four empires include: the Babylonian Empire, the Medo-Persian Empire, the Greek Empire and the Roman Empire. Is the prophecy of Daniel being fulfilled with the false Christ, the Beast occupying the temple of the Most High God and thereby bent on changing the law especially the Ten Commandments written with the finger of God (Exodus 31:18 (KJV), and the introduction of new rules like new moon from Luna to Sola, the Sabbath Day from Saturday to Sunday and some festivals such as Christmas (worship in honour of god of saturn, saturnalia) Easter (the goddess of sex and fertility).These are pagans festivals merged with introduced into Christian beliefs by Rome. Resurrection from the dead, was merged with the pagan celebration, and became known as Easter. The meaning of Easter was also changed to reflect its new Christian orientation.

The text therefore is based on extensive primary and particularly secondary research. It extracted from various theological and historical Christian books of different denominations and other religious groups about their stance on the clarity of various important phrases and terms being practised in the churches. It is thus to bring some awareness to the public and even to most of the church members in order to enhance their faiths and belies. The most compelling question engulfing the faith of many believers is whether Christians should observe Seventh Day Sabbath being observed by the Jews before the coming of Jesus Christ when He and His followers also observed.

Are Christians under the grace of Christ therefore have no need to observe the law of God which has been affirmed, blessed and summarised as 'Love' by Christ? Has the death of Christ abolished the Commandments in the Old Testament or did He come to die in order to remove the Original Sin brought into the world by one man (Adam)? As the Bible says 'the sin of one man (Adam) brought death into the earth and the Death and Resurrection of one man (Christ) brought life into the world.

If the Deity of Jesus Christ is removed from these new Bibles, do these Bible still retain the holiness and the authoritative Word of our Lord Jesus Christ?

Since Christ is coming for the second time, to judge the living and the death, will He judge people on how much faith and belief they have in Him or will He judge people on how much they have OBEYED His Commands. Jesus said 'If you LOVE me OBEY my commands.

The book attempts further, to provide responses to the queries posed for the awareness and thus to instil the importance of salvation and much faith into believers world-wide such as the commands of Jesus Christ in John 3:3-5 to be Born Again to enable believer to enter the Kingdom of heaven. Other prevailing issues for reflection include the fact that: (1) there is a misconception among many Christians that one does not need to be physically Baptised to become Born Again. And that a person just needs to believe and have faith and accept Christ with their mouth as a Personal Saviour thus saved satisfying the specific condition to enter heaven. If this is the case, then: (1) if we claim to have been 'Born Again' Christian, having believed and confessed faith with the mouth that Jesus is the Lord and a personal Saviour, why is Jesus Christ still coming for the second time to judge us of our sin (if so, which sin?), (2) If we all born in sin from birth, which requires forgiveness of this original sin, then when should it be reasonable for children raised in believing households reach the age of reason to confess with the mouth that Jesus is Lord, and thus believe in their heart that God raised Him from the dead in order to be saved as a 'Born Again' Christian? (3) Is physical Baptism a Necessity? (4) How true is Predestination? (5) Did Jesus Christ receive training for His Ministry? The prevailing issues raised in this book are paramount importance for our salvation because they give food for spiritual thought to engage us for serious studies of the Scriptures with reflection.

The Revd Dr Gabriel J Anan

INTRODUCTION

Jesus Christ is Unique

**Whatever has occupied mankind for so long,
it is worth knowing it.
Gabriel Anan**

**The important thing is to not stop questioning
Albert Einstein**

How Unique is Jesus Christ?

The text of this book is borne out of many interesting comments received from my previous book: "WHO'S THE TRUE CREATOR OF THE WORLD?". Some people would like to know more about how **unique and an extra ordinary person** is Jesus Christ. Many people also demanded an expansion on my statement on 23rd January 2024 interview that I had in the America TV with Logan Crawford about how the Roman Catholic Church replaced their sun-god, Sol Invictus-Mithra, with Jesus Christ and worshipping Him as their sun-god.

With regards to the uniqueness of Jesus Christ is that, He is both Perfect Divine and Perfect Man. Perfect Divine because He is the Holy Spirit. Perfect Man because He was born without the cursed and tainted human seed thus He has no sin.

Catholicism Influence

Unfortunately the Catholic Church introduced and promoted Jesus Christ throughout the world as a god/God and a Son of God referring to His Father in Heaven as god/God. The reason is that Catholicism replaced their sun-god **Sol Invictus/ Mithra** with Jesus as their **sun-god** and started worshipping Him on Sun-days. Some have stated that around the year 336-7 AD, **Pope Julius I** decided on the birth of Jesus Christ to be on 25th December, this idea paved the way to enable the Catholicism to join the yearly pagan gods celebration on 25th December. Catholicism introduced Christ-mass or **Christmas to be celebrated** yearly to fit in perfectly well with the yearly celebration of all the pagan gods on December 25. The yearly pagan gods Celebration is for paying homage to their chief god Tammuz who is said to have been born on December 25th in Babylon in the year 2600 BC for which all the gods have to agree to have been born on the same day in order for their worshippers to be celebrating this yearly festival on December 25th. In India this yearly Celebration of December 25th, is known as **BADA DIN** meaning in English language as **BIG DAY**, whilst in the Western world and other places it is known as Christ-mass or Christmas.

But the truth of the matter is that **Jesus is not born in December 25th to be calling and worshipping Him as god/God, this is blasphemy.** He is not to be reduced to the level of any lesser demonic spirit. So, to be calling Him a God/god is a **blasphemy** same as when the Pharisees equated Him with **Beelzebul** the demon, Jesus rebuked them saying to them that to say anything to Him as a son of the Man, He can forgive them but to Him as the Holy Spirit it is a **blasphemy** and their sins cannot be forgiven.

Another uniqueness of Jesus Christ is that, there is salvation in no one else, either a spiritual or human leader except Jesus Christ who is both Divine and Man without sin. Islam believes that, **Jesus Christ (Isa Al-Masih)**, is the final judge, not Muhammad. Jesus will return to judge the world, says (Sahil Bukhari 4:55:657). The 3 wise men from the East came to worshipped baby Jesus and presented Him with expensive gifts: **Gold, Frankincense and Myrrh** officially reserves for the Lords and Kings. Therefore whosoever believes in Him in worship and in prayer and accepts Him and His teachings shall be saved regardless of their beliefs because He came to the world for everybody and He is the Alpha and the Omega the Beginning and the Last.

Why the Jews rejected Him as their Messiah

Jesus was rejected by His own Jewish leadership because they did not accept that He is their Messiah because they would not accept His teachings on Love, forgiveness and pray for your enemies. They would not also accept that He was Man and Divine. Though Jesus challenged them that if they claimed He is the Son of Yahweh, why then would they not accept that He is the truth and speaks the truth? And He said to them it is because their Yahweh/God is a liar and a devil spirit. In this book, I have given full details of the questions posed, to justify the position of Jesus Christ. There are many true pieces of information also housed in the book especially the revelation of the True name and the Supreme Creator of the world which has eluded the world for so many centuries. For instance, many unscrupulous deities like Yahweh, Brahma and Mazda claimed to have created the world which is of course very deceptive. However, in order for Jesus to prove His true identity, Jesus Himself made many "I Ams" statements such as: "I am" the Son of Man. "I am" the Alpha and Omega and many others. Although Jesus Christ was born a virgin of the Holy Spirit through a woman, He came as a man therefore He has a male figure. Many scholars including the Archbishop of Canterbury the Most Reverend Justin Welby convincingly affirmed that god\God is neither male nor female because it is a spirit and not a divine. But Jesus Christ is born of the Holy Spirit through a woman and came as a man. He therefore went through the ritual of circumcision to prove that He is a Male. So He is a male and also Divine. And He further said this: "I am the Son of Man... and came to this earth as the Light of the world so that whosoever will believe in me will never remain in the darkness. This affirms that LIGHT and darkness can never co-exit. He also revealed to us that His Father and the Holy Spirit are Male and live in heaven above. Therefore to worship Him alone, you are certain of worshipping a male figure and the Holy Spirit and not any other spirits.

Justification of His Uniqueness

Jesus Christ was not born in any posh or well known hospital in Jerusalem or in any palace of any kingdom of the world. And yet, three (3) noble men from the East not only visited Him as a baby but worshipped and subsequently presented Him expensive gifts which were: **Gold, Frankincense and Myrrh.**

Although the names of the three (3) wise men who visited baby Jesus could not be really known but, they were the names of the magi because the Bible doesn't tell us. In fact, the Bible is silent on how many wise men visited Jesus. However, tradition has it that the three wise men who came to seek and honour the **infant Jesus were named Gaspar, Balthasar, and Melchior.**

The three wise men, also known as magi, were men belonging to various educated classes. *Our English word magician comes from this same root. But these wise men were not magicians in the modern sense of sleight-of-hand performers. They were of noble birth, educated, wealthy, and influential. They were philosophers, the counsellors of rulers, learned in all the wisdom of the ancient East. The wise men who came seeking the Christ child were not idolaters; they were upright men of integrity.*

They had apparently studied the Hebrew Scriptures and found there a clear transcript of truth. In particular, the Messianic prophecies of the Old Testament must have claimed their attention, and among these they found the words of Balaam: "A Star shall come out of Jacob; a Scepter shall rise out of Israel" (Numbers 24:17, NKJV). They certainly were acquainted with the prophecy of Micah: "But you, Bethlehem Ephrathah, though you are little among the thousands of Judah, yet out of you shall come forth to Me the One to be Ruler in Israel" (Micah 5:2, NKJV; see also Matthew 2:5, 6). They probably also knew and understood the time prophecy of Daniel regarding the appearance of the Messiah (see Daniel 9:25, 26) and came to the conclusion that His coming was near.

On the night of Christ's birth, a mysterious light appeared in the sky which became a luminous star that persisted in the western heavens (see Matthew 2:1, 2). Impressed with its import, the wise men turned once more to the sacred scrolls. As they tried to understand the meaning of the sacred writings, they determined to go in search of the Messiah. Like Abraham, they knew not at first where they were to go, but followed as the guiding star led them on their way.

Gifts of the three wise men

The tradition that there were three wise men arose from the fact that the Bible mentions three gifts: gold, frankincense and myrrh according to Matthew 2:11. However, the Bible doesn't say how many wise men made the journey to see the baby Jesus. The unfounded idea that they were also kings came from the imagery of

Jack Zavada

The Three Kings, or Magi, are mentioned only in the Gospel of Matthew 2:1-12. Few details are given about these men in the Bible, and most of our ideas about them actually come from tradition or speculation. Scripture does not say how many wise men there were, but it is generally assumed there were three since they brought three gifts: gold, frankincense, and myrrh.

The Three Kings

- The Magi were both real and symbolic. As real men, the three kings confirmed ancient prophecies about Jesus being the Messiah, and as symbols, they showed that he came to save all people, rich and poor, learned or unschooled, from anywhere in the world. These wealthy travellers were on the opposite end of the social and economic scale as the shepherds who had visited Jesus right after his birth.
- Many characters in Scripture go unnamed. They all point to Jesus Christ, the manifestation of Father's love for the human race. The Bible is a book about Jesus.
- There is a message in the title "Wise Men." Wise people acknowledge their need for a Saviour and

seek to find him. Foolish people, like Herod the Great, reject Jesus and even seek to destroy him.

The three Kings recognised Jesus Christ as the Messiah while he was still a child, and travelled thousands of miles to worship him. Matthew says only that these visitors came from "the east." **Scholars have speculated that they came from Persia, Arabia, or even India.**

They doggedly followed a star that led them to Jesus. By the time they met Jesus, he was in a house and was a child, not an infant, implying they arrived a year or more after his birth.

Three Gifts From Three Kings

The gifts of the Three Kings symbolise Christ's identity and mission: gold for a king, incense for the Lord, and myrrh used to anoint the dead. Ironically, the Gospel of John states that Nicodemus brought a mixture of 75 pounds of aloe and myrrh to anoint Jesus' body after the crucifixion.

The Three Wise Men with king Herod

The Lord honoured the wise men by warning them in a dream to go home by another route and not to report back to King Herod. Some Bible scholars think Joseph and Mary sold the wise men's gifts to pay for their trip to Egypt to escape Herod's persecution.

The Three Kings were among the wisest men of their time. Discovering that the Messiah was to be born, they organized an expedition to find him, following a star that led them to Bethlehem. Despite their culture and religion in a foreign land, they accepted Jesus as their Saviour.

Life Lessons

When we seek the Father with sincere determination, we will find him. He is not hiding from us but wants to have an intimate relationship with each of us.

These wise men paid Jesus the kind of respect only Lords deserves, bowing before him and worshiping him. Jesus is not just a great teacher or admirable person as many people say today, but the Son of the Living Father in Heaven.

After the Three Kings met Jesus, they did not go back the way they came. When we get to know Jesus Christ, we are changed forever and cannot go back to our old life.

Names of the Three Kings

Matthew reveals nothing of these visitors' ancestry. Over the centuries, legend has assigned them names: Gaspar, or Casper; Melchior, and Balthasar. Balthasar has a Persian sound. If indeed these men were scholars from Persia, they would have been familiar with Daniel's prophecy about the Messiah or "Anointed One." (Daniel 9:24-27, NIV).

The designation "Magi" refers to a Persian religious caste, but when this Gospel was written, the term was loosely used for astrologers, seers, and fortunetellers. Matthew does not call them kings; that title was used later, in legends. About 200 AD, nonbiblical sources started calling them kings, perhaps because of a prophecy in Psalm 72:11: ***"May all kings bow down to him and all nations serve him." (NIV) Because they followed a star, they may have been royal astronomers, advisers to the rulers.***

Was Jesus an Extraordinary Person?

This section explores the importance of Jesus Christ as a unique and an extra ordinary person ever lived. Michael D. Reynolds reflects on the character of Jesus Christ and His uniqueness. He stresses thus: the conventional notion about the character of Jesus of Nazareth is that he was grand, captivating, a paragon of virtue, and a teacher of concepts that all human beings should use to govern their lives. This view is shared at least in part even by many persons who do not worship the man. Because of these alleged traits, people regard Jesus as **unique.**

The present essay will examine the conventional view of Jesus by asking and answering a set of questions relevant to his character, avoiding customary presuppositions of exaltation. The answers of necessity must mostly be based upon the Gospels. These were written by eulogists, and subjected to elaboration and exaggeration in successive versions (Teeple 116, 207). They express ideas that would have astonished or appalled Jesus and his contemporaries, such as the notion of a trifid Lord. The Gospels do not present an accurate picture of their subject (ibid., chap. 1), but they are the only biographical material available. (The late, spurious biography to which the name John was attached will mostly be ignored. It was written to promulgate the author's concept of Jesus, and appended ideas from Greek philosophy to the dead man's cult [Teeple 187-90, 372-75].)

The Gospels are repetitive, and rather than citing every relevant passage, the existence of parallel passages in one or more of the other Gospels following the one cited will be indicated by *par,* unless there is a significant difference between the versions justifying explicit mention of the subsequent one(s).

1. Was Jesus free of faults of character?

Jesus is depicted as capable of petty pique (*Matthew* 21:18-19, par), and of violence (*Matthew* 21:12, par; *John* 2:15). He had no qualms about causing discord (*Matthew* 10:34, *Luke* 12:51-53). He told his followers to arm themselves (*Luke* 22:36, 38). Speaking in the third person, Jesus called for forcing people to submit to him (ibid., 14:23) and for killing those who did not (ibid., 19:27). Thus by explicit statements he excluded himself from the class of blessed peacemakers (*Matthew* 5:9).

Jesus and His disciples sometimes neglected the hygienic ritual of washing their hands before eating. This was important because diners put their hands into bowls used in common (*Matthew* 26:23, par). When people called attention to this fault, Jesus became angry, denigrated the custom of washing, and used the incidents as occasions for tirades against those who had remarked on the lapse, as well as others (*Matthew* 15:1-9; *Mark* 7:1-13; *Luke* 11:37-52; Teeple 295-96). In doing so, although he presented himself as a devout Jew, he insulted (*Luke* 11:45)[1] persons who were respected by many Jews for their piety and learning (*Matthew* 15:7-9, par, 23:1-33, par), and he did this even when he was a guest of the person he insulted (*Luke* 11:37-44).

2. Did Jesus express a complete or even forward-looking system of ethics?

Jesus' society and Jesus himself inherited a moral code that originated in a patriarchal Iron Age society. An allegation that he held ethical ideas more advanced than those of his Jewish contemporaries must be supported by one or more specific statements attributed to him. Interpreting an individual remark or act ascribed to Jesus as an expression of a modern moral principle, then inferring that he manifested that principle generally, is a semantic tactic, not a valid demonstration.

Jesus expressed unqualified approval of the "Mosaic" (Pentateuchal) law (*Matthew* 5:17-18) (although he is reported not to have adhered to it on several occasions [*Matthew* 12:1-4, par, 12:46-49, par; *John* 5:16-18, 8:3-10]). Nothing in the Gospels indicates that he would not have approved (for example) mutilations as punishments (*Exodus* 21:22-24), burning women alive (*Leviticus* 21:9), or not punishing a slave owner who beat a slave to death (*Exodus* 21:20-21).

Even persons who idolize Jesus manifest distress at his failure to say anything against slavery (Brace 42), and feel obliged to find excuses for him by devising specious arguments (ibid., 43-45). This is, however, only one aspect of a general fact. The moral ideas of Western civilization have advanced substantially during the past 2,000 years, especially since The Enlightenment (Pinker). If Jesus had been a supernaturally informed moralist, one might expect that he would have anticipated some of the moral progress of the future, such as abolition of slavery, rejection of subordination of women, abolition of judicial torture, or replacement of authoritarian governments with popular governments. But in the words attributed to Jesus, there is no hint of any moral ideas beyond those propounded by the moralists of his day, (Jewish and other) (McCabe). He did not express or even foreshadow modern moral principles such as these from the United Nations' Universal Declaration of Human Rights.

Article 1: All human beings are born free and equal in dignity and rights.

Art. 2: Everyone is entitled to all the rights and freedoms ... without distinction of any kind, such as race, colour, sex, language, religion [etc.].

Art. 4: No one shall be held in slavery or servitude.

Art. 5: No one shall be subjected to torture or to cruel, inhuman or degrading treatment or punishment.

Art. 16, section 2: Marriage shall be entered into only with the free and full consent of the intending spouses.

Art. 18: Everyone has the right to freedom of thought, conscience and religion; this right includes freedom to change his religion or belief.

Art. 21, sect. 3: The will of the people shall be the basis of the authority of government.

Art. 26: Everyone has the right to education.

Arts. 1 and 2 are contrary to the spirit Jesus exhibited when he likened non-Jews to dogs (*Matthew* 15:22-26; *Mark* 7:26-27).

Jesus' ethical principles included some of the good ones of his time, and his personal moral influence probably was positive. But he did not attain the ethical level of modern moralists. This creates a problem for thoughtful persons who assert that he was the complete and ultimate moralist. A common response is to allege that Jesus was the inspiration of all moral advances after his time. For those matters about which there is no record of his having said anything, devotees suppose that his general demeanour, or the implications of what he did say, somehow inspired future progress (Brace).[4] No convincing evidence is offered to support this thesis; it is a supposition.

Very many people after Jesus' time who said that they were his followers contravened the principles of love, mercy and justice that they attributed to him. Persons who allege that Jesus said nothing that promoted persecution by Christians (e.g., Brace 441) ignore quotations such as *Matthew* 10:21, par, 10:35 37, 12:30; *Luke* 12:51-53, 14:26, and 22:36, 38 that collectively express violent antagonism between the followers of Jesus and everyone else. Jesus' principle that the Father desires discord and violence on "his" behalf has been used by his followers ever since to justify imposition, persecution, and war.

3. Did Jesus offer any useful ideas for ameliorating the social problems of his day?

Jewish society in Palestine before, during, and after Jesus' life was replete with turmoil, dissension, and strife (Dujardin 249-68; Horsley; Teeple 101-4). For centuries, various powers had fought over Palestine. By Jesus' day, all the lands he traversed were ruled by tyrannical foreigners (Herod, king of Judea, was only half Jewish) (Teeple 40).

The lot of the Jewish peasants–the people from whom Jesus came–was precarious and oppressive. The capacity of the land for agriculture was limited, and ongoing warfare had damaged the agricultural resources. Jesus' own family, in which the parents had raised at least seven children (*Matthew* 13:55, par)[5], illustrates the problem of excessive population in relation to agricultural capacity.

The peasants were subjected to burdensome taxation, first in the form of tithes to support the Jewish priests and temple in Jerusalem (*Matthew* 17:24), and then by the occupying powers, whose principal interest in the land and people was to extract from them as much wealth as possible (Horsley 32-33, 55-58, 190). To meet these exactions and still be able to support themselves, peasants fell into debt, and some lost their land and became day labourers or tenant farmers. Partly as a result, brigandage was common.

These social conditions provided topics for the similes (parables) Jesus employed in his preaching (the anecdotes about the unmerciful servant, the workers in the vineyard, the wicked tenant farmers, and the good Samaritan). He was well aware of the problems of the peasantry. The subject of these parables, however, mostly was an imaginary afterlife. They did not address social problems. Jesus urged his disciples (*Luke* 12:33) and one rich man (*Matthew* 19:21, par) to give their possessions to the poor, but he himself seems to have recognised that such exhortations commonly were ineffective (ibid., 19:22-24, par). He did enunciate some specific, praiseworthy principles of charity (ibid., 25:34-40). These were not original (McCabe 286-87); and their moral force is vitiated by their being expressed not as behaviours worthy in themselves, but as valuable because they will be rewarded in an afterlife. Jesus did not address the causes of poverty and injustice.

Resistance to the excessive taxation had sometimes been violent before Jesus' time (Horsley 63-64). In his day evasion or overt refusal to pay probably were present (ibid., 55). "Paying taxes to Caesar was a religious offense as well as an economic burden" (ibid., 231). But when Jesus was forced to address the matter, he advocated acquiescing in payment of the Roman tax (*Matthew* 22:16-21, par). He is not recorded as having criticized the temple system with its taxes, except perhaps indirectly (ibid., 23:4). This although his hearers knew that their tithes were being used to accumulate wealth and not for the public good (Horsley 55, 60-61).

Jesus frequently spoke of *righteousness* (the translation of *dikaiosunë*), but the sense usually is *virtue* rather than *equitableness* or *justice*.[6] Protests against injustice and oppression were commonplaces of popular movements in

23

Palestine before and after his time (Horsley 30 43, 253-4). In his adopted role as an itinerant preacher among the poor, Jesus would have been remarkably obtuse if he had not criticized these things. But the Gospels record but one instance in which he explicitly denounced injustices: "devouring" widows' houses, by which apparently he meant appropriating them unjustly; "plundering;" and being negligent when acting as judge (*Matthew* 23:14, 23, 25; *Mark* 12:40; *Luke* 11:42, 20:47). Likewise, only a single occasion is recorded on which he may have decried oppression (*Matthew* 23:4, par; it is not clear to what "burdens" refers). He even exhibited toleration of injustice: the peasantry were subject to theft and violence by the rich and powerful; Jesus counselled them not to resist (ibid., 5:39-41, par). Submissiveness as a principle was reinforced by injunctions to be nonjudgmental and forbearing (*Luke* 6:37). (Jesus urged humility not as a social virtue meritorious in itself, but as a religious behaviour to be rewarded in the afterlife [e.g., *Matthew* 5:3, 23:11-12].)

An inevitable result of other worldliness is lack of interest in mundane matters that are not perceived as determining the nature of the afterlife. Secular welfare is one of these ignored subjects. It is noteworthy that when Jesus is recorded as speaking of injustice or oppression (previous paragraph), he does so for the purpose of denouncing groups of his contemporaries. His interest is in their flawed characters (which will affect their afterlives: *Matthew* 23:14, par, 33), not in the effects of their behaviour on other people. No instance was recorded in which Jesus proposed a specific course of action likely to ameliorate the social problems of his fellow countrypersons.

4. Did Jesus advocate or demonstrate a mode of life suitable for humankind?

In a single passage (*Mark* 6:3) Jesus is said to have been a *tektön*, which can mean either a woodworker or builder, or an unspecified craftsman. Traditionally Jesus has been thought to have been a carpenter, but recently some scholars have suggested that he was a stonemason.

Nowhere else in the Gospels, however, is there any mention of Jesus having worked (and in the parallel passage [*Matthew* 13:55] he is called "the carpenter's [or craftsman's] son," without mention of any occupation of his own). His early adult life is a blank and one supposes that he then was employed as a craftsman. But when, after a few fantastic tales about his infancy and childhood, he reappears at about age 30, he already is a vagabond. He and his followers obtain the necessities of life by charity from admirers (*Matthew* 26:18; *Mark* 11:2-3, 14:13-15; *Luke* 7:36, 10:7, 11:37, 14:1, 19:5, 29 30, 22:10-12), among whom women are prominent (*Matthew* 8:15, 27:55; *Mark* 15:41; *Luke* 8:2 3, 10:38). At times the group appears to have had no food (*Matthew* 12:1 2, par, 21:18 19, par) or shelter (ibid., 8:20, par). People's failure to offer them charity seems to have angered Jesus (ibid., 10:14-15, par). In keeping with a life of vagabondage, Jesus expressed the precept that one need not make an effort to procure the necessities of life (ibid., 6:25-34, par, 10:9-10, par). A life of wandering and subsisting on charity is not, of course, a model suitable for people in general to follow.

With respect to family relations, Ernst Haeckel observed that Jesus, with his gaze ever directed to "the beyond," ... thought as lightly of woman and the family as of all other goods of "this life." Of his infrequent contact with his parents and sisters the gospels have very little to say; but they are far from representing his relations with his mother to have been so tender and intimate as they are poetically depicted in so many thousands of pictures. (Haeckel 357)

(See *Matthew* 12:46-50, par; *Luke* 2:48-49; *John* 2:3-4.) Jesus refused to allow some people who wanted to become his followers to perform family duties first (*Matthew* 8:21 22; *Luke* 9:59-62). He had no qualms about disrupting families and destroying the love of family members for one another (*Matthew* 10:21, par, 10:35 36, 19:29, par; *Luke* 12:51-53, 14:26).

There is no evidence in the Gospels that Jesus married. His reported remarks about sexuality consists mostly of denunciations of coitus outside marriage (*Matthew* 15:19, par, 19:18, par) and of second marriages (ibid., 5:32, par). He seems to have thought that castration, or at least avoidance of coitus, was desirable, while acknowledging that this would not be accepted by all men (ibid., 19:11-12). Jesus is not reported to have said anything positive about sexuality.

5. Did Jesus contradict Himself?

The answer to this question is "repeatedly." The matter has been extensively addressed by Dennis McKinney in chapter 7 of his Encyclopedia of Biblical Errancy (McKinney), which should be consulted. (This chapter also contains observations about Jesus' character.)

6. Did Jesus have original ideas?

Jesus' moral precepts were the same as those expressed in the Jewish scriptures, and by contemporaries, both Jews and non-Jews (McCabe; Teeple 55-58, chap. 6).[7] This includes his several exhortations to love one's neighbor, a concept that Jesus each time (*Matthew* 5:43, 19:19, 22:36 and 39, par) attributed to an earlier source (*Leviticus* 19:18;

McCabe 282-83; Teeple 95-96).[8] The solitary injunction to "love your enemies, do good to them" (*Matthew* 5:44, par) also had precedents (*Proverbs* 25:21; McCabe 230-33), but perhaps none that made the self-contradictory plea to love a person whom one regards as an enemy. (Joseph McCabe observes that with this injunction Jesus asks his followers to be more magnanimous than his god [McCabe 299].) Jesus urged this and other benevolent behaviours not as abstract principles of ethics or to promote the welfare of individuals as members of society, but by stating that they would procure a "great reward" (*Matthew* 5:12, 19:29, par, 25:34; *Luke* 6:35-38, 14:14, 18:29-30) (see McCabe 236, note 1); "there never was a more utilitarian ethic in history than that of Jesus" (McCabe 305).

Jesus' reported use of immortality as an inducement (*Matthew* 19:29, par, 25:46; *Luke* 20:36), and postmortem "fire" as a threat (*Matthew* 5:22, 29-30, 13:42, 50, 18:8-9, 25:41; *Mark* 9:43 48; *Luke* 16:22-24) was not original. Long before his time some Jews had adopted the Egyptian-Persian notions of an afterlife in which people are assigned to a pleasant or an unpleasant residence depending upon the degree to which their behaviour conformed to the prevailing religion (Teeple 46-47, 248-51, 254 57).

Jesus is reported to have dined with tax collectors and (unspecified) sinners on two occasions (*Matthew* 9:10, *Luke* 19:1-6), and may have done so repeatedly, as suggested by *Matthew* 11:19, par. (He also accepted meals from Pharisees [*Luke* 11:37, 14:1].) He stated that his reason for this was that these people were more in need of hearing his call to repentance than others (*Matthew* 9:12, par). This can only mean that he regarded them as did the other Jews, as having less merit to enter the kingdom of heaven. He thought that by becoming his followers they could join the kingdom. Christians make much of Jesus' associating with such people; they are impressed because they view it as condescension by Jehovah. But nowhere does Jesus state that he has a special regard or love for sinful persons compared to others. (A possible reason for his associating with disapproved persons and the poor was that other Jews did not find his apocalyptic preaching credible or inspired. This would explain why he stated that "the first" would not receive the rewards he promised his lowly followers, "the last" [ibid., 19:30, par].) Nowhere does he express a principle that all humankind are kindred ("brotherhood of man") with which Christians credit him. His address is to his followers and his fellow Jews (ibid., 10:5-6).[9]

Jesus believed that the end of the world was imminent (*Matthew* 10:23, 16:27-28, par, 24:34 35, par; McCabe 304-5; Teeple 78-79, 233). This was the reason why a centre of his preaching was calling on his hearers to repent and seek **Yahweh's favour** (*Matthew* 4:17; *Mark* 1:15; Teeple 78 81, 92-93). This apocalyptic belief was not his own idea. It was widespread among his contemporaries (Horsley 16-20, 44-45, 194, 250; Teeple 62-64, 79-81). This popular anticipation of the end of the world can be attributed to people's inability to escape overwhelming social problems (see question 3), causing them to hope for relief by supernatural events (Horsley 19-20, 253-54).

7. Did Jesus offer a message to all humankind, or even to all the people of his society?

The evangelists report that Jesus imparted information obscurely (*Matthew* 13:18-23, par, 15:15-16, par, 16:6-12, par; but see *Mark* 5:33) and as secrets (*Matthew* 13:36-43; *Mark* 4:13-20, 34; *Luke* 24:45).[10] He acknowledged that he intentionally spoke obscurely (*Matthew* 13:10 13, par; *Mark* 4:10-12; *John* 16:25) and secretly (*Matthew* 10:27).

In these respects he compares unfavourably with Gautama Buddha, Confucius, Socrates, and other esteemed exponents of ethical principles who expressed their precepts openly and in a manner understandable by the public.

Some of Jesus' moral precepts were poorly conceived because contrary to human nature and impossible for most if not all people. "Love your neighbour as yourself," "love your enemies," and calls for self-mutilation (*Matthew* 5:29-30, 18:8-9, par, 19:12) are not realistic principles. These precepts would have seemed sound only to a select group of followers.

Jesus' purpose was to cause his fellow Palestinian Jews to prepare themselves for the impending end of the world (see the previous question). If he had intended to expound a moral message for other people, or for future generations, he could have, like Muhammad, found scribes to write down his words. Long after his death and after the creation of the Gospels, transcribers and editors added to the Gospels texts such as "the great commission" to proselyte everywhere (*Matthew* 28:19-20; *Mark* 16:15; *Luke* 24:47), which contradicted earlier commands (*Matthew* 10:5-6; *Luke* 10:1). Other than these additions, there is nothing in Jesus' purported words to indicate that he perceived himself as having a message for humankind.

8. Was Jesus Charismatic?

The Gospels state that Jesus attracted huge crowds (e.g., *Matthew* 4:25, 9:36, 13:2, 14:13-14, 15:30, 19:2) (note that the Gospel writers regard the men in the crowds as more important than the women [ibid., 14:21, par]). If Jesus was an extraordinarily popular person, however, it is remarkable that no record of his effect on the populace is found except in his postmortem eulogizing biographies. There is no evidence of any contemporary writer having been aware of his existence (Dujardin 262).

Although the Gospels report a few instances in which individuals not already members of Jesus' circle expressed a wish to follow him (*Matthew* 8:19; *Mark* 5:18, par; *Luke* 9:57 61), the men who were continuously devoted to him seem to have been limited to 12 apostles. (Regarding benefactors of Jesus and the apostles, see question 4.)

Beside the conventional one, there are views of Jesus that may explain his alleged popularity but do not attribute superhuman characters to him. Perhaps the most accurate idea of him is that he was a pious and sincere, but antiritualistic, Jew, mostly good-hearted, and much given to the common rabbinic device of speaking in similes; an itinerant preacher and visionary of a kind found in Palestine in his day (Dujardin 261-64; Horsley 160-87, 245). (The late gospel, but not the others, reports that he thought of himself as the Messiah [*John* 4:25-26] and divine [ibid., 8:23-24, 42, 58].) He was a man with the knowledge, beliefs, and hopes of his fellow Palestinian Jews. There are other perceptions of Jesus (e.g., McDonald 95 115), not all of which are favorable (see the next question).

9. Were the motives for Jesus' acts benevolent?

Jesus' motives were questioned as early as the early 18th century: The Egyptians ... maintained that the spirit of **god** could have commerce with a woman and make her fecund.

Jesus ... gave currency to this opinion, he thought it suited his designs. Considering how much Moses had made himself famous ... he undertook to build on this foundation, & got himself followed by some imbeciles. *The Treatise of the Three Imposters,* arts. 11, 12 (Anderson).

Hermann Reimarus may have been the first to observe that a plausible interpretation of the Gospel narratives is that Jesus' plan was to have the people in Jerusalem proclaim him king, fulfilling their idea of a Messiah anointed as the ruler of Israel (Reimarus chap. 2). His goal, that is, was to be a secular monarch during his lifetime. This purpose would have been quite reasonable in view of the history of popularly chosen Jewish "kings," right up to the time of Jesus' birth (Horsley 92-117). The sign reportedly affixed to the cross on which he was executed (*Matthew* 27:37, par) may have demonstrated his judge's awareness of such a plan.

The scanty biographical material about Jesus does not substantiate the opinion of his worshippers and others that he was uniquely virtuous, or that he was uniquely imposing and captivating. When Jesus' followers arrived at the supposition that he was in some way divine, he was invested with the characters that they desired their deity to possess: unbounded charity, mercifulness, and justness, and a bringer of peace (if victory were unattainable). And being divine he also, in their view, must have been imposing, capable of capturing people's attention and affection, and an exponent of exalted truths and principles.[11] Since that time, these alleged characters have been cited, in a circular argument, as evidence of his divinity.

Jesus did not express or even foreshadow important principles of present-day Western morality. But as ethical concepts have evolved during the past 2,000 years, progressively expressing humanism rather than theism, Christians have retroactively ascribed the later principles to Jesus.

During the course of history, many men have propounded a world view that gained them adherents, and have inspired their followers to exceptional actions. Many of these persons have been regarded as agents of deity, and some have been believed to be gods themselves. The fact that Jesus has had a large and long-lasting following need not be attributed to any unique character of his own, but to the circumstances existing in his day, and most importantly, to his having been made the central figure in a state religion that imposed itself and exterminated alternative sets of beliefs by the use of force.

[1] The King James translators had Jesus "reproach" the Pharisees, but the Greek verb *hubrizo* means "to insult, treat insolently, treat shamefully, damage someone's reputation," and connotes a deliberate, spiteful, and undeserved injury (as in *Luke* 18:32).

[2] In a document of a political body these principles are expressed as civil rights. Their basis, however, is ethics: all people *ought* to have freedom to act in certain ways, and no person *ought* to commit certain other acts.

[3] It should be noted that the religion founded on Jesus denied and opposed every one of these rights, and many Christians still oppose at least some of them. These facts contradict the assertion that after his death Jesus inspired moral progress.

[4] A single example of how Jesus' goodness is exaggerated: the Gospels report two interactions by him with children. They are his willingness to lay hands on them (*Matthew* 19:13-15, par) and his statements that one should welcome children while one is professing or invoking his name (ibid., 18:5, par), and that it is dangerous to put an obstacle in the way of children who believe in him (ibid., 18:6, par). (In the second instance, the child may be only a symbol of a new adult convert [McCabe 276]; cf. *Matthew* 10:42.)

These texts apprehend children only as recipients of Jesus' religious ideas. Christians cite them, however, as the basis of an allegation that Jesus had an extraordinary care for the general welfare of children. But he is not recorded as having spoken against the principle of the time that children are chattels of their father, or as having said that they have intrinsic rights as individual human beings.

[5] The Gospel authors consider Jesus' brothers, but not his sisters, worthy of being named individually. This suggests that his moral influence on those writers did not include a change in the cultural attitude that women are inferior to men.

[6] The word in *Matthew* 23:23 and par that often is translated as *justice* is *krisis,* which means a judgment, trial, or dispute, often with a connotation of condemnation (as in multiple other places in the Gospels). It does not denote "the principle of rectitude and just dealing of men with each other" (*Webster's New International Dictionary of the English Language,* 2nd ed.).

[7] The precept (*Matthew* 5:28) usually translated "any man who looks at a woman lustfully has already committed adultery with her in his heart," or similarly, has been alleged to be original with Jesus. The Greek text, however, is *pros to epithumēsai autēn*–"to lust after her," *pros* with the pronoun in the accusative case having the sense of "with a view to." Hence Jesus' meaning seems to have been that men should not look at women not their wives *for the purpose* of their own sexual arousal (erotic viewing as depicted in passages of *The Song of Songs* and *Proverbs* 5:18-19). If the woman were married, people including Jesus regarded such behaviour as a privilege of her husband.

[8] Of the words translated as *neighbour,* the Greek *plësion* means "[one who is] nearby" and the Hebrew *rea* means "friend, companion." In *Leviticus* 19:18 *neighbour* explicitly denotes fellow Jews ("your people"). These words do not refer to human beings in general.

[9] Jesus is reported to have preached to Samaritans, whom the Jews regarded as racially impure heretics (*John* 4:7-30, 39-42). He commanded his disciples, however, not to go to Samaritans (*Matthew* 10:5). He is said to have used a fictional Samaritan, in the role of someone who was not a Jew, to emphasise that his concept of a neighbour required kindness to fellow Jews (*Luke* 10:29-37). But he did not identify as neighbours non-Jews collectively.

[10] The notion of a divine teacher imparting secrets to selected followers is a basic doctrine of Gnosticism, which was a competitor of Christianity at the latter's beginning and produced an entire school of Christian belief and documents (Teeple chap. 24).

[11] An amusing but telling instance of the attribution of perfection to Jesus is the insistence by a Roman Catholic priest that Jesus must have had a perfect sense of humour, even though the priest knew no instance of this (Walsh 237-3).

Jesus was an extraordinary teacher. Crowds of people followed him everywhere. They wanted to see what he did. They also wanted to hear what he would teach them. Moses had said that Lord would send a great prophet. We can read what Moses said in Deuteronomy 18:15, 18. Now what Moses had said was true. Isaiah also said that the Messiah would say words of wise advice (Isaiah 9:6). The Gospels show us that this is true.

At one time Jesus got into a boat, and taught the crowds from it. The crowds were on the shore (Mark 4:1). On another occasion Jesus decided to take his disciples away from the crowds. They went away in a boat, but the crowds saw them. They knew where Jesus and the disciples were going. The crowds got to the place before them. When Jesus left the boat he saw the crowds. He thought that they were like sheep without a shepherd. (A shepherd is a person who looks after sheep.) So, Jesus taught the people many things (Mark 6:34).

At another time, Jesus was on a mountain when he taught the people. Everyone thought that he taught very well. He spoke with authority. Later, officials ordered soldiers to arrest Jesus. The soldiers returned without him. They said, 'No man ever spoke like this man' (John 7:46).

All the time, people spoke about what Jesus said. They had never heard anything like it before (Matthew 13:54, Mark 10:24-26, 11:18, John 7:15). His enemies sometimes tried to defeat Jesus with clever questions. Near the end of his ministry, they no longer did this. Jesus gave answers that defeated them all the time (Matthew 22:46). His answers often upset them.

Catholicism Influence

The book further explores the uniqueness of Jesus Christ the Saviour, who is both the Perfect Divine and Perfect man. He is Perfect Divine because He is the True and the Perfect Holy Spirit. He is Perfect Man because He was born without the cursed and tainted seed of a human being, thus without sin. The idea that Jesus is god/God or the Son of God was introduced and promoted by Roman Catholic Church throughout the world in the year about 336-7 BC. Pope Julius I decided on the birth of Jesus Christ as December

25th in the year 336 BC which fitted in perfectly well with the yearly pagan-gods' celebration of the December 25th. The celebration is known in India as BADA DIN meaning, BIG DAY in English.

It was the Catholicism that introduced Christ Mass-Christmas in order to join in the **yearly** pagan-gods celebration of the **December 25th** in paying homage to their chief god Tammuz who is said to have been born on 25th December in Babylon in the year 2600 BC. Catholicism replaced their sun-god Mithra with Jesus and has been worshipping Jesus on Sun-days as their sun-god. And yet Jesus Christ is definitely NOT born on 25th December and therefore, He is NOT to be called a god/God. In this respct, to call Jesus Christ a God/god is a **blasphemy** because He is NOT to be reduced to the level of the lesser spirit as a god/God. He is the Mighty Holy Spirit and a Saviour, and will **save** everyone who will accept Him as the True and the Supreme Creator of the world. And because of His uniqueness, **salvation** is found in Him alone. Jesus Christ is the Alpha and the Omega the Beginning and the End.

APPRECIATION TO CATHOLICISM

Whether cruelly or selfishly, wrongly or rightly, Crucifixion of Christ and the aftermath, if Catholicism had not introduced and promoted Jesus Christ into the world as occurred, the mission and the wonderful work of our Lord Jesus Christ would have been left in the desert without recognition especially His mission on salvation. This is because His own people the Jews rejected Him and His teachings of the truth for the benefits of human beings. The issue here is salvation would not depend on which denomination one belongs to as the Saviour Jesus Christ has made it clear that salvation belongs to anyone

who will do His Father's will. Our Lord Jesus Christ the Saviour Himself revealed in **Matthew 7:21-23 thus** that, on the **judgement Day**: ".... Not everyone that saith unto me Lord, Lord, shall enter into the kingdom of heaven; but he that doeth the **"WILL"** of my Father who is in heaven."

PART ONE

THE UNIQUENESS OF JESUS CHRIST

CHAPTER 1

HOW UNIQUE IS JESUS CHRIST?

Orthodox Christians believe that Jesus is the unique **Son of the Father** in human flesh. However, some unbelievers, who may or may not believe Jesus existed, do not believe that Jesus was necessarily a wise or a particularly good man. Others, such as Muslims, think that Jesus was a prophet, along with other prophets. Hinduism depicts Christ as one among many great gurus. Liberal Christians and many others hold Christ as a good human being and a great moral example.

In his essay 'Why I Am Not a Christian,' the agnostic Bertrand Russell wrote, 'Historically it is quite doubtful whether Christ ever existed at all, and if he did we know nothing about him.' As to Christ's character, he said, 'I cannot myself feel that either in the matter of wisdom or in the matter of virtue Christ stands quite as high as some other people known to history. I think I should put Buddha and Socrates above him in those respects' (Russell, *Why I Am Not a Christian*).

Divinity and Humanity

Christianity is unique among world religions, and Christ's true uniqueness is the centrepiece of Christianity. The truth about Christ is based primarily on the New Testament documents which have been shown elsewhere to be authentic. The New Testament record, especially the Gospels, is one of the most reliable documents from the ancient world. From these documents we learn that numerous facets of Christ are absolutely unique.

Jesus Christ was unique in that he alone, of all who ever lived, was both Divine and Man. The New Testament teaches the fully unified deity and humanity of Christ. The Nicene Creed (325) states the uniform belief of all orthodox Christianity that Christ was fully Divine and fully Man in one person. All heresies regarding Christ deny one or both of these propositions. This as a claim alone makes him unique above all other religious leaders or persons who have ever lived, and it can be backed up with factual evidence. Some of this evidence is seen in other aspects of Christ's uniqueness.

The Supernatural Nature of Christ.

Unique in Messianic Prophecies. Jesus lived a miracle-filled and supernaturally empowered existence from his conception to his ascension. Centuries before his birth, he was foretold by supernatural prophecy.

The Old Testament, which even the most ardent critic acknowledges was in existence centuries before Christ, predicted the *where* (Micah 5:2), the *when* (Dan. 9:26), and the *how* (Isa. 7:14) of Christ's entry into the world. He would be born of a woman (Gen. 3:15) from the line of Adam's son Seth (Gen. 4:26), through Noah's son Shem (Gen. 9:26–27), and Abraham (Gen. 12:3; 15:5). He would come through the tribe of Judah (Gen. 49:10) and would be the son of David (2 Sam. 7:12f.). The Old Testament predicted that Christ would die for our sins (Psalm 22; Isaiah 53; Dan. 9:26; Zech. 12:10) and would rise from the dead (Pss. 2:7; 16:10).

All of these supernatural prophecies were uniquely fulfilled in Jesus Christ. This is not true of any great religious leader or person who has ever lived, including Muhammad.

Unique in Conception. Christ was not only supernaturally anticipated; he was also miraculously conceived. While announcing his virgin conception, Matthew (1:22–23) points to the prophecy of Isaiah (7:14). Luke, a physician, records this miraculous inception of human life (Luke 1:26f.); Paul alludes to it in Galatians 4:4. Of all human conceptions, Jesus' stands as unique and miraculous.

Unique in Life. From his very first miracle in Cana of Galilee (John 2:11), Jesus' ministry was marked by its miracles (cf. John 3:2; Acts 2:22). These were not healings of delusional illnesses, nor were they explainable on natural grounds. They were unique in that they were immediate, always successful, had no known re lapses, and healed illnesses that were incurable by medicine, such as persons born blind (John 9). Jesus even raised several people from the dead, including Lazarus whose body was already to the point of rotting (John 11:39).

Jesus turned water to wine (John 2:7f.), walked on water (Matt. 14:25), multiplied bread (John 6:11f.), opened the eyes of the blind (John 9:7f.), made the lame to walk (Mark 2:3f.), cast out demons (Mark 3:10f.), healed all kinds of sicknesses (Matt. 9:35), including leprosy (Mark 1:40–42), and even raised the dead to life on several occasions (Mark 5:35f.; Luke 7:11–15; John 11:43–44). When asked if he was the Messiah, he used his miracles as evidence to support the claim saying, 'Go back and report to John what you hear and see: The blind receive sight, the lame walk, those who have leprosy are cured, the deaf hear, the dead are raised' (Matt. 11:4–5). This outpouring of miracles was set forth ahead of time by prophets as a special sign that Messiah had come (see Isa. 35:5–6). Nicodemus even said, 'Rabbi, we know you are a teacher who has come from the Father. For no one could perform the miraculous signs you are doing if the Lord were not with him' (John 3:2).

Unique in Death. Events surrounding Christ's death were miraculous. This included the darkness from noon to 3 p.m. (Mark 15:33) and the earthquake that opened the tombs and rent the temple veil (Matt. 27:51–54). The manner in which he suffered the excruciating torture of crucifixion was miraculous. The attitude he maintained toward his mockers and executioners was miraculous, saying, 'Father forgive them, for they do not know what they are doing' (Luke 23:34). The way in which he actually died was miraculous. As Jesus said, 'I lay down my life—only to take it up again. No one takes it from me, but I lay it down of my own accord' (John 10:18). At the very moment of his departure, he was not overcome by death. Rather, he voluntarily dismissed his spirit. 'Jesus said, 'It is finished.' With that, he bowed his head and gave up his spirit' (John 19:30).

Unique in the Resurrection. The crowning miracle of Jesus' earthly mission was the resurrection. It was not only predicted in the Old Testament (Psalms 2, 16), but Jesus himself predicted it from the very beginning of his ministry: He said, ' 'Destroy this temple, and I will raise it again in three days.' . . . But the temple he had spoken of was his body' (John 2:19, 21; Matt. 12:40–42; 17:9).

Jesus demonstrated the reality of his resurrection in twelve appearances over forty days to more than 500 people.

Unique in the Ascension. Just like his entrance into this world, Jesus' departure was also miraculous. After commissioning his disciples, 'he was taken up before their very eyes, and a cloud hid him from their sight. They were looking intently up into the sky as he was going, when suddenly two men dressed in white stood beside them' (Acts 1:10). Contrary to the view of some, this was not a 'parable' but a literal bodily ascension into heaven from which he will return in the same literal body to reign in this world (Acts 1:11; Rev. 1:7, 19–20). The great Christian creeds clearly emphasize the miraculous bodily ascension of Christ.

Unique in Sinlessness. Some of Jesus' enemies brought false accusations against him, but the verdict of Pilate at his trial has been the verdict of history: 'I find no basis for a charge against this man' (Luke 23:4). A soldier at the cross agreed saying, 'Surely this was a righteous man' (Luke 23:47), and the thief on the cross next to Jesus said, 'This man has done nothing wrong' (Luke 23:41).

For a description of what those closest to Jesus thought of his character, Hebrews says that he was tempted as a man 'yet without sinning' (4:15). Jesus himself once challenged his accusers, 'Which of you convicts me of sin?' (John 8:46), but no one was able to find him guilty of anything. This being the case, the impeccable character of Christ gives a double testimony to the truth of his claim. Jesus' sinlessness was unique.

The Character of Christ Is Unique.

Christ's character was unique in other ways. To a perfect degree he manifested the best of virtues. He also combined seemingly opposing traits.

In Exemplifying Virtues. Even Bertrand Russell, who fancied he saw flaws in Christ's character, confessed nonetheless that 'What the world needs is love, Christian love, or compassion.' But this belies a belief in what most others acknowledge, namely, that Christ was the perfect manifestation of the virtue of love.

Jesus' willing submission to the ignominious suffering and death by crucifixion, while he maintained love and forgiveness toward those killing him is proof of this virtue (Luke 23:34, 43). He alone lived perfectly what he taught in the Sermon on the Mount (Matt. 5–7). He did not retaliate against his enemies; instead, he forgave them. He rebuked his disciples for misusing the sword (Matt. 26:52), and miraculously reattached and healed the amputated ear of one of the mob who came to take him to his death (Luke 22:50).

Jesus was the perfect example of patience, kindness, and compassion. He had compassion on the multitudes (Matt. 9:36), to the point of weeping over Jerusalem (Matt. 23:37). Even though he justly condemned (in no uncertain terms) the Pharisees who misled the innocent (Matt. 23), he did not hesitate to speak with Jewish leaders who showed interest (John 3).

In Combining Seemingly Opposite Traits. One of the unique things about Christ is the way he brought together in his person characteristics that in anyone else would seem impossible. He was a perfect example of humility, to the extent of washing his disciples' feet (John 15). Yet he made bold claims to deity, such as, 'I and the Father are One' (John 10:30) and 'before Abraham was, I AM' (John 8:58; cf. Exod. 3:14). The claim, 'I am meek and lowly in heart' (Matt. 11:29) sounds arrogant, but he backed his words among little children (Matthew 18). Yet he was so strong as to overturn the tables of those who merchandised Father's house, cracking a whip to chase away their animals (John 2). Jesus was known for the virtue of kindness, yet he was severe with hypocrites who misled the innocent, (Matthew 23).

Life and Teaching. As Jesus himself declared, the substance of what he taught finds its roots in the Old Testament (Matt. 5:17–18). He condemned meaningless traditions and misinterpretations of the Old Testament (Matt. 5:21f., 15:3–5). Though the essence of what he taught was not new, the form and the manner in which he taught it was unique. The Sermon on the Mount employs a fresh teaching method.

The vivid parables, such as the good Samaritan (Luke 10), the prodigal son (Luke 15), and the lost sheep (Luke 15:4f.), are masterpieces of communication. Parables stand at the heart of Jesus' teaching style. By drawing on the lifestyles of the people to illustrate the truths he wished to convey, Jesus communicated truth and refuted error. Also, by speaking in parables he could avoid 'casting pearls before swine.' He could confound and confuse those who did not wish to believe (the outsider), yet illuminate those who did desire to believe (the insider). While the use of allegories and parables themselves was not unique, the manner in which Jesus employed parables was. He brought the art of teaching eternal mystery in terms of everyday experience to a new height. The 'laws of teaching' identified by modern pedagogues (Shafer, *Seven Laws*), were practiced perfectly in Jesus' teaching style.

The manner in which Jesus taught was unique. The Jewish intellectuals admitted, 'No one ever spoke the way this man does' (John 7:46). As he taught in parables, he was thronged by the multitudes (Matt. 13:34). As a lad, he impressed even the rabbis in the temple. For 'Everyone who heard him was amazed at his understanding and his answers' (Luke 2:47). Later, he confounded those who attempted to trick him so that 'No one could say a word in reply, and from that day on no one dared to ask him any more questions' (Matt. 22:46).

Christ is Superior to Moses

Jesus Christ was unique in every way. From his complete deity to his perfect humanity; from his miraculous conception to his supernatural ascension; from his impeccable character to his incomparable teaching–Jesus stands above all other religious or moral teachers.

Christ Is Superior to Moses. As a Jew himself, Jesus had no argument with Moses, the prophet who brought the Jewish law and led the Israelites out of Egyptian bondage to freedom as an independent nation. Moses and Jesus were prophets, and Jesus said that he did not come to abolish the law (found in the writings of Moses) but to fulfil it (Matt. 5:17). Jesus implies that Moses' words are words (compare Matt. 19:4–5 with Gen. 2:24). However, in many respects, we find that *Jesus is superior to Moses.*

Christ is a superior prophet to Moses. In Deuteronomy 18:15–19, Moses predicted that Lord would raise up a Jewish Prophet with a special message. Anyone who did not believe this prophet would be judged by the Lord. This passage has been traditionally interpreted as referring to

Messiah. Genesis 3:15 is also understood by many to refer to Jesus as the seed of the woman who would crush the head of the serpent.

Christ's revelation is superior to that of Moses. 'The Law was given through Moses; Grace and truth were realized through Jesus Christ' (John 1:17). While Moses set up the moral and social structures which guided the nation, the law could not save anyone from the penalty of their sins, which is death. As Paul says, 'by the works of the law no flesh will be justified in his sight; for through the law comes the knowledge of sin' (Rom. 3:20). The revelation which came through Jesus, though, was one in which the sins which the law made known are forgiven, 'being justified as a gift by his grace through the redemption which is in Christ Jesus' (Rom. 3:24). Christ's revelation builds on the foundation of Moses by solving the problem of which the law made us aware.

Christ's position is superior to that of Moses. Moses is the greatest of the Old Testament prophets, but Jesus is more than a prophet. As the Epistle to the Hebrews says, 'Moses was faithful *in* all his house as a servant, for a testimony of those things which were to be spoken later; but Christ was faithful as a Son *over* his house' (Heb. 3:5–6). ***While Moses served Yahweh/god, Jesus was declared to be the Son of the Father with the right to rule over all servants.***

Christ's miracles are superior to those of Moses. Moses performed great miracles, but Christ's miracles were greater in degree. Moses lifted the bronze serpent to give healing to those who would look, but in this he was merely following instructions. He never made the blind to see, or the deaf to hear. Also, there is nothing in Moses' ministry to compare with the resurrection of Lazarus or of Christ.

Christ's claims are superior to those of Moses. Moses never made a claim to be the Father and did nothing other than fulfil his role as a prophet. Jesus did claim to be the Lord and predicted his own resurrection to prove it.

Christ Is Superior to Muhammad. Muhammad, the founder of Islam agreed with Jesus and Moses that the Father is one, that He Created the universe, and that he is beyond the universe. There is considerable agreement over the events of the first sixteen chapters of Genesis, to the point where Hagar was cast out from Abram's house. After this, the Bible focuses on Isaac while Islam is concerned with what happened to their forefather, Ishmael. The teaching of Muhammad may be summarized in the five doctrines:

1. Allah is the one true Lord. 2. Allah has sent many prophets, including Moses and Jesus, but Muhammad is the last and greatest. 3. The *Qur'an* is the supreme religious book, taking priority over the Law, the Psalms, and the Injil (Gospels) of Jesus. 4. There are many intermediate beings between the Lord and us (angels), some of whom are good and some evil. 5. Each man's deeds will be weighed to determine who will go to heaven and hell at the resurrection. The way to gain salvation includes reciting the Shahadah several times a day ('There is no Lord but Allah; and Muhammad is his prophet.'), praying five times a day, fasting a month each year, almsgiving, and making pilgrimages to Mecca.

Christ offers a superior message. Jesus made superior claims to those made by Muhammad. Jesus claimed to be the Lord. Muhammad claimed only to be a mere man who was a prophet. If Jesus, then, is not the Lord, then he is certainly no prophet. Jesus offered a superior confirmation for his claims. Jesus performed numerous miracles. Muhammad performed no miracles and admitted in the *Qur'an* that Jesus did many. Only Jesus died and rose from the dead.

Christ offers a better way of salvation. Unlike the Allah of Islam, the Father of the Bible reached out to us by sending his Son to earth to die for our sins. **Muhammad offered no sure hope for salvation**, only guidelines for working oneself into Allah's favour. ***Christ provided all that is needed to get us to heaven in his death***, 'For Christ also died once for all, the just for the unjust, in order that he might bring us to God' (1 Peter 3:18).

Christ offers a superior model life. Muhammad spent the last ten years of his life at war. As a polygamist he exceeding even the number of wives (four) he had prescribed for his religion. He also violated his own law by plundering caravans coming to Mecca, some of whom were on pilgrimage. He engaged in retaliation and revenge, contrary to his own teaching.

Jesus Is Superior to Hindu Gurus. In Hinduism a *guru* is a teacher. The Hindu scriptures cannot be understood by reading; they must be learned from a guru. These holy men are worshiped even after their deaths as supposed incarnations of the gods. What they teach is that humans need liberation from the endless cycle of reincarnation (*samsara*) which is brought on by *karma*, the effects of all words, deeds, and actions in the present and all former lives. Liberation (*moksha*) is obtained when the individual expands his being and consciousness to an infinite level and realizes that *atman* (the self) is the same as *Brahman* (the one absolute being from which all multiplicity comes).

In other words, each Hindu must realize personal godhood. Such a realization can only be achieved by following *Jnana Yoga*– salvation by knowledge of the ancient writings and inward meditation; *Bhakti Yoga*–salvation by devotion to one of the many deities; *Karma Yoga*– salvation by works, such as ceremonies, sacrifices, fasting, and pilgrimages, which must be done without thought of rewards. Each of these methods will to some extent include *Raja Yoga*, a meditation technique involving control over the body, breathing, and thoughts.

Hinduism as it is actually practiced consists largely of superstition, legendary stories about the gods, occult practices, and demon worship.

Christ teaches a superior worldview. Jesus teaches a theistic worldview. But pantheism, the realization of **godhood**, is the heart of Hinduism.

Christ's teaching is morally superior. Orthodox Hinduism insists that suffering people be left to suffer, because it is their destiny, as determined by *karma.* Jesus said, 'Love your neighbour as yourself.' He defined neighbour as anyone in need of help. John said, 'But whoever has the world's goods, and sees his brother in need and closes his heart against him, how does the love of the Father abide in him?' (1 John 3:17). Also, many, if not most, gurus use their esteemed position to exploit their followers financially and sexually. The Bagwan Sri Rajneesh accumulated dozens of Rolls Royces as gifts from his followers. The Beatles became disenchanted with the Maharishi Mahesh Yogi when they learned that he was much more interested in the body of one of the women in their party than with any of their spirits. They admitted, 'We made a mistake.' Even the respected guru **Mahatma Gandhi** slept with women other than his wife.

Jesus gives a superior path to enlightenment. While the gurus are necessary to understand the sacred writings of *Bhagavad Gita* and the *Upanishads*, there is no esoteric or hidden truth in the Bible that must be explained apart from ordinary understanding. Christian meditation is not an effort to empty the mind, but rather to fill it with the truth of Scriptural principles (Psalm 1). Inward meditation is like peeling an onion; you keep tearing off layer after layer until, when you reach the middle, you find that there is nothing there. Meditation on the Lordd's Word begins with content and opens up the meaning until it yields contentment of soul.

Christ teaches a better way of salvation. The Hindu is lost in the karmic cycle of reincarnation until he reaches *moksha* and is left to work the way out of this maze alone. Jesus promised that we would be saved by faith (Eph. 2:8–9; Titus 3:5–7), and that we could know that our salvation is guaranteed (Eph. 1:13–14; 1 John 5:13).

Christ Is Superior to Buddha. Siddhartha Gautama (*Buddha* is a title meaning 'enlightened one') is inferior to Christ. Buddhism began as a reformation movement within Hinduism, which had become a system of speculation and superstition. To correct this, Gautama rejected the rituals and occultism and developed an essentially atheistic religion (though later forms of Buddhism returned to the Hindu gods). His basic beliefs are summed in the Four Noble Truths:

1. Life is suffering. 2. Suffering is caused by desires for pleasure and prosperity. 3. Suffering can be overcome by eliminating desires. 4. Desire can be eliminated by the Eightfold Path.

The Eightfold Path is both a system of religious education and the moral precepts of Buddhism. It includes (1) right knowledge ('Four Noble Truths'), (2) right intentions, (3) right speech, (4) right conduct (no killing, drinking, stealing, lying, or adultery), (5) right occupation (which causes no suffering), (6) right effort, (7) right mindfulness (denial of the finite self), and (8) right meditation (*Raja Yoga*).

The goal of all Buddhists is not heaven or being with the Lord, for there is no Lord in Gautama's teaching. Rather they seek nirvana, the elimination of all suffering, desires, and the illusion of self-existence. While a liberal branch of Buddhism (Mahayana Buddhism) now has deified Gautama as a savior, Theravada Buddhism stays closer to Gautama's teachings and maintains that he never claimed divinity. As to his being a savior, it is reported that Buddha's last words were, 'Buddhas do but point the way; work out your salvation with diligence.' As a variant form of Hinduism, Buddhism is subject to all of the criticisms mentioned above. Jesus' teaching is superior. Further:

Christ fills life with more hope. Jesus' teaching is superior to Buddha's in that Jesus taught hope in life, while Buddhism sees life only as suffering and selfhood as something to be eradicated. Jesus taught that life is a gift of God to be enjoyed (John 10:10) and that the individual is to be honored supremely (Matt. 5:22). Furthermore, he promised hope in the life to come (John 14:6).

Christ offers a better way of salvation. The Buddhist also teaches reincarnation as the means of salvation. However, in this form the self or individuality of the soul is eradicated at the end of each life. So even though you live on, it is not you as an individual who has any hope of attaining nirvana. Jesus promised hope to each man and woman as an individual (John 14:3) and said to the thief on the cross beside him, 'Today you shall be with me in paradise' (Luke 23:43).

Jesus is a better Christ. Jesus claimed and proved to be the Father in human flesh. Buddha was a mere mortal man who died and never rose again. Jesus, however, rose bodily from the grave. Gautama simply wanted to bring his 'enlightenment' to others to help them to nirvana, where all desires and individual existence is lost.

Christ Is Superior to Socrates. Although Socrates never started a religion, he has attracted a great following. Socrates never wrote anything, but Plato, his disciple, wrote a great deal about him, although these accounts may be as much Plato's ideas as the thought of Socrates. Plato presents Socrates as a man convinced that the Lord has appointed him to the task of promoting truth and goodness by making humans examine their words and deeds to see if they are true and good. Vice, in his opinion, was merely ignorance, and knowledge led to virtue. He is credited as the first person to recognize a need to develop a systematic approach to discovering truth, though the system itself was finally formulated by Aristotle–a disciple of Plato's.

Like Christ, Socrates was condemned to death on the basis of false accusations from authorities who were threatened by his teaching. He could have been acquitted if he had not insisted on making his accusers and judges examine their own statements and lives, which they were unwilling to do. He was content to die, knowing that he had carried out his mission to the end, and that death, whether a dreamless sleep or a wonderful fellowship of great men, was good.

Christ has a superior basis for truth. Jesus, like Socrates, often used questions to make his hearers examine themselves, but his basis for knowing the truth about human beings and the Father was rooted in the fact that he was the all-knowing the Lord. **Jesus said of himself, 'I am the way, the truth, and the life.'** He was, in his very being, the fount from which all truth ultimately flowed. Likewise, as the Father, He was the absolute Goodness by which all other goodness is measured. He once asked a young man to examine his words by saying, 'Why do you call me good? No one is good except the Father alone.' Jesus was the very truth and good which Socrates wanted to understand.

Christ gives more certain knowledge. While Socrates taught some true principles, he often was left to speculate about many important issues, such as what happens at death. Jesus gave a sure answer to such questions, because he had certain knowledge of the human destination (John 5:19–29; 11:25–26). Where reason (Socrates) has insufficient evidence to make a definite conclusion, revelation (Jesus) gives answers which might never be anticipated.

Christ's death was more noble. Socrates died for a cause and did so with courage, which is certainly to be commended. However, Jesus died as a substitute for others (Mark 10:45) to pay the penalty that they deserved. Not only did he die for his friends, but also for those that were, and would remain, his enemies (Rom. 5:6–7). Such a demonstration of love is unequaled by any philosopher or philanthropist.

Christ's proof of his message is superior. Rational proofs are good when there is sound evidence for their conclusions. But Socrates cannot support his claim to be sent by the Father with anything that compares to the miracles of Christ and his resurrection. Pagan prophets and prophetesses, such as the Oracle of Delphi, do not compare with the precise biblical prediction and miracles. In these acts there is a superior proof that Jesus' message was authenticated by the Father as true.

Christ Is Superior to Lao Tse (Taoism). Modern **Taoism is a religion of witchcraft, superstition, and polytheism,** but it was originally a system of philosophy, and that is how it is being presented to Western culture today. Lao Tse built this system around one principle which explained everything in the universe and guided it all. That principle is called the Tao. There is no simple way to explain the Tao. The world is full of conflicting opposites–good and evil, male and female, light and dark, yes and no. All oppositions are manifestations of the conflict between *Yin* and *Yang*. But in ultimate reality *Yin* and *Yang* are completely intertwined and perfectly balanced. That balance is the mystery called the Tao. To understand the Tao is to realize that all opposites are one and that truth lies in contradiction, not in resolution.

Taoism goes beyond this to urge living in harmony with the Tao. A person should enter a life of complete passiveness and reflection on such questions as, 'What is the sound of one hand clapping?' or 'If a tree falls in the forest when no one is there to hear it, does it make a sound?' One should be at peace with nature and avoid all forms of violence. This system of philosophy has many similarities with Zen Buddhism.

Christ brings superior freedom. Jesus allows humans to use their reason. In fact, he commands them to do so (Matt. 22:37; cf. 1 Peter 3:15); Taoism does not, at least on the highest level. Taoism engages in the claim that 'Reason does not apply to reality.' That statement itself is self-defeating, for it is a reasonable statement about reality. It is either true or false about the way things really are, and not contradictory, yet it claims that ultimately truth lies in contradiction. Jesus commanded: 'Love the Lord your Father with all your heart, and with all your soul, *and with all your mind*. This is the great and foremost commandment' (Matt. 22:37–38, emphasis added). The Father says, 'Come now, and let us reason together,' (Isa. 1:18). Peter exhorts us to 'give a reason for the hope that you have' (1 Peter 3:15b).

Jesus encouraged the use of freedom to choose, never imposing himself on the unwilling (Matt. 23:37). Taoism asks each follower to set will on the shelf; to give up the power to change things. Jesus says that each person has a choice and that this choice makes the difference. Each chooses to believe or not believe (John 3:18), to obey or disobey (John 15:14), to change the world or be changed by it (Matt. 5:13–16).

Jesus allows each person the freedom to be saved. Taoism offers only a way to resign oneself to the way things are. Christ offers a way to change both who we are and what we are, so that we might know the joys of life. Rather than accepting death as an inevitable end, Christ provides a way to conquer death by his resurrection. Lao Tse can make no such claim.

Christ is absolutely unique among all who ever lived. He is unique in his supernatural nature, in his superlative character, and in his life and teaching. No other world teacher has claimed to be the Father. Even when the followers of some prophet deified their teacher, there is no proof given for that claim that can be compared to the fulfllment of prophecy, the sinless and miraculous life, and the resurrection. No other religious leader (except some who copied Christ) offered salvation by faith, apart from works, based on acting to take away the guilt for human sin. No religious or philosophical leader has displayed the love for people that Jesus did in dying for the sins of the world (John 15:13; Rom. 5:6–8). Jesus is absolutely unique among all human beings who ever lived.

The Uniqueness of Jesus Christ

Each year as we approach the Christmas season and the threshold of a new year, I have found it rewarding to reflect on the uniqueness of our Saviour, the Lord Jesus Christ. As one who believes in the authority and inspiration of the Scripture there is the hope and conviction that the return of Christ is not only imminent, but that even those momentous events described in <u>Matthew 24</u> and <u>Revelation 6-18</u> cannot be far away. The world, for the most part, however, does not hold to such a belief. The world celebrates Christmas without Christ and this grows more blatant as the years go by. And not only that, but many today resent the singing of carols or any sort of religious emphasis during the season of the year. Some have even suggested changing the name of the season to some secular, nondescript name. In fact, do we not now live in a age in which only one prejudice is tolerated—anti-Christian bigotry?

Michael Novak, the eminent columnist, once said that today you can no longer hold up to public pillorying and ridicule groups such as African-Americans or native Americans or women or homosexuals or Poles, and so on. Today, the only group you can hold up to public mockery is Christians. Attacks on the Church and Christianity are common. As **Pat** once put it, "Christian-bashing is a popular indoor sport."

But this should not surprise us. The world view, which more and more Americans have opted for, even if by default, is that of secular humanism with its hope in mankind, not the Divine-man, Christ Jesus. Ironically, coupled with this world view is a certain despondency, disappointment, and discontentment with the job mankind is doing. This has opened the door for the New Age movement and its confidence in mankind, but also its belief in what amounts to demonic powers, the powers that are behind all the religions of the world, the cults, and occult. The world has always had its religious leaders and false messiahs. Christ warned that in the last days many false messiahs would arise, which, as John tells us will culminate in the Antichrist (1 John 2:18, 22; 4:3).

Of the religions of the world, Christianity is unique because it stems from the uniqueness of Jesus Christ, the greatest man who ever lived. In Jesus, we have One who has virtually changed every aspect of human life, but sadly, most people are completely oblivious to the reality of how He has so completely impacted the world. Certainly one of the great tragedies of the Christmas holidays each year is not just the commercialisation of His birth, but the way it is trivialised even when people do speak of His birth and Christmas as an expression of the "spirit of giving." As **Kennedy** points out, tragic it is that people have forgotten Him to whom they owe so very much.

Jesus says in Revelation 21:5, "Behold, I make all things new." (Behold! [*idou* in Greek]: "Note well," "look closely," "examine carefully.") Everything that Jesus Christ touched, he utterly transformed. He touched time when he was born into this world' He had a birthday and that birthday utterly altered the way we measure time.

The person, work, and life of Jesus Christ stands as irrefutable evidence against the secular world view and all the religions of the world regardless of their makeup. No one else is qualified or capable to meet the needs of fallen humanity or restore that which was lost by Adam in the fall of man. A striking illustration of this is seen in Revelation 5:1-11. A careful study of the context and content of Revelation 6-19 suggests that the seven-sealed book, which only Christ can open, contains the story of mankind losing his lordship over the earth to Satan, the usurper, and its recovery through the Divine-man Saviour, the Lion who is also the Lamb. He alone is able to accomplish what no one else in the universe can, and, based on His death as the Lamb and His resurrection as the Redeemer/Saviour, He recovers what was lost through the judgments of the sealed book.

Thus, as we consider the uniqueness of Christ, we also need to recognize this uniqueness demands our allegiance and commitment as believers. It demands that we rearrange our priorities and stand as luminaries in a dark and dismal world holding forth the message of the unique Christ, the Divine-man Saviour of the World. Jesus Himself sought to impress this mindset on His disciples when He stated, "You are the salt of the earth, ... You are the light of the world ..." (Matt. 5:13-16).

In the person of Jesus Christ, we have one so unique that His life cannot be explained by natural processes. His person and life defy the natural. The uniqueness of Jesus Christ presents evidence, as Josh McDowell has so well written "demands a verdict," that this Divine-Man is not only unique, but the Saviour of the world. To properly consider the uniqueness of Christ, let's first consider the uniqueness of Christianity.

The Uniqueness of Christianity

Alone of all the beliefs of mankind, be they religious or political or philosophical, "Christianity (including its Old Testament foundation) is **based upon historical acts and facts.** Other religions are centred in the ethical and religious teachings of their founders, but Christianity is built on the great events of creation and redemption.

The Moslem faith is based on the teachings of Mohammed, Buddhism is based on the teachings Buddha, Confucianism on the teachings of Confucius, Marxism on the teachings of Marx, and evolution on the teachings of Darwin. Not one of these is based on the observation of historical data or facts, but on the teachings and theories of men. Remember, evolution is based on theory—not on observable data.

Christianity, however, is founded, not on what Jesus taught (and this distinction is vital to grasp) but on **who** Jesus is and on **what** Jesus accomplished. Of course, as Christians, we stand firmly on His teachings. No one ever spoke and taught like Jesus, but ultimately, the value of **what He said** was dependent upon **who He was** and **what He did** and the abundant historical evidence that authenticated His life and words. This gave the teachings of Christ authority and placed them alone in the category of absolute truth. The truthfulness of Jesus and His teachings stand on the validity of historical records which are subject to investigation and examination.

All other beliefs are based on the teachings and ideas of those who were nothing more than mere men. No matter how brilliant, charismatic, or powerful they may be, there is no guarantee of their objectivity, accuracy or ultimate ability to deliver what they have promised.

The uniqueness of Christianity, however, ultimately depends on the uniqueness of its central figure—the Lord Jesus Christ. Some try to place Christ among the great religious leaders of history, as one among many, but this is grotesque and absurd. Either He was who He said He was and who history demonstrates Him to be, or, as someone has put it, He was on par with 'a man who thinks he is a poached egg.' Christ's uniqueness is so great that no one, absolutely no one, can compare with Him.

But there is another evidence of the uniqueness of Christianity as an outgrowth of the life, death, and resurrection of Christ. It is the awesome impact of Christ through the church on mankind and history. In his excellent book, *What If Jesus had Never Been Born?*, Kennedy give an overview of some of the positive contributions Christianity has made throughout the centuries. Following this overview, he develops this in great detail. Here are a few highlights:

- o Hospitals, which essentially began during the Middle Ages.
- o Universities, which also began during the Middle Ages. In addition, most of the world's greatest universities were started by Christians for Christian purposes.
- o Literacy and education for the masses. Capitalism and free enterprise.
- o Representative government, particularly as it has been seen in the American experiment. The separation of political powers. Civil liberties.
- o The abolition of slavery, both in antiquity and in more modern times.
- o Modern science. The discovery of the New World by Columbus.
- o The elevation of women. Benevolence and charity; the good Samaritan ethic.
- o Higher standards of justice. The elevation of the common man.
- o The condemnation of adultery, homosexuality, and other sexual perversions. This has helped to preserve the human race, and it has spared many from heartache. High regard for human life.The civilising of many barbarian and primitive cultures. The codifying and setting to writing of many of

the world's languages. Greater development of art and music. The inspiration for the greatest works of art.

o The countless changed lives transformed from liabilities into assets to society because of the gospel. The eternal salvation of countless souls!

These are some of the many contributions brought about by the preaching of the message of the gospel of salvation in Christ. Such happened because of the spiritual change that Christ brings into the hearts of men. After summarising these contributions, **Kennedy** concluded:

When Jesus Christ took upon Himself the form of man, He imbued mankind with a dignity and inherent value that had never been dreamed of before. Whatever Jesus touched or whatever he did transformed that aspect of human life. Many people will read about the innumerable small incidents in the life of Christ while never dreaming that those casually mentioned "little" things were to transform the history of humankind.

The Anticipation of His coming

The fact of fulfilled prophecy is a unique feature of Christianity. The coming of Jesus Christ was prophesied in minute detail regarding His lineage, nature, place of birth, where He would be raised, His career, purpose, the specific manor and nature of His death, His resurrection, and many other fulfilled prophecies. And all of these prophecies were made hundreds of years before His birth or first advent.

THE NATURE OF HIS BIRTH

His birth was, of course, the most unique birth in all of human history. Though ancient mythology was filled with tales of demi-gods who were supposed to be the progeny of lustful unions between women and gods (demons), there was nothing even close to the narrative of the birth of Jesus Christ.

Christ's birth stands alone in history. By the miraculous work of the Holy Spirit, God Himself took up residency in a virgin's womb in embryonic form so that after a natural nine-month pregnancy, she gave birth to a son who was also God's Son. He was the God-man Savior—not a God-indwelt man. He was both true and genuine humanity and undiminished deity united in one Person forever. No other birth was like this in fact or fiction.

As a result of this unique birth, Christ was able to bypass the curse of sin and the curse of Jeconiah so that He was uniquely qualified as the sinless One to both go to the cross to die as the Lamb of God and to reign on the throne of His father David as the Lion of the tribe of Judah (Rev. 5).

THE UNIQUENESS OF HIS PERSON

This is found, as mentioned above in the divine/human natures of Christ—two natures united in one person. The Bible makes the claim that Jesus Christ is both God and Man. As God He created all things (Jn. 1:1; Col. 1:16). As man He was sinless and came as the sinless substitute to die for mankind's sin. But the declaration of Scripture and the evidence of His life affirm that He was not half man and half God, but **totally man** and **totally God** united in one Person.

He is God's indescribable and unfathomable gift to the world. He is the most unique Person of the universe. No other religious leader has ever seriously made such a claim for no other could support it by their life.

THE UNIQUENESS OF HIS LIFE

His life is unparalleled in beauty, scope, character, and effect. No one ever spoke like Jesus Christ, did the things He did, or made the claims He made.

In view of Christ's mighty words and works, and the perfect and sinless person men found Him to be, the claims He made cannot be dismissed. People cannot, in all honesty to the historical evidence, dismiss Christ's claims as those of a mad man or reject Him as a fraud. Modern skeptics try to attribute his miracles and claims to simply the character of his life. But they do this simply because of their prejudice against the light (truth) and against the miraculous, not because there is a lack of bona fide historical evidence.

THE UNIQUENESS OF HIS DEATH

His death is also unique, not because He was crucified, but because it was prophesied in Psalm 22 long before death by crucifixion was known in Palestine. Second, it is unique because of the manner in which he died, displaying his sinless and holy character. And third, because of the miracles surrounding his death—the darkness, the earthquake, and the opening of the graves. After seeing Christ on the cross and the events of that day, the Roman centurion who had seen hundreds die on a cross said, "truly this was the Son of the Father."

THE UNIQUENESS OF HIS RESURRECTION

Other religious and philosophical leaders have come and gone, risen and fallen, but none have come back from the dead to carry on their work as did Jesus Christ. This too is unique, not only because Jesus Christ stands alone in this respect, but because of the Old Testament predictions and the incontrovertible evidence for the historical fact of the resurrection—the empty tomb, His post-resurrection appearances, and the transformed lives of his disciples, not to mention the continuation of Christianity in the face of the greatest adversity.

The fact is, men reject Jesus Christ, His birth, miracles, and resurrection not because of a lack of evidence, but (1) because they have never really researched the evidence with an open mind, or (2) do not want to submit to his authority and claims, or (3) because they have a basic anti-supernatural philosophy, a prejudice against the miraculous, or both.

They approach history with a preconceived notion and then adjust the evidence accordingly. In other words, before they even begin their historical examination they have determined the content of their results.

Many historians approach history with certain presuppositions and these presuppositions are not historical biases but rather philosophical prejudices. Their historical perspective is rooted within a philosophical framework, and the metaphysical conviction usually determines the "historical" content and results. The "modern" researcher, when presented with the historical evidence for the resurrection, will usually reject it, but not because of historical examination.

The response will often be: "Because we know there is no Creator"; or "The supernatural is not possible"; or, "We live in a closed system"; or "Miracles are not possible"; etc.... All too often it is the offshoot of *philosophical speculation* and not historical homework.

An illustration of what McDowell is talking about is the Jesus Seminar which recently claimed to search for the

'Jesus of history' who they claim is different from the 'Jesus of faith.' It is the view of those involved in the Jesus Seminar that the historical Jesus was a bright, witty, countercultural man who never claimed to be the Son of the Lord, while the Jesus of faith is a cluster of 'feel-good' ideas that help people live right but are ultimately based on wishful thinking. In discussing the Jesus Seminar, Strobel quotes Dr. Luke Timothy Johnson and writes:

Johnson systematically skewers the Jesus Seminar, saying it "by no means represents the cream of New Testament scholarship," it follows a process that is "biased against the authenticity of the gospel traditions," and its results were "already determined ahead of time." He concludes, "This is not responsible, or even critical, scholarship. It is a self-indulgent charade."

He goes on to quote other distinguished scholars with similar opinions, including Dr. Howard Clark Kee, who called the Seminar "an academic disgrace," and Richard Hayes of Duke University, whose review of *The five Gospels* asserted that "the case argued by this book would not stand up in any court.

What makes Christ' person unique? It is His virgin birth as the Son of Man, the incarnation, the birth of the Divine-man. Only the virgin birth can give an adequate answer to the phenomena of the uniqueness of Jesus Christ.

(1) In Christ's life and ministry, he demonstrated who He was—the Divine-man, the only begotten of the Father, full of grace and truth. He also declared His purpose—to die for our sin.

(2) In His death on the cross, Christ accomplished that purpose. He bore our sin in His sinless body on the tree. He died as our substitute, and took our judgment.

(3) By His resurrection, the Father proved the value of His Son's death and the sinlessness of His Person. It proved Him to be the unique Divine-man.

As ordained in the eternal counsels of the Father, historically for man, it all began in the fullness of time (Gal. 4:4) when Mary gave birth to her firstborn son, Jesus. But this was no ordinary birth. Rather, it was the result of the power of the Holy Spirit (Matt. 1:20; Luke 1:35). Though anticipated in the prophets for hundreds of years, it all began with that first Christmas when the Son of the Father became flesh and began to dwell among men.

Luke 2:1-14. Now in those days a decree went out from Caesar Augustus to register all the empire for taxes. **2:2** This was the first registration, taken when Quirinius was governor of Syria.**2:3** Everyone went to his own town to be registered.**2:4** So Joseph also went up from the town of Nazareth in Galilee to Judea, to the city of David called Bethlehem, because he was of the house and family line of David. **2:5** He went to be registered with Mary, who was promised in marriage to him, and who was expecting a child. **2:6** While they were there, the time came for her to deliver her child.**2:7** And she gave birth to her first-born son and wrapped him in strips of cloth and laid him in a manger, because there was no place for them in the inn.

2:8 Now in that region there were shepherds out in the field, keeping guard over their flock by night. **2:9** An angel of the Lord appeared to them, and the glory of the Lord shone around them, and they were absolutely terrified.**2:10** But the angel said to them, "Do not be afraid; for take note, I proclaim to you good news of a great joy that will be for all the people: **2:11** to you is born today in the town of David a Saviour, who is Christ the Lord. **2:12** This will be the sign for you: you will find a baby wrapped in strips of cloth and lying in a manger." **2:13** Suddenly a multitude of the heavenly host appeared with the angel, praising the Lord and saying,

2:14 "Glory to the Father in the highest, and on earth peace among people with whom he is pleased!"

The following well known anonymous composition of the nineteenth century beautifully demonstrates the uniqueness of Jesus Christ, the Saviour of the World.

One Solitary Life

He was born in an obscure village, the child of a peasant woman. He grew up in another village, where He worked in a carpenter shop until He was thirty. Then for three years He was an itinerant preacher. He never wrote a book. He never held an office. He never had a family or owned a home. He didn't go to college. He never visited a big city. He never travelled two hundred miles from the place where he was born. He did none of the things that usually accompany greatness. He had no credentials but Himself.

He was only thirty-three when the tide of public opinion turned against Him. His friends ran away. One of them denied Him. He was turned over to His enemies and went through the mockery of a trial. He was nailed to a cross between two thieves.

While He was dying, His executioners gambled for His garments, the only property he had on earth. When He was dead, He was laid in a borrowed grave through the pity of a friend. Nineteen centuries have come and gone, and today He is the central figure of the human race.

All the armies that ever marched, all the navies that ever sailed, all the parliaments that ever sat, all the kings that ever reigned, put together, have not affected the life of man on this earth as much as that one solitary life.

The Father is a missionary Father who created human beings in His image and for a relationship with Him.

Scripture explains how humanity chose to rebel against the Father. And He has been pursuing the restoration of His relationship with us. The Father has chosen a people to join with Him in seeking restoration of relationship with all of humanity.

Jesus Is The Word

Consequently, Jesus Christ came as the Word in human form to model the Divine's heart for humanity. Through His death and resurrection, He paid the debt for our sins. In fact, He makes it possible for all who will believe to be transformed into ambassadors of the Father. In turn, they become a part of initiating reconciliation with peoples of every tribe, nation, and language.

So, we can better understand World Mission and how it relates to the Church and our lives by exploring the following;

Jesus and the Post-Modern World

In reality, we live in a postmodern world that believes there is no absolute truth and that truth is relative. So, how in this postmodern pluralistic culture, can we present the uniqueness of Jesus Christ?

For us, as disciples of Jesus Christ, the Word is our guide in our journey and ministry.

In fact, in the Word is the uniqueness of Jesus Christ is evident.

The Father of the Bible is the only Father who manifested Himself through His own son, Jesus Christ (John 3:16).

He is different from all false gods (Jeremiah 10:6; Deuteronomy 6:4; 1 Corinthians 8:4-6).

Jesus is not one of the many ways to the Father—He is the only way.

No one can come to Father except through Jesus Christ (John 14:6; Acts 4:12).

He is the only One who has been conceived by the Holy Spirit and born of a virgin (Isaiah 7:14; Matthew 1:18-25; Luke 1:26-38).

Jesus is the only One who is eternal (Colossians 1:17; John 1:1-3; John 8:57).

He is the only One who is Father incarnate, Father in human flesh (John 1:1-18; Hebrews 1:1-3; Hebrews 2:14-18; Philippians 2:5-11; 1 Timothy 2:5-6).

Jesus is the only One who is the visible image of the invisible Father, who is fully Divine and fully man (Colossians 1:15-20; Colossians 2:9).

He is the only One who lived a sinless life that qualified Him to become the Saviour (2 Corinthians 5:21; Hebrews 4:15; Hebrews 7:23-28).

Jesus is the only One who forgives sin—something that the Father alone can do (Mark 2:5-7).

He is the only One who has conquered death (1 Corinthians 15:3-8).

Jesus is the only One who will come back to judge the world (2 Timothy 4:1; Revelation 19:11).

Jesus and the Lausanne Movement

"The Lausanne Movement" describes the uniqueness of Jesus Christ in this way: "We affirm that there is only one Saviour and only one gospel . . . Jesus Christ, being Himself the only Divine-man, who gave Himself as the only ransom for sinners, is the only mediator between the Father and people."

"We are called to proclaim Christ in an increasingly pluralistic world . . . In the first century too there were 'many gods and many lords.' Yet the apostles boldly affirmed the uniqueness, indispensability and centrality of Christ. We must do the same."

"The Lausanne Movement is determined to bear a positive and uncompromising witness to the uniqueness of our Lord, in His life, death, and resurrection, in all aspects of our evangelistic work including inter-faith dialogue."

In fact, the only true Son is our living, triune Father. He has revealed Himself in the Bible to all of humanity.

What the Scriptures Say About Jesus

The Scriptures of the Old and New Testaments tell us clearly that God is eternally one and, as the living and sovereign One, **He differs fundamentally from all false gods**

(Deuteronomy 6:4; Psalm 115:3-7; Isaiah 44:6; Jeremiah 10:6; 1 Corinthians 8:4-6).

In His tri-personal nature as Father, Son, and Holy Spirit, Father is one perfect and complete community of love in Himself who has fulfilled His redemptive plan in the person of His only begotten Son, Jesus (Genesis 1:1; John 1:1; John 15:26; I John 4:9; 2 Corinthians 13:13).

The Father created humankind in His own image (Genesis 1:27).

He is the Creator, Redeemer, Sustainer, and Renewer, the origin and ultimate purpose and goal of every human being. For this reason, the Father calls all humanity to acknowledge Him and believe in Him, to worship, and to share His life (Ecclesiastes 11:9; 2 Corinthians 5:10; Psalm 46:11).

The Father has spoken to us through Jesus Christ the Son as His special revelation of salvation (Hebrews 1:2). By the initiation of the Father (John 1:1-2; John 3:16), through His incarnation by the Holy Spirit, and by His atoning death, Christ reconciled the humanity to the Father and redeemed us from the destructive powers of sin, death, and the Devil (2 Corinthians 5:19; Ephesians 1:7; Hebrews 2:14).

The Uniqueness Of Jesus Christ

The uniqueness of Jesus Christ, the only Son of the Father, demands a response.

In reality, the necessity of personal belief, is at the heart of the Christian Gospel. So, Christ fulfils and completes all the aspirations of humanity. He comes as the Second Adam to restore sinful humanity and a broken world. When people come to know Christ, they discover meaning and purpose, and their full identity is regained. While a decision to accept the free offer of salvation is crucial to evangelism, it must also affirm that this unique Saviour offers not merely salvation as a work, but He also offers Himself in a transformational way. In fact, the whole purpose of the Christian life is to become like Jesus.

Jesus The Only Way To The Father

By Christ's bodily resurrection and ascension to heaven, the Father has confirmed Him as the only Mediator between Himself and humanity, and He has appointed Him the universal Lord over all powers and authorities as well as Judge Uird of our world hasn't heard the Good News of Jesus. Yet. Global Disciples refers to these as "least-reached" people, and fewer than 10% of all missionaries work among these groups. We live in a time where many of these people are within reach of a local church. Through our simple and effective strategy of training and coaching, **believers share the Gospel in their own nations and cultures. Jesus said, "Go and make disciples of all nations,"** and we're committed to doing just that. If you are looking for a Christian mission organization to partner with to become a better disciple *and help make disciples, connect with us today*

Intertwined between the pages of the Word is a love story. A story that is wrapped in grace and forgiveness, offering hope and redemption to all mankind. It's amazing how the birth of a baby changed the course of history and became a fulfillment of prophecy.

Our Lord Jesus Christ has a story like no other.

But what makes Jesus so unique? What makes His story differ from all other deities and religious leaders?

These are questions many ask as they come into the Christian faith or ponder at some point in their faith journey. Jesus being the Son of the Father in human form, but, fully divine, can be a difficult concept for anyone to wrap their head around.

Not to mention, the world has many views on who Jesus is. As believers, we know Jesus as a part of the Trinity. He came to this earth as a man to live a perfect life, providing an example for us to live by, and granting us salvation (John 10:15).

But how do we know that Jesus was more than a good man, prophet, or great guru?

First, we must recognise that Christianity is unlike any other world religion. **Where every other religion focuses on merit and what must be done here on earth to get into good graces with their god, Christianity focuses on Christ.**

Jesus Christ is the *only way* to the Father (John 14:6).

The Christian faith also recognizes that we are all sinners and are not good enough on our own, yet Christ stepped in to save us from our sinful selves. Romans 5:8 tells us that the Father demonstrates His love for us through Christ's sacrifice on the cross.

So, who is Jesus, what makes Him so unique, and why is it so important to understand who He is?

The Unique Character of Jesus

Jesus is the humble servant, the best storyteller and the teacher. Full of compassion, exuding grace and touching hearts with His unfailing love.

Jesus' character is beautifully displayed throughout the gospels as we see His disciples and followers honour, respect, and seek His wisdom. But His followers didn't start out so loyal and admiring. They were merely commoners, simple and mostly uneducated.

Before they encountered Jesus, they were arrogant and hot-tempered fishermen. Then there was the misfit tax collector, a mischievous thief, and even a traitor. I'm guessing it was a pretty rowdy and lively bunch. Yet, Jesus chose them!

Throughout the three years of extensive and intimate training, we see Jesus' character come to life. We see His humble nature, His patience, kindness, and goodness poured upon His beloved disciples. What would have been difficult for any normal man, we see Jesus' loving and gentle nature draw these 12 vastly different men together, bonding them in unity like brothers.

As we read the stories of those that had a personal and deep-seated relationship with Him, we see how Jesus chose the lowly. Sought out the poor. Healed the sick, restored the weak and hurting, and got acquainted with the lonely and lost. His mission was vastly different than the ways of the world.

John 1:1-4 **should say this to us, "In the beginning was the Word, and the Word was One. He alone was the Divine in the beginning. Through him all things were made; without him nothing was made that has been made. In him was life, and that life was the light of all mankind."**

Jesus is the Word. He alone is the One from the beginning of time.

Just as a marriage is joined by two individual people and becomes one flesh (Mark 10:8), our Father, Son, and the Holy Spirit are a united front.

Jesus is a Son of the Father, unlike any other deity is the One full of grace and Truth (John 1:14). He is the One that seeks to have a relationship with us (James 4:8).

He is the One that grants us gifts in order to spread His message (1 Peter 4:10). The One that brought salvation to all people (Titus 4:16) and proclaimed to be the Son of the Father (1 John 5:20).

That is the unique character of our Lord Jesus Christ!

A Unique Life of Jesus

Jesus didn't have your typical birth story. He made His appearance as an innocent baby in a lowly stall in Bethlehem. What appeared to be humble beginnings shows the nature of His character (Luke 2:6-7).

Yet, when the echoes of His first cry pierced this broken and shattered world, angels rejoiced, shepherds looked up to the heavens, and three wise men made the long and rigorous trek to see and worship the long-awaited Messiah (Luke 2:15, Matthew 2:1-2).

Jesus had entered the earth in human form. Then the teaching andexamples of how to live this life began. Throughout the New Testament, we see how Jesus came in man form to relate to us, build a personal relationship with us, train us in His ways, and to ultimately save us by offering a redemption plan.

We see the Father's hand in everything, from the teaching as a young boy in the church of Bethlehem (Luke 2:47) to the last words uttered on the cross — "it is finished" (John 19:13) and "Father, into your hands I commit my spirit" (Luke 23:46).

Jesus knew this life would not be any easy one and that He would experience pain and suffering. He knew He would be an outcast and misunderstood by many.

He knew He would be tempted by the deceiver. Yet, He still came as an innocent baby and grew to be a sinless man as part of a much bigger plan and greater purpose. His unique life teaches us that He is one with the Father.

Jesus Christ Lives!

The King of the Jews, **the title Jesus claimed, and the words that were displayed upon His fatal cross. While this unjust sentence to death by royal and religious enemies, who denied His status, calling Him a blasphemer, was utter torture, it marked the beginning of a new life.**

As Jesus hung on a cross between two thieves, it appears so insolent, yet we know that the Father is purposeful in everything He does. This was no coincidence. Maybe it was to spread one last message to the people (and to us) of His undeniable role in the trinity.

Just as we saw in His humble beginnings, Jesus also reveals His character in His humble departure as He surrounds Himself around sinners. Then shows mercy to the thief which asked to be remembered (Luke 23:40-42).

As the skies grow dim, Jesus cries out, asking why Jews have forsaken Him (Matthew 27:6). This is the pivotal point at which Jesus has taken on *all* the sins of the world — past, present, and future. The sin distances Him from the Father, yet it had to be done. It is a fulfilment of prophecy.

As dark as that day was, it was filled with hope for all mankind.

This is where we meet Jesus on the pages of His Word, and He reveals His love story for us. He rescues us from the darkness (sin) and turns it into light through His selfless sacrifice. Hope and healing are freely given. Grace abounds. The debts of our sins have been paid in full.

Jesus offers us a new life — through Him!

Every other religious leader's tomb you visit has a body inside, but Jesus' tomb is empty. Every other religion has a list of good deeds to perform or a level of achievement you must obtain to be enough. With Jesus, we are enough. This is what makes Jesus so unique.

He lived a perfect life. He died a purposeful death. And He currently lives at the right hand of the Father. Jesus — the greatest love story ever told!

PART TWO

THE TRUE IDENTITY OF JESUS CHRIST

CHAPTER 2

WHO IS TRUE JESUS?

I n order to prove His true identity, Jesus Himself made many "I am" statements such as: "I am" the Alpha and Omega, although *Cindi McMenamin* adds that Jesus had said many significant words that are recorded in the Gospels. Yet, there are seven statements Jesus made in the book of John that were particularly pivotal to His ministry, Old Testament prophesies, and His claims of who He was. They were also particularly significant to the first-century Jewish listener who would've better understood the context of what Jesus was saying.

Jesus Christ identifies Himself with "I Ams"

The Yahweh had centuries earlier revealed Himself to Moses with the decisive statement, **("IAM") BUT AS WHO OR WHAT?** *BECAUSE JESUS DECLARED WHO HE IS SUCH AS "I AM THE ALPHA AND OMEGA"(Revelation 22: 13-14)*. Throughout the Old Testament, others added to His name "I AM" – translated Yahweh or Jehovah – by giving Him names that clarified His character, based upon His provision and His miracles. Scripture declares the Father's names as Jehovah-Jireh (the Lord, My Provider), Jehovah Rapha (the Lord Heals), Jehovah Nissi (the Lord, My Banner), Jehovah Shalom, (the Lord, Our Peace), Jehovah Raah (the Lord, My Shepherd), and more.

Then, centuries later, Jesus used the same name (I AM) in the Gospel of John to describe Himself when He said to the Samaritan woman "I...am *He*" (John 4:26), when he told His frightened disciples as He walked on the surface of the waters toward their boat in a storm "It is I" (John 6:20), and when He reaffirmed to His followers, "I am *He*" (John 13:19).

The Father further defined for us who He was in the Book of John through Jesus's seven "I am" statements.

What Are the "I Am" Statements of Jesus?

Jesus made these seven resounding statements throughout the Gospel of John:

1. **"I am the bread of life**. He who comes to Me shall never hunger, and he who believes in Me shall never thirst" (John 6:35). Jesus also reiterated this statement in John 6:41, 48, and 51.

2. **"I am the light of the world.** He who follows Me shall not walk in darkness, but have the light of life" (John 8:12).

3. **"I am the door of the sheep.** All who ever came before Me are thieves and robbers, but the sheep did not hear them. I am the door. If anyone enters by me, he will be saved and will go in and out and find pasture" (John 10:7-9).

4. **"I am the good shepherd.** The good shepherd gives His life for the sheep...I am the good

shepherd; and I know my sheep, and am known by My own." (John 10:11, 14).

5. **"I am the resurrection and the life.** He who believes in Me, though he may die, he shall live" (John 11:25).

6. **"I am the way, the truth, and the life.** No one comes to the Father except through Me" (John 14:6).

7. **"I am the true vine** and My Father is the vinedresser... I am the vine, you are the branches. He who abides in Me, and I in him, bears much fruit; for without Me you can do nothing" (John 15:1-5).

What Is the Significance of Each "I Am" Statement in the Bible?

Jesus' "I am" statements were particularly significant to the Jewish listeners within the context of *when* he said them or *where* He said them. He was continually pointing their eyes toward Himself as the Lord in light of the Old Testament Scriptures that prophesied His coming.

"I am the bread of life."

Jesus said this shortly after He had fed the five thousand and the people wanted more free food. But Jesus didn't want to keep filling their stomachs. He wanted them to see that physical food only satisfied hunger temporarily, but He was the One who could satisfy them spiritually. He was saying He is the bread that *provides* life.

Manna satisfied the physical needs of the Israelites in the wilderness, but only for a while. Christ satisfies our spiritual needs forever. Those who believe in Jesus have life. The manna in the wilderness satisfied temporary hunger and those who ate of it eventually died. Jesus provides the bread of life that leads to life everlasting.

"I am the Light of the world."

Jesus made this statement during the Feast of Tabernacles. At this feast, a huge candelabra was lit in the women's court of the temple. It reminded the Israelites of the pillar of fire that guided their ancestors during the wilderness wanderings. Jesus made this statement just after forgiving, rather than condemning, a woman caught in adultery whom the Pharisees had brought before Jesus in the middle of His teaching.

Jesus was letting them know that in a world darkened by sin, He is holy (His light contrasts the darkness) and He offers the light and guidance to those stumbling in sin. The people knew the Old Testament Scripture "For the Lord is a sun and shield; the Lord will give grace and glory..." (Psalm 84:11). In that instance, Jesus was epitomising the character of the Lord as a sun (which provides light), a shield (which protects), and grace (which forgives) for the glory of the Lord.

"I am the door of the sheep."

This statement of Jesus' was made during a discourse with Israel's religious readers in which Jesus in so many words declared them to be unfit shepherds of the nation. According to the Nelson Study Bible, "Shepherds guided their flocks into stone enclosures each night to protect them. These structures had no doors. The shepherd would sit or lie in the opening to prevent predators from attacking. Thus Jesus was describing His care and constant devotion to those who are His." This statement also reinforces what

He said in <u>John 14:6</u> about being the only way to come to the Father. The only way to get into the Father's "sheepfold" or "family" or "dwelling" is to go through Jesus – the door or entryway.

"I am the good shepherd."

With this statement, Jesus described His sacrificial love for His people. He was letting the Israelites know that, unlike a hired man who will run and leave a flock unprotected in order to save his own life when the wolf threatens the sheep, He will not abandon His sheep, but will keep watch over His people. In <u>John 10:15-16</u>, Jesus said "I lay down My life for the sheep. And other sheep I have which are not of this fold; them also I must bring, and they will hear My voice, and there will be one flock and one shepherd." This was a prophetic utterance about His coming sacrificial death to save both the Jews and <u>Gentiles</u> who would believe in His name. In <u>Psalm 23</u>, David referred to the Lord as his shepherd, and in this passage, Jesus refers to Himself as the ultimate Good Shepherd who was about to give His life for His sheep and fulfill His Father's plan of <u>salvation</u> for all people.

"I am the resurrection and the life."

Jesus spoke this crowning statement of hope to His grieving friend, Martha, after her brother, Lazarus, had died. In the next verse He clarified His statement by saying, "And whoever lives and believes in Me shall never die. Do you believe this?" (<u>John 11:26</u>). Death brought a sense of despair, hopelessness, and finality until Jesus spoke those glorious words, and then demonstrated them by bringing His dead friend back to life. Shortly afterward, Jesus showed the world that He had conquered the grave when He, Himself, rose to life three days after His death for the sins of all who would believe. According to 1 Corinthians 15:55, death no longer holds its sting because Jesus has overcome the grave. All who are in Christ will live forever.

"I am the way, the truth, and the life."

When the disciples were confused about Jesus' statements about heaven, Thomas asked what all of them must have been thinking: "Lord, we do not know where You are going, and how can we know the way?" Jesus said to him, "I am the way, the truth, and the life. No one comes to the Father except through Me" (John 14:5-6). Jesus was reiterating that all roads do *not* lead to heaven. There are *not* many paths or religions to the Lord. Jesus is the *only* way to forgiveness, the *only* source for truth and knowledge about the Lord, and the *only* route to eternal life. Jesus offers to spiritually dead people the very life of the Lord. And there are no other options. This statement was significant to those of His day who were trying to gain access to the Lord's favour through the Law and their good works. And it is significant to us today because we are surrounded by many beliefs and religions claiming access to the Father and a way to *earn* His favour and eternal life, apart from Jesus alone.

"I am the true vine."

Jesus said this to His followers in the Upper Room on the night of His arrest and impending death. The Old Testament contains many references to Israel as Yahweh/ god's vine (Psalm 80:8; Isaiah 5:1-7; Ezekiel 15; Hosea 10:1). But because of the nation's unfruitfulness, Jesus came to fulfill the Father's plan. By abiding in or dwelling with or attaching ourselves to Christ, we enable His life to flow in and through us. Then we cannot help but bear fruit that will honour the Father. In this metaphor, He is the gardener. In

Him, and in His nurturing, tending, and pruning, you and I can grow to our potential and bear much fruit. Jesus was saying "Stick close to Me and you will be able to accomplish much for My Father's glory."

Why Are Jesus' Statements Important?

Jesus wasn't just exercising positive self-talk when He made these bold statements. He was letting the first century Jews, who were familiar with their Yahweh/god elevated as the uppercase letter "G"-God's definition of Himself in Genesis1;1. Yahweh said "I am" but did not say who he was. This is for them to know that He Jesus is the true Creator of the World as in John 1:1 and that He is also the incarnate, the Messiah they were waiting for, the Most High Lord in the flesh. If anyone else had made these statements it would have been blasphemy (That is what Jesus was accused of by the Jewish leaders, who then arranged to have Him crucified for such "blasphemy." Yet that plot was ultimately ordained by the Lord to fulfil prophesy that Jesus would be crucified for the sins of all who would believe in His name).

Jesus fulfilled and affirmed numerous Old Testament prophesies about Himself through these statements. It's also important to consider that He knew who He was, and He wanted us to clearly know, too. He can't be minimised to merely our "ticket to heaven" but must be seen as our daily sustenance, our direction, our protector, our sacrificial Saviour, our victory over death, our access to the Father and eternal life, and our vitality and strength.

Do *yo*u know Jesus as not just a great teacher, not just a miracle worker, not just your Saviour, but as the Great I Am in the flesh who became your sustenance, light, hope, salvation, and strength? Jesus said, "And you shall know the truth, and the truth shall make you free" (John 8:32).

Experience the truth and freedom of knowing who Jesus really is, and its significance to you personally and to a hurting world that needs Him.

What everyone must know about Jesus Christ

after looking at what the New Testament has to say about the Person of Jesus Christ, we can make a number of observations and identity.

1. Jesus Was Fully Divine

From the totality of Scripture, we find that Jesus Christ was fully Divine. The Bible says that He is the eternal Divine who has always existed, and always will exist. He is the Father's Son, the Second Person of the Holy Trinity. The Bible gives both direct and indirect evidence to this.

2. Jesus Was Fully Human

Though Jesus was Divine the Son for all eternity, He became human at a certain point in history. Indeed, He came to a specific nation as a member of the human race. While He was supernaturally conceived, everything about His birth, childhood, and humanity was normal.

In other words, He was not super-human. Christ experienced all the things other human beings experience. This means that Jesus was human in every sense of the term. Yet, there is one main difference between Jesus and the rest of us; He never sinned. Jesus went through His entire life without once breaking the laws of the Father. Therefore, while Jesus Christ was a human being, He was also perfect humanity.

3. The Incarnation Is a Mystery That We Cannot Completely Understand

How the Father could become human being with two natures, yet living in only One Person is not completely understandable to us. Father and the Son becoming like one of us is certainly a mystery; a mystery the Bible does not attempt to explain. Our responsibility is to accept what the Bible says about Jesus' deity as well as His humanity. In doing so, we must recognise that we will never fully understand this truth. It is important that we realise this.

4. Jesus Is Prophet, Priest and King

Jesus Christ has three offices; Prophet, Priest, and King. When the Son came to earth the first time, He came in the role of a prophet. He spoke the Father's truth to the people. However, His words were rejected. He was crucified on the cross of Calvary. His death on the cross was for the sins of the world. In other words, He died as our substitute.

Three days after His death on the cross, Jesus Christ rose from the dead. After appearing to certain people for some forty days, the risen Christ then ascended into heaven. Today, He intercedes for believers as our Great High Priest. He is the One through whom we pray. It is because of Jesus' role as our High Priest, that our prayers to the Father are heard.

Jesus' coming to earth is not the last time the world will see Him. There will come a time when He will return to earth. When Jesus returns a second time, He will return as King. He will set up His everlasting kingdom that will have no end.

This is a brief summary of what the Bible says about the identity of Jesus. While there are many other things we would like to understand about Him Scripture gives us sufficient information so that we can know who He is, what He has done on our behalf, and what He expects from us.

What Should We Conclude about the Identity of Jesus Christ?

After looking at what the New Testament teaches about Jesus Christ, there are a number of observations and conclusions which we can make concerning who He is.

From the Bible, we find that Jesus Christ was fully Devine and fully human. He is the living Devine, and the Son of the Father, who became human at a certain time in history. Before He came to this earth He had only one nature, a divine nature. When He came to this earth He took upon Himself something which He did not previously have, a human nature.

While this is the teaching of Scripture, it is not totally understandable to us. In other words, it is a mystery as to how the Devine could become a human. Our responsibility is not so much to understand this truth but rather to believe it. Scripture also teaches that the Son of the Father has three basic offices; at of a Prophet, Priest, and King.

Jesus Christ was a prophet, or a spokesman for thr Father, at His First Coming. He spoke the Father's truth to the people. Unfortunately, His prophetic words were rejected. Instead of receiving Him as the Promised Messiah, they put Him to death. However, death could not hold Him. Jesus came back from the dead three days after His death. He rose from the dead in a glorified body never to die again.

Presently, Jesus Christ is our Great High Priest. This means that He is interceding for us to the Father. It is because of Him, and what He has done, that we are able to have our prayers answered. When Jesus returns to the earth, He will return as King of Kings. At the time of His return, Jesus will set up His everlasting kingdom. He will remain King for all eternity.

This briefly sums up what the Bible says about the identity of Jesus Christ. Though we have many unanswered questions about Him what the Scripture does tell us is certainly sufficient. Our responsibility, therefore, is to learn what we can about Him and then act upon the things which we know are true. This is how we can live a life which is pleasure

Bottom of Form

13 Bible Verses about The I Am's Of Christ Most Relevant Verses.

John 4:26 Verse Concepts Jesus *said to her, "I who speak to you am He." John 6:35. Verse Concepts

Jesus said to them, "I am the bread of life; he who comes to Me will not hunger, and he who believes in Me will never thirst. John 8:23 Verse Concepts. And He was saying to them, "You are from below, I am from above; you are of this world, I am not of this world.nJohn 8:58 Verse Concepts

Jesus said to them, "Truly, truly, I say to you, before Abraham was born, I am. John 9:5 Verse Concepts. While I am in the world, I am the Light of the world." John 10:7 Verse Concepts. So Jesus said to them again, "Truly, truly, I say to you, I am the door of the sheep.

John 10:36 Verse Concepts do you say of Him, whom the Father sanctified and sent into the world, 'You are blaspheming,' because I said, 'I am the Son of the Father? John 11:25 Verse Concepts

Jesus said to her, "I am the resurrection and the life; he who believes in Me will live even if he dies, John 13:13 Verse Concepts. You call Me Teacher and Lord; and you are right, for so I am. John 14:6 Verse Concepts

Jesus *said to him, "I am the way, and the truth, and the life; no one comes to the Father but through Me. John 15:1 Verse Concepts "I am the true vine, and My Father is the vinedresser. Revelation 1:8 Verse Concepts "I am the Alpha and the Omega," says the Lord, "who is and who was and who is to come, the Almighty." Revelation 1:17 Verse Concepts

When I saw Him, I fell at His feet like a dead man. And He placed His right hand on me, saying, "Do not be afraid; I am the first and the last.

With the various recipients of miracles and/or crowds whom Jesus commands to "say nothing to anyone" (Mark 1:43) or "to tell no one" (7:36), the secrecy motif functions somewhat differently. As soon as Jesus appears on the scene, word starts spreading like wildfire about his teaching and miracles. With this comes all kinds of theories about who he is, including "Elijah . . . [or] one of the prophets from old" (6:15), a resurrected John the Baptist (6:14; 8:28), and/or a Davidic king who will reestablish Jerusalem's monarchy (11:10).

Thus, on the heels of various miracles, it seems Jesus commands silence with two objectives. First, he may be attempting to prolong his ability to travel due to ever-growing crowds (e.g. <u>Mark 6:53–56</u>). Indeed, regularly in Mark we see how Jesus seeks solitude but is thwarted by crowds—"he could not be hidden" (7:24). Second, he may have been mitigating the spread of (mis)information about him, to avoid raising the suspicions of his opponents (e.g., 6:14), and prevent things from spiraling out of hand before the right time. Ironically, however, "the more he charged them, the more zealously they proclaimed it" (7:36)!

In other words, for outsiders the secrecy motif relates to concealing who Jesus is—and *isn't*—until the proper time has arrived for his true revealing.

For Insiders (Disciples)

With Jesus' disciples the commands to silence take a different shape. The first instance comes after Peter proclaims Jesus to be "the Christ" (<u>Mark 8:29</u>)—at which Jesus "charged them to tell no one about him" (8:30). The second comes after the transfiguration scene (9:2–8)—at which Jesus "charged them to tell no one what they had seen" until after his resurrection (9:9). Both scenes feature a pivotal revelation of Jesus's identity: "Christ" (8:29, spoken by Peter) and "my beloved Son" (9:7, spoken by the Father).

For outsiders the secrecy motif relates to concealing who Jesus is—and *isn't*—until the proper time has arrived for his true revealing.

Why the command to silence?

At this stage in Jesus' ministry, he has begun to speak "plainly" (<u>Mark 8:32</u>) to his disciples so that they might understand "what was to happen to him" (10:32). Three times Jesus makes clear that his messianic mission—contrary to popular opinion—will entail rejection, death, and resurrection (8:31; 9:31; 10:33–34). Yes, he's a miracle worker, and the "Christ," and the "Son of Man." But the big "reveal" is that he came to die for sin.

The problem: the disciples simply don't get it. Peter rebukes Jesus, resulting in a counter-rebuke (Mark 8:32–33); "they did not understand the saying" (9:32); and James and John squabble about future privilege (10:35–41). Indeed, throughout Mark the disciples prove slow-minded and hard-hearted (4:13; 6:52; 8:17; 9:19).

Thus, Jesus commands them to be silent because they—despite his plain self-revealing—still struggle with incomprehension. For insiders, the secrecy motif highlights not how Jesus keeps his identity a secret, but rather how they have failed to grasp what he has revealed to them. It's not Jesus who is concealing truth, but their own hearts.

This makes Mark 16:8 all the more fitting: even after his resurrection, the female disciples "said nothing to anyone, for they were afraid." Mark's story ends with silence.

In sum, Jesus' commands to silence seem aimed at controlling the spread of *information* about Jesus as well as its *timing*: he is the Messiah and divine Son, but that is only fully revealed at his death and resurrection. Until then, the misunderstandings result in shrieking demons, spiraling crowds, and obtuse statements by the disciples.

But what about us as readers of Mark's Gospel? We know from the outset that Jesus is "Christ" as well as

"Son of the Father" (<u>Mark 1:1</u>). And we know how the story ends.

Yet we, too, struggle with incomprehension. We, like the crowds, may be attracted to the wonder-working Jesus and ignore his call to suffer. We, like the disciples, may want a "Christ" of our own design but not the dying one on the cross. We, too, may feel the inward pinch to "say nothing to anyone" about the Son of ther Father.

Let the secrecy motif of Mark, then, remind us that the secret is no more.

APPRECIATION TO CATHOLICISM

Whether wrongly or rightly, selfishly or otherwise, if Catholicism had not introduced and promoted Jesus Christ into the world as occurred, the mission and the wonderful work of our Lord Jesus Christ would have been left in the desert without recognition which have enabled Him to carry out His mission for salvation. This is because His own people the Jews rejected Him and His teachings of the truth for the benefits of human beings. The issue here is salvation would not depend on which denomination one belongs to as the Saviour Jesus Christ has made it clear that salvation belongs to anyone who will do His Father's will. Our Lord Jesus Christ the Saviour Himself revealed in **Matthew 7:21-23 thus** that, on the **judgement Day**: ".... Not everyone that saith unto me Lord, Lord, shall enter into the kingdom of heaven; but he that doeth the **"WILL"** of my Father who is in heaven."

PART THREE

THE REJECTION OF JESUS CHRIST BY THE JEWS

---- ❦ ----

CHAPTER 3

WHY DO MOST JEWS REJECT JESUS AS THEIR MESSIAH?

One of the saddest stories in the Bible is the story of the Jews rejecting their own Messiah. After spending millennia desperately waiting and anticipating His arrival, most Jews didn't recognise Him. The Jews of Jesus' time had studied the Old Testament Scriptures and knew who the Messiah was supposed to be: a political leader that expelled their enemies out of their territory, re-established the Jewish nation, and brought peace and prosperity back to them as chosen people. But that is not what Jesus came for. Although the prophecies of political peace are yet to be fulfilled in the millennial kingdom, Jesus' purpose on earth was to bring personal peace between people and the Father. Even more shocking, that peace was to be offered to the Gentiles just as freely as to the Jews.

If Jesus the person was incongruous to the Jews' idea of their Messiah, His teaching was more so. For the most part, Jesus taught a rather strict form of Judaism, enforcing narrow divorce laws and emphasising that He did not come to destroy the law. There were a few teachings, however, that devout Jews found hard to swallow.

The first was that He could forgive sins. Jews believe the forgiveness of sins is a much more involved process than one man's word. They also believe that if sins are forgiven so easily, it will only lead to more sin.

Secondly, Jesus' teaching to love our enemies and pray for them. This is anathema to the long-suffering Jews who have been persecuted so harshly by so many. It also sounds contradictory to laws in the Old Testament, such as Deuteronomy 17:7, which says to purge evil "from your midst." The disconnect was that Jesus was talking about personal relationships (which He had come to restore), not national policy (which the Jews thought He had come to restore). It is good and appropriate for a nation to have and enforce laws, and to go to war for just causes. Jesus taught that our own dealings should be filled with grace and mercy.

The Jews do not Accept the Teachings of Jesus especially on peace and the forgiveness.

Jews also do not accept Jesus' teaching that He is the only way to the Father. With a religious system based on restitution and sincere repentance, Jews have no need of an intermediary to reach the Fathe. They also don't understand the nature of forgiveness and salvation. Since they do not believe mankind has a sin nature, they do not believe any reasonable, attentive person can sin so much they cannot find forgiveness through their own effort.

The Jews rejected Jesus as Messiah

The Jews rejected Jesus as Messiah because it was absolutely inconceivable to them that the Lord came down as a man and dwelt among them. It was impossible that Lord should have a physical form, and complete heresy for any man to claim He was the Lord. Their pride in their strict adherence to theYahweh's law of the Old Testament blinded them to Who Jesus is.

Yahweh blinded the Jews to reject Jesus as their Messiah.

Since their release from Babylon the Jews have been worshipping their **Yahweh/god**. They knew the law and followed it. They waited expectantly for **Yahweh's Messiah**—a military leader who would herald a new age of prosperity. Something about that mindset made it historically imperative that belief in Jesus should *not* take hold over the Jewish population. Perhaps it would have curtailed the spread of the gospel to the Gentiles. Or maybe the in-place religious and political leaders would have influenced the budding Christianity too much. Paul says in Romans 9:30-32:

What shall we say, then? That Gentiles who did not pursue righteousness have attained it, that is, a righteousness that is by faith; but that Israel who pursued a law that would lead to righteousness did not succeed in reaching that law. Why? Because they did not pursue it by faith, but as if it were based on works. They have stumbled over the stumbling stone.

Their zeal for the law blinded them to the law-giver, as Romans 10:3 says, "For, being ignorant of the righteousness of Yahweh/god, and seeking to establish their own, they did not submit to righteousness." This is an old theme in the history of Israel, as the Old Testament can attest.

Most Jews today still reject Jesus, taking old habits and justifying them with modern philosophies. If there is no sin nature, there is no need for a sacrifice purer than human effort and intent. "Messiah" no longer means a single person, but a force through history that will revenge the Jewish people and restore Israel as a mighty power. If Jews had followed Jesus' pacifist ways, there would be no more Jews. There is also a great deal of tension regarding Jews and the crucifixion of Jesus. Many from the Christian church have blamed Jews, most viciously, for Jesus' horrible death. This is erroneous, as Jesus voluntarily laid down His life as a sacrifice for the sin of all mankind. But the corporate memory of a persecuted people is long, and violence in the name of "Jesus" has left a mark on Jewish thought.

Still, not all Jews, then or now, reject Jesus. The apostles were Jewish, and it's estimated that there are a quarter-million Messianic Jews in the U.S. today. And Israel as a nation still has a role to play. In the millennial kingdom, the Father will once again look to Jews who accept Jesus to be saved just like anyone else who would accept Jesus as their Lord and Saviour. Jews will flock to Israel (Ezekiel 34:11-13). They will come to accept Jesus as their Messiah (Zechariah 12:10) would be saved (Ezekiel 11:17). And Jesus will rule the world from Jerusalem (Isaiah 2:4), **bringing peace** to the nations (Isaiah 11:6-9). The Jews' rejection of Jesus is only until the "fullness of the Gentiles has come in" (Romans 11:25). May that be soon.

Further, the Jews rejected Jesus because He failed, in their eyes, to do what they expected their Messiah to do—destroy evil and all their enemies and establish an eternal kingdom with Israel as the preeminent nation in the world. The prophecies in Isaiah 53 and Psalm 22 describe a suffering Messiah who would be persecuted and killed, but the Jews chose to focus instead on those prophecies that discuss His glorious victories, not His crucifixion.

The commentaries in the Talmud, written before the onset of Christianity, clearly discuss the Messianic prophecies of Isaiah 53 and Psalm 22 and puzzle over how these would be fulfilled with the glorious setting up of the kingdom of the Messiah. After the church used these prophecies to prove the claims of Christ, the Jews took the position that the prophecies did not refer to the Messiah, but to Israel or some other person.

The Jews believed that the Messiah, the prophet which Moses spoke about, would come and deliver them from Roman bondage and set up a kingdom where they would be the rulers. Two of the disciples, James and John, even asked to sit at Jesus' right and left in His kingdom when He came into His glory. The people of Jerusalem also thought He would deliver them. They shouted praises to the Father in Heaven for the mighty works they had seen Jesus do and called out, "Hosanna, save us," when He rode into Jerusalem on a donkey (Matthew 21:9). They treated Him like a conquering king. Then, when He allowed Himself to be arrested, tried, and crucified on a cursed cross, the people stopped believing that He was the promised prophet. They rejected their Messiah (Matthew 27:22).

Note that Paul tells the church that the spiritual blindness of Israel is a "mystery" that had not previously been revealed (Romans chapters 9–11). For thousands of years, Israel had been the one nation that looked to the Father while the Gentile nations generally rejected the light and chose to live in spiritual darkness. Israel and her inspired prophets revealed Yahweh as monotheism—one elevated from

"god to God" who was personally interested in mankind's destiny of heaven or hell, the path to salvation, the written Word with the **plagiarised-Ten Commandments**. Yet Israel rejected her prophesied Messiah, and the promises of the kingdom of heaven were postponed. A veil of spiritual blindness fell upon the eyes of the Jews, who previously were the most spiritually discerning people. As Paul explained, this hardening on the part of Israel led to the blessing of the Gentiles who would believe in Jesus and accept Him as Lord and Saviour.

Two thousand years after He came to the nation of Israel as their Messiah, Christ is still (for the most part) rejected by the Jews. Many Jews today (some say at least half of all living Jews) identify themselves as Jewish but prefer to remain "secular." They identify with no particular Jewish movement and have no understanding or affiliation with any Jewish biblical roots. The concept of Messiah as expressed in the Hebrew Scriptures or Judaism's "13 Principles of Faith" is foreign to most Jews today.

But one concept is generally held as universal: Jews must have nothing to do with Jesus! Most Jews today perceive the last 2,000 years of historical Jewish persecution to be at the hands of so-called "Christians." From the Crusades, to the Inquisition, to the pogroms in Europe, to Hitler's Holocaust—Jews ultimately believe that they are being held responsible for the death of Jesus Christ and are being persecuted for that reason. They, therefore, reject Him today.

There are many Jews in the United States turning to Jesus Christ

The good news is that many Jews are turning to Christ today. The Father of Jesus in Heaven **and not, the Yahweh/**

god, shall save the believing Jews to Himself. In the United States alone, some estimates say that there are over 100,000 Jewish believers in Jesus, and the numbers are growing all the time.

Why Was Jesus Rejected at Nazareth? BY LAURA J. DAVIS

Have you ever wondered why the people in Jesus' hometown of Nazareth rejected him over a few little words? He had just finished reading the following to them:

> "The spirit of the Lord is upon me; because He hath anointed me to bring good tidings unto the humble; He hath sent me to bind up the brokenhearted, to proclaim liberty to the captives, and the opening of the eyes to them that are bound; To proclaim the year of HaShem's good pleasure."

> Isaiah 61:1-2, JPS

Now here is the interesting thing about these verses: In the Tanakh, the verses above are similar to what Jesus would have initially read. But in the Christian Bible, a few words are changed and added, which I have highlighted:

> "The Spirit of the Lord is upon me, because he hath anointed me to preach the gospel to the poor; he hath sent me to heal the brokenhearted, to preach deliverance to the captives, and recovering of sight to the blind, to set at liberty them that are bruised, to preach the acceptable year of the Lord."

> Luke 4:18-19, KJV

You will notice in the KJV that this phrase was added: "To set at liberty them that are bruised."

And you will also see in the NIV that one verse is entirely missing:

> **"The Spirit of the Lord is on me because he has anointed me to proclaim good news to the poor. He has sent me to proclaim freedom for the prisoners and recovery of sight for the blind, to set the oppressed free, to proclaim the year of the Lord's favour."**

> **Luke 4:18-19, NIV**

Why was Jesus rejected?

Naturally, my main question as to the changes and omissions is: why? Why would the NIV translators leave out the fact that Jesus came to "heal the brokenhearted?" Or why would the KJV add "*to set at liberty them that are bruised*?" Why would the translators of the New Testament change any of the words of Isaiah 61 at all? I have no answer for that, but I include these verses here to show you why it is so crucial to not rely on any one translation.

If you are studying the Old Testament, I highly recommend using the **Jewish Publication Society's 1917 edition of the Tanakh,** as it is the most reliable and, in cases like today's verses, ideal for cross-references.

Getting back to the verses at hand, after Jesus finished reading to the people, he said, **"Today this Scripture is fulfilled in your hearing."** And of course, everyone who heard him was impressed with this statement. In their minds, they thought he was going to help people by seeing what he could do to make their lives easier. They were thinking in physical terms. Being under oppressive Roman rule, they believed Jesus was going to do something about it. They didn't get the deeper picture of what he was saying, and they also missed the significance of where he stopped reading.

Why Did Jesus Stop Reading?

Jesus stopped in the middle of verse two. Why? Because what he was saying was a proclamation to all that the Lord was among them. The Messiah had come and was in their midst, **"To proclaim the year of HaShem's good pleasure."** The time had finally arrived for all to meet and receive their Messiah. Which was why Jesus didn't finish the verse, because if he had, he would also have been proclaiming **"The day of vengeance of our Lord; to comfort all that mourn."** He didn't come the first time to bring judgment or vengeance. He came to save us and bring salvation. That's why he didn't finish the verse. But look closely at his words and what he was saying:

> *"HaShem hath anointed me to bring good tidings unto the humble."*
>
> *Isaiah 61:1, JPS*

Most translations of Luke 4:18–19 say that the Lord had anointed Jesus to "preach *the gospel to the poor"* or *"proclaim good news to the poor."* They had changed the meaning of the Hebrew word `anav*, which means "humble, meek, lowly, or poor," and lost the original intent when they translated it from Hebrew to Greek. They used the word *ptōchos* instead, which means "poor, destitute, or indigent." So when Jesus said he had been anointed to preach good news to the poor, he meant the meek, the humble, those who realized they were not worthy in the Lord's eyes—the poor in spirit.

Who was Jesus Trying to Reach?

When Jesus preached his famous <u>Sermon on the Mount</u>, the first thing he said was, "Blessed are the poor in spirit" (Matthew 5:3). This is what he meant when he read <u>Isaiah 61:1-2</u>. He was anointed by HaShem to bring good news to those who saw their sin, regretted it, and wished there was a way to make themselves right with the Lord. Which is why the rest of what he said was so incredible! Just listen to what Jesus is offering for those who are poor in spirit:

- *"He hath sent me to bind up the brokenhearted."* "Bind up" literally means to "heal, bind, or bandage." In other words, Jesus came to fix those who are brokenhearted over their sin and who have lost hope of any reconciliation with the Lord. It's not about how your husband's infidelity betrayed your heart. This is about **spiritual** brokenness. Despair over sin, in particular.

- *"To proclaim liberty to the captives."* Jesus isn't promising freedom to those in prison for their crimes. He is promising freedom to all whose sin keeps them eternally separated from the Lord.

- *"And the opening of the eyes to them that are bound."* With freedom comes insight. Those who are bound in sin will have their eyes opened to see that only Jesus can set them free.

But when Jesus saw how the people were reacting to his words, he realized they didn't understand his meaning. So he needed to get their attention, and so he said, "**Verily, I say unto you, no prophet is accepted in his own country**" (Luke 4:24).

Imagine that you have known Jesus since he was a little boy. Your children grew up playing with him. Now here he is reading the Scriptures on the Sabbath, and you are impressed and delighted that he has chosen to serve the people.

But then you sit up, and you cock your head a little and think to yourself, "Did he just say he was a prophet?" So now you are listening a little closer. Then Jesus does the unthinkable. He compares everyone in the synagogue to the faithless Jews of Elijah and Elisha's time and suggests it would be Gentiles instead who would enjoy the blessings of Lord because the Jews would reject their prophet (Luke 4:25–27). Well, that got their attention big time. They were angry. How dare Jesus suggest that people like those idol-worshipping Romans would experience the Father's blessings? The **Jews were Yahweh/god's chosen p**eople, not the Gentiles

But the Jews were famous for rejecting the prophets the Lord sent them. Jesus knew their hearts, and he was aware that a vast majority of them would reject him. And in time, Jesus' prophecy would come true, when the Jewish nation, under the guidance of the Sanhedrin, would reject him as their Messiah by having him crucified. **But this rejection started in his hometown.**

Jesus wasn't trying to antagonize people on purpose. That wasn't his intent because, at other times, he dealt gently with people who were aware of their guilt and wanted to find forgiveness. **But this was his hometown.** These were "his people," so to speak. He knew their hearts, and like the Jews of Jeremiah's time, they believed they were saved simply because they were Yahweh/god's chosen people. Whether they sinned or not was irrelevant.

Are You Ignoring Lord's Voice?

Sometimes we act the same way when Lord is trying to talk to us. We ignore His voice or that inner warning when we know we have done wrong. Or we rush headlong into doing things our own way, even though we know better. We may even get caught up like the crowds in Nazareth who rushed to throw Jesus off a cliff (Luke 4:28–29). Or by accepting new teachings or doctrines without first checking them out against Scripture.

Jesus made his reasons clear for why he came:

- To bring good tidings to the humble
- To bind up the broken-hearted
- To proclaim liberty to the captives
- To open the eyes of those who are bound

These blessings come to all who recognize their sin and their need for a Saviour. Despite what many celebrity preachers claim, Jesus did not come to make us rich, nor did he come to make us feel better about ourselves. The gospel has nothing to do with "feel good" doctrines but has everything to do with recognising our sin and acknowledging that Jesus is the only way to be healed and made right with the Lord. Once you do that, everything else falls into place

Why Was Jesus Rejected in His Hometown?

"He went away from there and came to his hometown, and his disciples followed him. And on the Sabbath he began to teach in the synagogue, and many who heard him were astonished, saying, 'Where did this man get these things? What is the wisdom given to him? How are such mighty works done by his hands? Is not this the carpenter, the son of Mary and brother of James

and Joses and Judas and Simon? And are not his sisters here with us?' And they took offense at him. And Jesus said to them, 'A prophet is not without honour, except in his hometown and among his relatives and in his own household.' And he could do no mighty work there, except that he laid his hands on a few sick people and healed them. And he marveled because of their unbelief." - *Mark 6:1-6*

After Jesus restored Jairus' daughter to life with his healing touch, he and the disciples departed Capernaum and traveled 25 miles south to Nazareth. For Jesus, this was a homecoming, a chance to see his family and the friends with whom he was raised. We might expect the town to be excited about his visit and welcome Jesus as a local celebrity. After all, they would have heard all about how he taught with authority, healed diseases, drove out demons, and even calmed a storm. That's a fairly impressive resume!

And yet, the people of Nazareth greeted Jesus with skepticism and outrage. Others might be empowered by the Lord to perform such works, but this was Mary's Son. He grew up down the street, and they knew he was just a carpenter. While today we value the opportunity to achieve, advance, and make a new way in the world, the people of Jesus' day were defined by their families and their upbringing. Jesus did not come from a line of teachers and preachers; he was not a scribe or a priest. And so, the people took offense at what he was doing and who he claimed to be. They felt entitled to define Jesus according to their terms. In response to their unbelief, Jesus quoted the proverb about a prophet having no honor in his hometown. Not only did those words describe Jesus' reception in Nazareth, they foretold the rejection he would face in the future. Jesus knew that his popularity would be short-lived, that the religious leaders and teachers would continue to oppose and persecute him. In the meantime, the townspeople were unmoved and, as a result, Jesus could not do mighty works in their midst. Mark tells us he was only able to heal a few sick people during his visit.

There is irony in that last statement. The fact that anyone was healed by the laying on of hands was truly amazing, yet there was so much more Jesus could have done if only they had believed. Jairus and the hemorrhaging woman would attest that faith led to miracles. Jesus was looking for followers who would recognize their helplessness and turn to him with faith, hope, and expectation. Instead, the people of his hometown disparaged and dismissed him. As a result, they missed out on the joy and power of the kingdom and mighty works of Jesus. How does your skepticism keep you from experiencing the full and awesome power of Jesus? Have you sought to understand and define him from your earthly perspective? Faith is about surrender and trust.

Nazareth; or, Jesus Rejected by His Friends

And all they in the synagogue, when they heard these things, were filled with wrath, and rose up, and thrust him out of the city, and led him unto the brow of the hill whereon their city was built, that they might cast him down head long. But he passing through the midst of them went his way Luke 4:28-30.

JESUS had spent several years in retirement in the house of his reputed father at Nazareth. He must have been well known: the excellency of his character and conduct must have attracted notice. In the meantime He left Nazareth and went to be baptised by John in Jordan, and began at once his work of preaching and working wonders. The inhabitants of Nazareth, no doubt, often said one to another, "He will be sure to come home and see his parents; when he comes, we will all go to hear what the carpenter's son has to say." There is always an interest in hearing one of the lads of the village when he becomes a preacher, and this interest was heightened by the hope of seeing wonders, such as he had wrought at Capernaum. Curiosity was excited, everybody hoped and trusted that he would make Nazareth famous among the cities of the tribes; perhaps he would settle down there, and attract a crowd of customers to their shops by becoming the great Physician of Nazareth, the great Wonder-worker of the district. By-and-by, when it so pleased him, the famous Prophet came to his own city, and, when the Sabbath drew near, the interest grew very intense, as men asked the question, "What think you, will he be at the synagogue tomorrow? If he shall be there, he must by some means be induced to speak." The ruler of the synagogue, sharing in the common opinion, at the proper point of the service, when he saw Jesus present, took up the roll of the prophet and passed it to him, that he might read a passage, and then speak according to his own mind upon it. All eyes were opened; no sleepy people were in the synagogue that morning, when he took the roll, unfolded it like one who was well accustomed to the book, opened it at a passage most pertinent and applicable to himself, read it, standing, thus paying respect to the word by his posture; and then, when he had folded up the book, he took his seat, not because he had nothing to say, but because it was the good practice in those days for the preacher to sit down and the hearers to stand, a method much to be preferred to the present one in some respects, at any rate when the preacher is lame, or the hearers drowsy. The passage which Jesus read to them, I have said, was very suitable and applicable to himself; but the most remarkable point perhaps in it was not so much what he read, as what he did not read; for he pause 1 almost in the middle of a sentence: "To proclaim," said he, "the acceptable year of the Lord," and there he stopped. The passage is not complete unless you read the next words, "and the day of vengeance of our Our Lord" wisely ceased reading at those words, probably wishing that the first sermon he should deliver should be altogether gentle, and have in it not so much as a word of threatening. His heart's desire and prayer for them was that they might be saved, and that instead of a day of vengeance it might be to them the acceptable year of the Lord. So he folded the book, sat down, and then began his exposition by opening up his own commission. He explained who the blind were, who the captives were, who the sick and wounded and bruised were, and after what sort the grace of our Lord provided liberty and healing and salvation; they were all wonder struck; they had never heard any one speak so fluently and with so much force, so simply, and yet so nobly. All eyes were fastened, and everybody was astonished at the speaker's style and matter. Soon a buzz went round the synagogue, for each man said to his fellow, "Is not this the carpenter's son? is not his mother called Mary? and his brethren, James, and Joses, and Simon, and Judas? And his sisters, are they not all with us? Whence then hath this man all these things?" They were astonished and envious too. Then the speaker, feeling that it was not the object of his ministry to astonish people, but to impress their hearts, changed his subject, and charged with tremendous vigour upon their consciences; for if men will only give the minister their wonder, they have given him nothing. We desire you to be convinced, and converted, and short of this, we fail. Jesus turned from a subject so glowing with interest, so fruitful with every blessing, seeing that to them it was no more than pearls to swine, and he spoke to them personally, pointedly, somewhat cuttingly, as they thought. "Ye will surely say unto me this proverb, Physician, heal thyself: whatsoever we have heard done in Capernaum, do also here in thy country;" and then he plainly told them that he did not recognise their claims, that albeit he might have been bred in that district, and have lived with them, yet he did not recognise from that reason any obligation to display his power to suit their pleasure; and he gave an instance in point; he showed that Elijah (when Lord, "the father of the fatherless, and the judge of the widow," would bless a widow) was not sent to bless a widow of Israel, but a Gentile woman, a Syrophenician, one of the accursed Canaanites. To none of the widows of Israel "was Elias sent, save unto Sarepta, a city of Sidon, unto a woman that was a widow." Then, again, he mentioned that Elisha, the servant of Elijah, when he had healing to give to lepers, did not heal Israelitish lepers, he healed not even those lepers who came with the good news that the Syrian host had fled, but he healed a stranger from a far country, even Naaman. Thus the Saviour set forth the doctrine of sovereign grace; thus he declared himself to be free to do as he would with his own; and this, with other circumstances connected with the sermon, so excited the anger of the entire congregation, that those eyes which had looked upon him with wonder at first, now began to glare like the eyes of beasts, and those tongues which were ready to have given him applause, began to howl forth indignation. They rose up at once to slay the preacher; the curiosity of yesterday was turned into the indignation of to-day; and whereas, a few hours ago they would have welcomed the prophet to his own country, they would now think, "Crucify him! crucify him!" too good for him. They drag him out of the synagogue, breaking up their own worship, forgetful of the holiness of the day to which they paid such wonderful respect, and they haled him forth to cast him, as malefactors sometimes were from lofty rocks, from the brow of the hill whereon their city was built. He evaded them and escaped, but what a singular termination to such a beginning! Why, you and I would have said, What a fruitful field have we here! The best of preachers, and one of the most desirable of audiences — a people all attentive, every ear open, almost every mouth open, so wonder-struck are they with him, with his mode of address, and with what he has to say! There will be innumerable conversions here. Nazareth will become the stronghold of Christianity. It will be the very metropolis of the new faith. But no such thing: such is the perversity of human nature, that where we expect much, we get but little, and the field which should have brought forth wheat a hundredfold, yields nothing but thorns and thistles.

My design is, as the Lord may help me, to make an application of this narrative to the hearts and consciences of some now present, who are doing with the Saviour somewhat in the same manner as these men of Nazareth did with him in the days of his flesh. We shall consider, first of all, who were these rejectors of Christ; secondly, why this rejection; and thirdly, what came of it.

WHO WERE THESE REJECTORS OF CHRIST?

I ask the question because I am persuaded that they have their types and representatives here at the present moment.

They were, dear friends, first of all, those who were nearest related to the Saviour. They were the people of his own town. Ordinarily, you would expect fellow townsmen to show a man the most kindness. He was come unto his own, and though his own received him not, this was a subject of wonder that they should not do so. Now, there are some in this house this morning who are not Christians: they are no with Christ, and consequently they are against him; but still they are the nearest related to Christ of any unconverted people in the world, because from their childhood they have attended religious worship, they have joined in the songs, and prayers, and services of the Lord's house; moreover, they are fully persuaded of the authenticity and divinity of the word of the Father and they have no doubt but what the Saviour was sent from the Father, and that he can save, and is the appointed Saviour. They are not troubled with doubts, sceptical thoughts do not perplex them; they are, in fact, Agrippas, almost persuaded to be Christians. They are not Christians, but they are the nearest related to Christians of any people living upon the face of the earth. You would naturally expect that they would be the best people to preach to, but they have not proved to be so. They have not proved to be so in my case, for some such attending here are less likely to be brought to decision than those who are afar off. You know to whom I refer, for some of you, as you look me in the face, might well think, "Master, in saying so, thou rebukest us also."

These people of Nazareth, again, were those who blew most about Christ. They were well acquainted with his mother and the rest of his relatives. They knew his whole pedigree. They could tell at once that Joseph and Mary were of the tribe of Judah; probably could tell why they came from Bethlehem, and how it was that they once sojourned for a while in Egypt. The whole story of the wondrous child was known to them. Now, surely these people, not needing to be taught the rudiments, not requiring to be instructed in the very elements of the faith, must have been a very hopeful people for Jesus to preach to; but alas! They did not prove to be so. I have many here who are wonderfully like them. You know the whole story of the Saviour, and have known it ever since your childhood. More than that, the doctrines of the gospel are theoretically well understood by you. You can discuss gospel truths, and you delight to do so, for you take a deep interest in them. When you read the Scripture, it is not to you a dark, mysterious volume, which you cannot at all comprehend, but you are able to teach others which are the first principles of the truth; and yet, for all that, how strangely sad it is, that, knowing so much, you should practise so little. I am afraid that some of you know the gospel so well, that for this very reason it has lost much of its power with you, for it is as well known as a thrice-told tale. If you heard it for the first time, its very novelty would strike you, but such interest you cannot now feel. It is said of Whitfield's preaching, that one reason of its great success was, that he preached the gospel to people who had never heard it before. The gospel was to the masses of England in Whitfield's day, very much a new thing. The gospel had been either expunged from the church of England and from Dissenters' pulpits, or where it remained, it was with the few within the church, and was unknown to the masses outside. The simple gospel of "believe and live," was so great a novelty, that when Whitfield stood up in the fields to preach to his tens of thousands, they heard the gospel as if it were a new revelation fresh from the skies. But some of you have become gospel-hardened. It would be impossible to put it into a new shape for your ears. The angles, the corners of truth, have become worn off to you. Sundays follow Sundays, and you come up to this Tabernacle — you have been here long — you take your seats and go through the service, and it has as much become as mete a routine with you as your getting up and dressing yourselves of a morning. The Lord knows I do dread the influence of routine upon myself; I fear lest it should get to be a mere form with me to deal with your souls, and I pray the Lord he may deliver you and me from the deadly effect of religious routine. It were better if some of you would change your place of worship, rather than sleep in the old one. Go and hear somebody else, if you have heard me long and obtained no blessing. Sooner than get to sit in those pews and perish under the word, lulled by the gospel which is meant to arouse you, go elsewhere, and let some other voice speak to your ear, and let some other preacher see what the Lord may do by him. O may the Spirit of the Lord but save you, and it shall be equal joy to me whether you be saved under some one else, or under my own word. Yet here is the matter: it is sad indeed that men so nearly related to Christianity, who know so much about Christ, should yet reject the Redeemer.

Again, these were people who supposed that they had a claim upon Christ. They did not feel that it would be a great kindness on the part of the Lord Jesus to heal their sick. They no doubt argued, "He is a Nazareth man, and of course he is in duty bound to help Nazareth." They considered themselves as being in a sort his proprietors, who could command his powers at their own discretion. Our Saviour rejected that idea, and would not wear their yoke. I have sometimes feared that you who are children of godly parents, or seat-holders, or subscribers to various religious objects, in your hearts imagine that if any are to be saved, surely it must be yourselves, yet your claim has no basis to rest upon. I would to the Lord that ye were not only almost, but altogether saved, every one of you; but perhaps the very fact that you think you have a claim upon grace, may be the stone which lies in your path, because you think, "Surely Jesus Christ will cast an eye of favour upon us, even if others perish!" I tell you he will do as he wills with his own, and publicans and harlots will enter into the kingdom of heaven before some of you, if you think that you have any right to mercy; for the mercy of the Lord is the Lord's sovereign gift, and he will have you know it to be so. He has said it, said it as with a voice of thunder, "I will have mercy on whom I will have mercy, and I will have compassion on whom I will have compassion." If you kick against his sovereignty, you shall stumble at a stone upon which you shall be broken. Oh, but if you can feel you have no claim upon Lord, if you can put yourself into the position of the publican who dared not lift up so much as his eyes towards heaven, but smote upon his breast, saying, "Lord be merciful to me a sinner," you are in a position in which the Lord can bless you, consistently with the dignity of his own sovereignty. O take up the position which grace accepts. Beggars, and such you must be, must not be choosers. He who asks for grace, must not set himself up to dictate to the Lord; he who would be saved, though he be unworthy, must come to the Lord upon the footing of a suppliant, and humbly plead that for mercy's sake, the Lord's love would be manifested towards him. I fear that there may be a spice of this kind of spirit in the minds of some of you, and if so, you are the people who have rejected Christ. Hear, O heavens, and give ear, O earth! We call the skies, and the round earth to witness, here are those that are near to being Christians, who know the gospel by the letter of it, and who think they have a claim upon the Saviour, who yet remain disobedient to the divine command, "Believe and live:" they turn upon their heel and reject the Saviour, and will not come unto him that they might have life. Hear it, I say, O heavens, and be astonished, O earth!

WHY THEY THUS REJECT THE MESSIAH.

The reasons will be applicable to some of you, ye unconverted people, who are sitting here. Sometimes the Spirit of the Lord comes with a melting power over an audience, and makes men feel the truth which is meant for them. Pray, my dear brethren in Christ, that such may be the case now; that our unconverted friends, who give us so much concern because of their enmity to Jesus, maybe impressed with the remonstrances now addressed to them. Why did they reject Christ? I think they did so under a very complex feeling, not to be accounted for by one circumstance. Several things went to make up their wrath and enmity. The fire of their anger fed upon several kinds of fuel.

In the first place, I should not wonder but what the groundwork of their dissatisfaction was laid in the fact that they did not feel themselves to be the persons to whom the Saviour claimed to have a commission. Observe, he said, in the eighteenth verse, that he was "anointed to preach the gospel to the poor." Now, the poorest ones in the synagogue may have felt pleased at that word; but as it was almost a maxim with the Jewish doctors that it did not signify what became of the poor—for few but the rich could enter heaven—the very announcement of a gospel for the poor must have sounded to them awfully democratical and extreme, and must have laid in their minds the foundation of a prejudice. He meant, of course, the "poor in spirit," whether they are poor in pocket or not, for those are the poor whom Jesus comes to bless; but the use of expressions so contrary to all that they had been accustomed to hear made them bite their lips, while they said within themselves, "We are not poor in spirit; have not we kept the law?" Did not some of them say, "We have worn our phylacteries, and made broad the borders of our garments; we have not eaten except with washen hands; we have strained out all gnats from our wine; we have kept the fasts, and the feasts, and we have made long prayers, why should we feel any poverty of spirit?" Hence they felt there was nothing in Christ's mission for them. When he next mentioned the broken-hearted, they were not at all conscious of any need of a broken heart. They felt heart-whole, self-satisfied, perfectly content. What is the use of a preacher? Who is to preach to the broken-hearted when all his hearers feel that they have no cause to rend their hearts with repentance? Then when he spoke of captives, they claimed to have been born free and not to have been in bondage to any man; they rejected with scorn the very idea that they needed any liberator, for they were as free as free could be. When Jesus farther spake of the blind — "Blind!" said they, "does he insult us? We are far-seeing men — blind 1 Let him go and preach to some of the outcasts who have become blinded, but as for us, we can see into the very depths of all mysteries. We need no instruction and opening of eyes from him." When at last he spake of those who had been bruised, as though they had been beaten with stripes for their sins — "We have no sins," said they, "for which we should be braised; we have been honourable, upright people, and never have been chastened by the scourge of the law; we want no liberty for them that are bruised. What is the acceptable year of the Lord to us, if it is only for bruised captive ones? We are not such." At a glance you perceive, my brethren the reason why in these days Jesus Christ is rejected by so many church-going and chapel-going people. Here you see the reason why so many of your respectable attendants at our places of worship reject salvation by grace; it is because they do not feel that they need a Saviour. They think that they are rich and increased in goods, and have need of nothing; but they know not that they are naked, and poor, and miserable. They claim to be intelligent, thoughtful, and enlightened; they do not know that until a man sees Christ he walks in darkness and is stone blind, and beholdeth no light. They are not bruised, they say. The Lord perhaps has left them, because it was of no avail to bruise them; and why should they be smitten any more? They only revolt more and more. Because they feel no smarts of conscience, no terrors of the Lord's law, therefore Jesus Christ is a root out of a dry ground to them. They despise him, as the healthy man laughs at the physician, and as the man that is rich cares not for the alms of the benevolent. Ah I but my dear friends, let me remind you that if you do not feel your need of a Saviour, that need exists for all that, though you do not see it. You were born in sin and shapen in iniquity, and no baptismal waters can wash away your defilement. Beside this, you have sinned from your youth up in heart, and word, and thought; and you are condemned already, because you have not believed on the Son of the Father. Although you may not have been openly wicked, yet there is a text which I must needs bring to your remembrance — "The wicked shall be turned into hell with all the nations that forget the Lord." That last list includes you, my hearer— you who forget, and postpone, and trifle, who wait for "a more convenient season;" you who live with the gospel before you, and yet do not comply with its commands, but say to your sins, "I love you too well to repent of you," and to your self-righteousness, "I am too fond of this foundation to leave it to build upon the foundation which Lord has laid in the person of his dear Son. Ah! my dear hearers, it is the self-conceit which makes the empty bag think itself full, which makes the hungry man dream that he has feasted and is satisfied. It is self-righteousness which damns the souls of thousands. There is nothing so ruinous as this presumptuous self-confidence, I pray the Lord may make you feel yourself to be undone, ruined, lost, cast away, and then there is no fear of your rejecting Christ, for he that is perfectly bankrupt is willing to accept a Saviour; he that has nothing of his own, falls flat before the cross, and takes gladly the "all things" which are stored up in the Lord Jesus. This is the first and perhaps the greatest reason why men reject the Saviour.

But, secondly, I entertain little doubt but what the men of Nazareth were angry with Christ because of his exceedingly high claims. He said, "The Spirit of Jehovah is upon me." They started at that. Yet they might be willing to admit that he was a prophet, and so, if he meant it in that sense, they would be patient, but when he said, "The Lord hath anointed me to preach," and so on, claiming to be no other than the promised Messiah, they shook their heads, and murmuringly said, "He claims too much." When he placed himself side by side with Elijah and Elisha, and claimed to have the same rights and the same spirit as those famous ones, and by inference compared his hearers to the worshippers of Baal in Elijah's day, then they felt as if he set himself up too high, and put them down too low. And here, again, I see another master reason why so many of you good people, as you would be thought to be, reject my Lord and Master. He sets himself too high: he asks too much of you: he puts you down too low. He tells you you must be nothing, and he must be everything. He tells you that you must give up that idol god of yours, the world, and the pleasures thereof, and that he must be your Master, and not your own wills. He tells you that you must pluck out the right eye of pleasure, if it comes in the way of holiness, and rend off the right arm of profit rather than commit sin. He tells you that you must take up your cross and follow him without the camp, leaving the world's religion and the world's irreligion, being no longer conformed to the world, but becoming in a sacred sense a Nonconformist to all its vanities and maxims, customs and sins. He tells you that he must be the Prince Imperial in your souls, and that you must be his willing servants and his loving disciples. These are claims too high for human nature to yield to them; and yet, dear hearer, remember that if you do not yield to them, a much worse thing awaits you. Kiss the Son, kiss his sceptre now, I say. Now bow down and acknowledge him, for if not, beware "lest he be angry, and ye perish from the way, when his wrath is kindled but a little." Those who kiss not the sceptre of silver, shall be broken with the rod of iron. They who will not have Christ to reign over them in love, shall have him to rule over them in terror in the day when he puts on the garments of vengeance, and dyes his vesture in the blood of his foes. Acknowledge him as he is covered with his own blood, lest you have to acknowledge him when he is covered with yours! Accept him while you may, for you will not be able to escape from him when those eyes, which are like eyes of fire, shall flash devouring flame upon his adversaries! Alas! this is a fruitful source of mischief to the sons of men: they cannot give King Jesus his due, but would fain thrust the Lord of glory into so great, so good a King!

Thirdly, another reason might be found in the fact that they were not for receiving Christ until fie had exhibited some great wonder. They craved for miracles. Their minds were in a sickly state. The gospel which they did want, they would not have; the miracles which he did not choose to give, they eagerly demanded. Oh! how many there are nowadays who must see signs and wonders, or else they will not believe 1 I know you, young woman, you have set in your heart this before you, "I must feel as John Bunyan felt— the same horror of conscience, the same gloom of soul, or else I never will believe in Jesus." But what if you never should feel it, as probably you never may? Will you go to hell out of spite with the Lord, because he will not do for you just what he did for another? A young man yonder has said to himself, "If I had a dream, as I hear So-and-so had, or if there should happen to me some very remarkable event in providence, which should just meet my taste; or if I could feel to-day some sudden shock of I know not what, then I would believe." Thus you dream that my Lord and Master is to be dictated to by you! You are beggars at his gate, asking for mercy, and you must needs draw up rules and regulations as to how he shall give that mercy. Think you that he will ever submit to this? My Master is of a generous spirit, but he has a right royal heart, and he spurns all dictation, and maintains his sovereignty of action. But why, dear hearer, do you crave for signs and wonders? Is it not enough of a wonder that Jesus bids you trust him, and promises that you shall be saved at once? Is not this enough of a sign that Lord has proposed so wise a gospel as that of "Believe, and live"? Is not this enough— is not the gospel its own sign, its own wonder, and its own proof, because he that believeth hath everlasting life? Is not this a miracle of miracles, that "the Lord so loved the world that he gave his only begotten Son, that whosoever believeth in him might not perish"? Surely that precious word, "Whosoever will, let him come and take the water of life freely," and that solemn promise, "Him that cometh unto me, I will in nowise cast out," those are better than signs and wonders. A truthful Saviour ought to be believed. He never did lie. Why will you ask proof of the veracity of one who cannot lie? The devils themselves declared him to be the Son of the Father; but will you stand out against him? Sovereign, mighty, irresistible grace, come and conquer this wickedness in the hearts of men, and make them willing to trust Jesus, whether they see signs and wonders or not.

Again, and perhaps this time I may hit the head of the nail in some cases, though I suppose not in many in this place: part of the irritation which existed in the minds of the men of Nazareth was caused by the peculiar doctrine which the Saviour preached upon the subject of election. I question whether that was not at bottom the real sting of the whole matter; he laid it down that the Lord had a right to dispense his favours just as he pleased; that in doing so he often selected the most unlikely objects: that for instance, a widow away in idolatrous Sidon, had her wants supplied in famine, while the widows of Israel were left without meal: that at another time under Elisha, when the Lord would heal a leper, he left the Israelitish lepers to die, but a leper who came from the idolatrous land of Assyria, and who had been accustomed to bow in the house of Rimmon, received healing. Now, they did not like this, and I suppose even in this congregation, though you are pretty well accustomed to strong statements upon the sovereignty of the Father, and we are not ashamed to preach predestination and election as clearly as we preach any doctrine, yet there are some who are mightily uneasy when, the doctrine is mooted, and feel as if they could almost slay the preacher, because the doctrine is so offensive to human nature. Everywhere you will notice that the Church of Rome has not half the hatred to

Luther:
Calvinism.

It is the doctrine of grace, which is the soul of Calvinism, that is the poison of Popery; it cannot endure the truth that the Lord will save where he wills; that he has not given salvation into the hands of priests, nor given it to our own merit or our own will to save us. The Lord holds the keys of the casket of grace, and distributes as he pleases. This is the doctrine which makes men so angry, that they know not what to say of it; but, my dear hearer, I trust this is not the reason why you refuse to believe in Jesus, for if it be, it is a most foolish reason, for while this is true, there is yet another truth that "Whosoever believeth in Jesus Christ, shall not perish." While it is true that the Lord will have mercy on whom he will have mercy, it is equally true that he wills to have mercy, and has already had mercy on every soul that repenteth of its sin, and that puts its trust in Jesus. Wherefore cavil at a truth because you cannot understand it? Why kick ye against the pricks to your own wounding, when the pricks remain as sharp as ever, and will not be moved by all your kicking. The Lord of Hosts hath purposed it to stain the pride of all glory, and to bring into contempt all the excellency of the earth: "It is not of him that willeth, nor of him that runneth, but of the Lord that showeth mercy." The Lord will bring down the high tree, dry up the green tree, and make the dry tree to flourish, that no flesh may glory in his presence, but that the Lord may be exalted. Bow, then, to sovereign grace! Should he not be King? Who else should rule but the Lord? And if he be a King, has he not a right to forgive the felon condemned to die, and yet give no reason to you? Leave that question, and all others, and come to Jesus, whose open arms invite you. He saith, "Come unto me, all ye that labour and are heavy laden, and I will give you rest." If you wait till you have solved all difficulties, you will never come at all. If you refuse Christ till you understand all mysteries, you will perish in your sins. Come while the gate is opened and while the lamp holds out to burn, and he hath said it, "Him that cometh unto me, I will in nowise cast out."

I must still mention another reason for the quarrel of the Nazarenes with our Lord: it was probably because they loved not such plain, personal speaking as the Saviour gave them. Some hearers affect great delicacy. You must not call a spade a "spade;" it is an "agricultural implement," and only to be spoken of in dainty terms. But our Lord used no fine talk, He was a plain speaking man, and he spoke to men plainly. He knew that men would go to hell, let him be as plain as he might, and therefore he would not let them have the excuse that they could not understand the preacher. He put the truth so clearly that not only could they understand it, but they could not misunderstand it if they tried. His preaching was most personal. "Ye will say." He did not speak about Capernaum, but all about Nazareth, and this helped also to make them angry.

Once again, he gave a hint that he meant to bless the Gentiles. Elijah had fed and Elisha had healed a Gentile, and this undoubted fact made the Jew set his teeth, for he feared that the monopoly of blessing was to cease, and that gifts of grace were to be given to others besides the sons of Israel. A Gentile dog was to be admitted into the family, to be permitted not only to eat the crumbs that fell from the table, but to be changed into a child: the Jews could not bear it. Now, there is a great deal of this monopolising spirit among self-righteous people. Why, I have heard people say — shocked I have been to hear it — "Oh! they are having meetings for getting together these girls off the street. It is no use — you may try; it is no use trying to reform them. And then here are other people looking after these low characters, going into those nasty back slums. Well, if people get there, they ought to be there; we ought not to lower ourselves to look after such good-for-nothing people. There is the church, if they do not choose to go, let them stop away." turn up their noses at old Jewish monopolising of the gospel; as if these people were not as good as you, for all their sins and for all their poverty; for though their vice may happen to be outward, it is not a whit more detestable than the pride of some people which makes a boast of a self-righteousness which does not exist. I do not know which the Lord looks upon with the greatest abhorrence, the open sinner or the openly good living person whose inward pride stands out against the gospel. It matters nothing to the physician whether he sees the eruption outside the skin or knows it to be inside; perhaps he thinks it may be harder to get at the second than at the first Now, our Lord Jesus Christ will have you to know, however good you are, that you must come to him just as the vilest of the vile must come. You must come as guilty — you cannot come as righteous; you must come to Jesus to be washed; you must come to him to be clothed. You think you do not want washing; you fancy you are clothed, and covered, and beautiful to look upon; but oh! the garb of outward respectability, and of outward morality, often is nothing but a film to hide an abominable leprosy, till the Lord's grace changes the heart. The Lord requireth truth in the inward parts, and in the hidden part he will make us to know wisdom; but this superficial England of ours is perfectly satisfied with outside gentility, and you may be as rotten as you will within the heart. The living God will have no pretence, you must be born again. This doctrine, again, is one which people cannot endure, and all hard things will they say of the preacher, and for this reason they reject Christ, but in so doing they reject their own mercy, they reject the only hope of heaven, and they seal their own destruction.

And now, WHAT CAME OF IT?

This came of it. First of all, they thrust the Saviour out of the synagogue, and then they tried to hurl him down the brow of the hill. These were his friends, good, respectable people: who would have believed it of them? You saw that goodly company in the synagogue who sang so sweetly, and listened so attentively, would you have guessed that there was a murderer inside every one of their coats? It only needed the opportunity to bring the murderer out; for there they are all trying to throw Jesus down the hill. We do not know how much devil there is inside any one of us; if we are not renewed and changed by grace, we are heirs of wrath even as others. The description which is given in the Romans, that second chapter, that awful chapter, is a truthful picture of every child of Adam. He may look respectable; he may seem to be a lamb, and to be so quiet that a weaned child might play on the cockatrice's den; but he is a deadly cockatrice for all that. The snake may sleep, and you may play with it, but let it wake, and you will see that it is a deadly thing. Sin may lie dormant in the soul, but there may come a time when it will wake up; and there may come a time in England when those good people who hang on to the skirts of Christ, and attend our places of worship, may actually develop into persecutors. It was so in England. The people who used to hear the gospel at the close of Henry the Eighth's day — the people that were so pleased to hear Hugh Latimer under Edward the Sixth, were quite as ready to carry a fagot under Queen Mary, and to burn the servants of the Lord. My dear friends, your opposition to Christ may not take that active form, but unless you are converted you are enemies to Jesus. You deny it! I ask you why then do you not believe in him? Why do you not trust him? You are not opposed to him, why do not you yield to him? But so long as you do not trust him, I can only set you down as his enemy. You give this clearest proof of it, that you will not even be saved by him. If there were a man drowning, and another man put out his hand, and he said, "No, I will not be saved by you, I would sooner be drowned," what a proof that would be of enmity! What proof could be surer That is your case, you refuse to be saved by Christ's grace. Oh, what an enemy of Christ at the bottom of your heart you must be!

But what came of it? Why, though they thus thrust him out, they could not hurt the Saviour. The hurt was all their own. Christ did not fall from the hill; he escaped by his miraculous power: and the gospel will not be hurt even though you reject it, and do worse than reject it — set yourself in opposition to it. Jesus Christ glides through the midst of his enemies uninjured. Through the persecutions of Nero, and Diocletian, the true Christ of the Lord went on his way. Through all the burnings of Mary, and the hangings of Elizabeth, right on through the times of Claverhouse and his dragoons, the good old gospel remained unconquered by its foes. It abides still to this very day the same: it escapes from all the anger of its most virulent foes. But what became of them? Well, they had rejected Christ, and he left them, left them unhealed because of their unbelief — that will be your case. And now it is one thousand eight hundred and sixty years ago, and the souls of all these men of Nazareth have appeared before the judgment-seat; and in a few more years, when the great trumpet shall sound, all those men who tried to throw him down the brow of the hill will have to look at him; and they will see him seated where they cannot grasp him, nor abuse him, nor cast him down. What a sight it will be for them! Will they say to one another, "Is not this Joseph's son?" When they see him sitting on the throne of his glory, and all his holy angels with him, will they say, "His mother, is she not with us, and his brothers and his sisters?" Will they then say to him, "Physician, heal thyself"? Oh, what a change will come over those brazen brows! How for every sneer there will be a blush, and for each word of anger there will be cries, and weeping, and wailings, and gnashings of teeth! My hearers, the same thing will happen to you. Within a few more years, you and I will have mixed our bones with mother earth, and then after that shall come a general resurrection, and we shall live and stand in the latter days upon the earth, and Christ will come in the clouds of heaven, and you who heard the gospel and despised him, what will you say? Have your apology ready, for you will soon be called upon to say why judgment should not be pronounced upon you. You cannot say you did not know the gospel, or that you were not warned of the result of rejecting it: you have known, what more could you have known? But your heart would not receive what you knew. When the Lord begins to say, "Depart, ye cursed," what claim will you have not to be numbered with that accursed company? It will be in vain to say, "We have eaten and drunk in thy presence, and thou hast taught in our streets," for that will be an aggravation that the kingdom of heaven came so nigh unto you, and yet you received it not. And when the thunderbolts are launched, and he who was once the Lamb so full of mercy, shall shine forth as the Lion of the tribe of Judah, full of majesty, that thunderbolt shall be winged with extra force and speed with this tremendous fact — that you rejected Christ, that you heard him, but turned a deaf ear to him; that you neglected the great salvation, and did despite to the Spirit of grace. As I cannot even hope to find words that can have the force of the Lord's own language, I shall close this sermon by reading you these few words, which I beg you to lay to your heart. They are in the first chapter of Proverbs, at the twenty fourth verse: "Because I have called, and ye refused; I have stretched out my hand, and no mail regarded; but ye have set at nought all my counsel, and would none of my reproof: I also will laugh at your calamity; I will mock when your fear cometh; when your fear cometh as desolation, and your destruction cometh as a whirlwind; when distress and anguish cometh upon you. Then shall they call upon me, but I will not answer; they shall seek me early, but they shall not find Eme: for that they hated knowledge, and did not choose the fear of the Lord: they would none of my counsel: they despised all my reproof. Therefore shall they eat of the fruit of their own way, and be filled with their own devices."

PART FOUR

IMPORTANCE OF EFFECTIVE PRAYER

CHAPTER 4

THE PURPOSE OF PRAYING TO CHRIST

This chapter accesses the compelling question about the reasons some prayers are answered very quickly, some take a long time whilst others virtually unanswered. And yet Jesus Christ assures the believers with faith to Ask, Seek and Knock in Matthew 7: 7-11 and that whosoever "Asks and it will be given to you; seek and you will find; knock and the door will be opened to you. For everyone who asks receives; the one who seeks finds; and to the one who knocks, the door will be opened.

"Which of you, if your son asks for bread, will give him a stone? Or if he asks for a fish, will give him a snake? If you, then, though you are evil, know how to give good gifts to your children, how much more will your Father in heaven give good gifts to those who ask him!

In 1John 5: 14-15 we hear further revelation on prayer, "This is the confidence we have in approaching Jesus: that if we ask anything according to his will, he hears us. And if we know that he hears us—whatever we ask—we know that we have what we asked of him.

One of the most important questions believers want an answer from the Creator Father is the **"WILL"** that the Saviour Jesus Christ demands of them to do in order to be saved, this is because **SALVATION** is paramount for every believer to enter the Kingdom of the Father. The seriousness of knowing what the **"WILL"** is and thus how to do the **WILL** of the Father in heaven to be saved is very crucial instead of having faith in Christ the Saviour. This is affirmed in **Matthew 7: 21-23** as described below. What kind of prayer that the Father says "YES" to? And if He says "YES" the next question is how quickly? And if no why not, and if not very often then what must be the reason? What kind of prayers the Lord would answer? Must we blame the Father for not answering our prayer because we serve Him? This is the issue.

As described earlier, the one most crucial question on salvation is the kind of the heavenly Father's **"WILL"** required to be done in order to be saved demanded by Christ the Saviour. The question is what is the **'WILL'** of the Creator Lord that needs to be done in order to be saved, as stressed by Our Lord Jesus Christ the Saviour Himself, as in **Matthew 7:21-23?** Jesus Christ revealed that, on the **judgement Day**: '…. Not everyone that saith unto me Lord, Lord, shall enter into the kingdom of heaven; but he that doeth the **"WILL"** of my Father which is in heaven', in the King James Version of the Bible. The importance of doing the **"WILL"** of the Father in heaven has also been stressed by Our Lord Jesus Christ when He gave the **Lord's Prayer** to His Disciple that … thy **"WLL"** be done on earth as it is done in heaven" The author, in this respect, has methodically put together a popular thought for pondering without provoking thought. However people may suggest not another book on **salvation**, surely! But, yes, with the difference. The book, in its critical sense, enquires into the most popular belief held by many Christians that, to be **saved** is by being Born Again in **John 3: 3-5**, paying tithes, being baptised as in **Mark 16: 15-16** (whoever believes and is **baptised** will be saved), and many others but above all, it's by faith and not by work. But, as indicated above, it's by doing the '**WILL**' of the Father, is the most crucial. In this respect, I carried out a survey to gather some reliable information with regards to this prevailing matter as stressed by our Lord Jesus Christ the Saviour regarding the **"WILL"** of the Father.

What is the 'WILL' of the Father in heaven that requires to be done, in order to be saved in Matthew 7: 21-23? So the book is for the reader to have an open mind with critical thought. The querying of the statue quo is being demanded because my old professor insists thus: "If you don't question ideology you would die of ignorance."

Knowing and Understanding
The Miracles of Jesus

The most important key to a vibrant prayer life is to understand our spiritual authority in Christ as explained in the Scriptures. The only way to do that is to become intimately familiar with the Bible. Even a few minutes a day in the Word of the Father will add strength and authority your prayers. The miracles of Jesus are miraculous deeds attributed to Jesus in Christian and Islamic texts. The majority are faith healings, exorcisms, resurrections, and control over nature. In the Gospel of John, Jesus is said to have performed seven miraculous signs that characterize his ministry, from changing water into wine at the start of his ministry to raising Lazarus from the dead at the end. For many Christians and Muslims, the miracles are actual historical events. Others, including many liberal Christians, consider these stories to be figurative. Since the Enlightenment, many scholars have taken a highly skeptical approach to claims about miracles. In most cases, Christian authors associate each miracle with specific teachings that reflect the message of Jesus. In *The Miracles of Jesus*, H. Van der Loos describes two main categories of miracles attributed to Jesus: those that affected people (such as Jesus healing the blind man of Bethsaida), or "healings", and those that "controlled nature" (such as Jesus walking on water). The three types of healings are cures, in which an ailment is miraculous remedied, exorcisms, in which demons are cast out of victims, and the resurrection of the dead. Karl Barth said that, among these miracles, the Transfiguration of Jesus is unique in that the miracle happens to Jesus himself.

According to Craig Blomberg, one characteristic shared among all miracles of Jesus in the Gospel accounts is that he delivered benefits freely and never requested or accepted any form of payment for his healing miracles, unlike some high priests of his time who charged those who were healed. In Matthew 10:8 he advised his disciples to heal the sick without payment and stated, "Freely ye received, freely give."

It is not always clear when two reported miracles refer to the same event. For example, in the healing the centurion's servant, the Gospels of Matthew and Luke narrate how Jesus healed the servant of a centurion in Capernaum at a distance. The Gospel of John has a similar but slightly different account at Capernaum and states that it was the son of a royal official who was cured at a distance.

Cures

The largest group of miracles mentioned in the New Testament involves cures. The Gospels give varying amounts of detail for each episode, sometimes Jesus cures simply by saying a few words, at other times, he employs material such as spit and mud. And as per Luke 4:40, "…all those who…were sick…were brought to Him, and He laid His hands on every one of them and healed them."

Blind people

The canonical Gospels contain a number of stories about Jesus healing blind people. The earliest is a story of the healing of a blind man in Bethsaida in the Gospel of Mark.

Mark's gospel gives an account of Jesus healing a blind man named Bartimaeus as Jesus is leaving Jericho. The Gospel of Matthew has a simpler account loosely based on this, with two unnamed blind men instead of one (this "doubling" is a characteristic of Matthew's treatment of Mark's text) and a slightly different version of the story, taking place in Galilee, earlier in the narrative. The Gospel of Luke tells the same story of Jesus healing an unnamed blind man but moves the event in the narrative to when Jesus approaches Jericho.

The Gospel of John describes an episode in which Jesus heals a man blind from birth, placed during the Festival of Tabernacles, about six months before his crucifixion. Jesus mixes spittle with dirt to make a mud mixture, which he then places on the man's eyes. He instructs the man to wash his eyes in the Pool of Siloam. When the man does this, he is able to see. When asked by his disciples whether the cause of the blindness was the man's sins or his parents' sins, Jesus states that it was due to neither.

Lepers

A story in which Jesus cures a leper appears in Mark 1:40–45, Matthew 8:1–4 and Luke 5:12–16. Having cured the man, Jesus instructs him to offer the requisite ritual sacrifices as prescribed by the Deuteronomic Code and Priestly Code and to not tell anyone who had healed him. But the man disobeyed, increasing Jesus's fame, and thereafter Jesus withdrew to deserted places but was followed there.

In an episode in the Gospel of Luke Luke 17:11–19, while on his way to Jerusalem, Jesus sends ten lepers who sought his assistance to the priests, and they were healed as they go, but the only one who comes back to thank Jesus is a Samaritan.

Paralytics

Healing the paralytic at Capernaum appears in Matthew 9:1–8, Mark 2:1–12 and Luke 5:17–26. The Synoptics state that a paralytic was brought to Jesus on a mat; Jesus told him to *get up and walk*, and the man did so. Jesus also told the man that his sins were forgiven, which irritated the Pharisees. Jesus is described as responding to the anger by asking whether it is easier to say that someone's sins are forgiven, or to tell the man to *get up and walk*. Mark and Luke state that Jesus was in a house at the time, and that the man had to be lowered through the roof by his friends due to the crowds blocking the door.

A similar cure is described in the Gospel of John as the healing the paralytic at Bethesda[21] and occurs at the Pool of Bethesda. In this cure Jesus also tells the man to take his mat and walk.

Women

The curing of a bleeding woman appears in Mark 5:21–43, Matthew 9:18–26 and Luke 8:40–56, along with the miracle of the daughter of Jairus. The Gospels state that while heading to Jairus's house, Jesus was approached by a woman who had been bleeding for 12 years and that she touched Jesus's cloak (fringes of his garment) and was instantly healed. Jesus turned about and, when the woman came forward, said, "Daughter, your faith has healed you, go in peace".

The Synoptics describe Jesus as healing the mother-in-law of Simon Peter when he visited Simon's house in Capernaum, around the time of Jesus recruiting Simon as an Apostle (Mark records the event occurring just after the calling of Simon, while Luke records it just before). The Synoptics imply that this led other people to seek out Jesus.

Jesus healing an infirm woman appears in Luke 13:10–17. While teaching in a synagogue on the Sabbath, Jesus cured a woman who had been crippled by a spirit for eighteen years and could not stand straight at all.

Other healing

The healing of a man with dropsy is described in Luke 14:1–6. In this miracle, Jesus cured a man with dropsy at the house of a prominent Pharisee on the Sabbath. Jesus justified the cure by asking, "If one of you has a child or an ox that falls into a well on the Sabbath day, will you not immediately pull it out?"

In the healing of the man with a withered hand,[25] the Synoptics state that Jesus entered a synagogue on Sabbath and found a man with a withered hand, whom Jesus healed, having first challenged the people present to decide what was lawful for Sabbath—to do good or to do evil, to save life or to kill. The Gospel of Mark adds that this angered the Pharisees so much that they started to contemplate killing Jesus.

The miraculous healing the deaf mute of Decapolis only appears in the Gospel of Mark. Mark states that Jesus went to the Decapolis, met a man there who was deaf and mute, and cured him. Specifically, Jesus first touched the man's ears, then touched his tongue after spitting, and then said, "Ephphatha!", an Aramaic word meaning "be opened".

The healing of Malchus was Christ's final miracle before his resurrection. Simon Peter had cut off the ear of the High Priest's servant, Malchus, during the scene in the Garden of Gethsemane. Jesus restored the ear by touching it with his hand.

The miraculous healing of a centurion's servant is reported in Matthew 8:5–13 and Luke 7:1–10. These two Gospels narrate how Jesus healed the servant of a centurion in Capernaum. John 4:46–54 has a similar account at Capernaum but states that it was the son of a royal official who was healed. In both cases the healing took place at a distance.

Jesus healing in the land of Gennesaret appears in Matthew 14:34–36 and Mark 6:53–56. As Jesus passes through Gennesaret all those who touch his cloak are healed.

Matthew 9:35–36 also reports that after the miracle of Jesus exorcising a mute, Jesus went through all the towns and villages, teaching in their synagogues, proclaiming the good news of the kingdom and healing every disease and sickness.

Exorcisms

Exorcism in Christianity and New Testament

According to the three Synoptic Gospels, Jesus performed many exorcisms of demoniacs. These incidents are not mentioned in the Gospel of John and appear to have been excluded due to theological considerations.The seven major exorcism accounts in the Synoptic Gospels which have details, and imply specific teachings, are:

- Exorcism at the Synagogue in Capernaum, where Jesus exorcises an evil spirit who cries out, "What do you want with us, Jesus of Nazareth? Have you come to destroy us? I know who you are—the Holy One of the Father!".

- Exorcism of the Gerasene demoniac or "Miracle of the (Gadarene) Swine": Jesus exorcises a possessed man (changed in the Gospel of Matthew to two men). When Jesus asks the demon's name (finding the name of the possessing demon was an important traditional tool of exorcists), he is given the reply Legion, "…for we are many". When the demons asked to be expelled into a nearby group of pigs rather than be sent out of the area, Jesus obliges, but the pigs then run into the lake and are drowned.

- Exorcism of the Syrophoenician woman's daughter, appears in Matthew 15:21–28 and Mark 7:24–30. A Gentile woman asks Jesus to heal her daughter, but Jesus refuses, saying that he has been sent only to "the lost sheep of the house of Israel". The woman persists, saying that "dogs eat of the crumbs which fall from their masters' table". In response Jesus relents and informs her that her daughter has been healed.

- Exorcising the blind and mute man, appears in Matthew 12:22–32, Mark 3:20–30, and Luke 11:14–23. Jesus heals a demon-possessed man who was blind and mute. People are astonished and ask, "Could this be the Son of David?"

- Exorcising a boy possessed by a demon, appears in Matthew 17:14–21, Mark 9:14–29, and Luke 9:37–49. A boy possessed by a demon is brought forward to Jesus. The boy is said to have foamed at the mouth, gnashed his teeth, become rigid and involuntarily fallen into both water and fire. Jesus's followers could not expel the demon, and Jesus condemns the people as unbelieving, but when the father of the boy questions if Jesus could heal the boy, he replies "everything is possible for those that believe". The father then says that he believes and the child is healed.

- The miracle of Jesus exorcising at sunset appears in the Synoptic Gospels just after healing the mother of Peter's wife, in Matthew 8:16–17, Mark 1:32–34 and Luke 4:40–41. In this miracle Jesus heals people and cast out demons.

- The miracle of Jesus exorcising a mute appears in Matthew 9:32–34 immediately following the account of the miracle of Jesus healing two blind men. A man who is demon-possessed and could not talk is brought to Jesus, who exorcises the demon, and the man is able to speak.

There are also brief mentions of other exorcisms, e.g.:

- Jesus had cast seven devils out of Mary Magdalene. (Mark 16:9, Luke 8:2)

- Jesus continued to cast out devils even though Herod Antipas wanted to kill him. (Luke 13:31–32)

Resurrection of the dead

All four canonical gospels describe the resurrection of Jesus; three of them also relate a separate occasion on which Jesus calls a dead person back to life:

- Daughter of Jairus. Jairus, a major patron of a synagogue, asks Jesus to heal his daughter, but while Jesus is on the way, Jairus is told his daughter has died. Jesus tells him she was only sleeping and wakes her with the words Talitha kum!

- The Young Man from Nain. A young man, the son of a widow, is brought out for burial in Nain. Jesus sees her, and his pity causes him to tell her not to cry. Jesus approaches the coffin and tells the man inside to get up, and he does so.

- The Raising of Lazarus. A close friend of Jesus who had been dead for four days is brought back to life when Jesus commands him to get up.

Control over nature

The Gospels include eight pre-resurrection accounts concerning Jesus' power over nature:

- Turning water into wine at a wedding, when the host runs out of wine, the host's servants fill vessels with water at Jesus' command, then a sample is drawn out and taken to the master of the banquet who pronounces the content of the vessels as the best wine of the banquet.

- The miraculous catch of fish takes place early in Jesus's ministry and results in Saint Peter, Saint Andrew, James, son of Zebedee and John the Apostle joining Jesus as his apostles.

- Feeding the multitude – Jesus, praying to the Father and using only five loaves of bread and two fish, feeds thousands of men, along with an unspecified number of women and children; there are even a number of baskets of leftovers afterward.

- Walking on water – Jesus walks on water.

- Calming the storm – during a storm, the disciples woke Jesus, and he rebuked the storm causing it to become calm. Jesus then rebukes the disciples for lack of faith.

- Finding a coin in the fish's mouth is reported in Matthew 17:24–27.

•- Cursing the fig tree – Jesus cursed a fig tree, and it withered.

Post-resurrection miracles attributed to Jesus are also recorded in the Gospels:

- A miracle similar to the miraculous catch of fish, also called the catch of 153 fish to distinguish it from the account in Luke, is reported in the Gospel of John but takes place after the Resurrection of Jesus.

The Book of Mormon, one of the religious texts of the Church of Jesus Christ of Latter-day Saints, records multiple miracles performed by Jesus. Sometime shortly after his Ascension, the Book of Mormon records that Jesus miraculously descends from heaven and greets a large group of people who immediately bow down to him. Jesus offers this invitation: "Arise and come forth unto me, that ye may thrust your hands into my side, and also that ye may feel the prints of the nails in my hands and in my feet, that ye may know that I am the Lord of Israel, and the Lord of the whole earth, and have been slain for the sins of the world" 3 Nephi 11:8–17.

In addition to descending from heaven, other miracles of Jesus found in the Book of Mormon include the following. Healing the "lame, or blind, or halt, or maimed, or leprous, or that are withered, or that are deaf, or that are afflicted in any manner"3 Nephi 17:7–10.

- Providing bread and wine as emblems of his sacrifice and death to the multitude when neither had been brought 3 Nephi 20:3–7.

- Changing the nature of three of his called twelve disciples in the Book of Mormon so that they could live until his Second Coming and the other nine that they would live until the age of 72 and be taken "up to his king

ere widely believed in around the time of Jesus. The demigods such as Heracles (better known by his Roman name, Hercules), Asclepius (a Greek physician who became a god) and Isis of Egypt all were thought to have healed the sick and overcome death (i.e., to have raised people from the dead). Some thought that mortal men, if sufficiently famous and virtuous, could do likewise; there were myths about philosophers like Pythagoras and Empedocles calming storms at sea, chasing away pestilences, and being greeted as gods, and similarly some Jews believed that Elisha the Prophet had cured lepers and restored the dead. The achievements of the 1st century Apollonius of Tyana, though occurring after Jesus's life, were used by a 3rd-century opponent of the Christians to argue that Christ was neither original nor divine (Eusebius of Caesaria argued against the charge).

The first Gospels were written against this background of Hellenistic and Jewish belief in miracles and other wondrous acts as signs—the term is explicitly used in the Gospel of John to describe Jesus's miracles—seen to be validating the credentials of divine wise men.

Traditional Christian interpretation

Many Christians believe Jesus's miracles were historical events and that his miraculous works were an important part of his life, attesting to his divinity and the Hypostatic union, i.e., the dual natures of Jesus as Divine and Man. They see Jesus' experiences of hunger, weariness, and death as evidences of his humanity, and miracles as evidences of his divinity.

Christian authors also view the miracles of Jesus not merely as acts of power and omnipotence, but as works of love and mercy, performed not with a view to awe by omnipotence, but to show compassion for sinful and suffering humanity. And each miracle involves specific teachings.

Since according to the Gospel of John. it was impossible to narrate all of the miracles performed by Jesus, the Catholic Encyclopedia states that the miracles presented in the Gospels were selected for a twofold reason: first for the manifestation of Lord's glory, and then for their evidential value. Jesus referred to his "works" as evidences of his mission and his divinity, and in John 5:36 he declared that his miracles have greater evidential value than the testimony of John the Baptist.[43] John 10:37–38 quotes Jesus as follows:

Do not believe me unless I do what my Father does. But if I do it, even though you do not believe me, believe the miracles, that you may know and understand that the Father is in me, and I in the Father.

In Christian teachings, the miracles were as much a vehicle for Jesus' message as his words. Many emphasise the importance of faith, for instance in cleansing ten lepers, Jesus did not say: "My power has saved you," but said:

Rise and go; your faith has saved you.

Similarly, in the miracle of walking on water, Apostle Peter learns an important lesson about faith in that as his faith wavers, he begins to sink.

Christian authors have discussed the miracles of Jesus at length and assigned specific motives to each miracle. For example, authors Pentecost and Danilson suggest that the miracle of walking on water centred on the relationship of Jesus with his apostles rather than their peril or the miracle itself. In their view, the miracle was specifically designed by Jesus to teach the apostles that when encountering obstacles, they need to rely on their faith in Christ, first and foremost.

Authors Donahue and Harrington argue that the healing of healing of Jairus's daughter teaches that faith, as embodied in the bleeding woman, can exist in seemingly hopeless situations and that through belief, healing can be achieved, in that when the woman is healed, Jesus tells her, "Your faith has healed you".

THE REVD DR GABRIEL J. ANAN, PHD

Liberal Christianity

Liberal Christians place less emphasis on miraculous events associated with the life of Jesus than on his teachings. The effort to remove superstitious elements from Christian faith dates to intellectual reformist Christians such as Erasmus and the Deists in the 15th–17th centuries. In the 19th century, self-identified liberal Christians sought to elevate Jesus's humane teachings as a standard for a world civilisation freed from cultic traditions and traces of pagan belief in the supernatural. The debate over whether a belief in miracles was mere superstition or essential to accepting the divinity of Christ constituted a crisis within the 19th-century church, for which theological compromises were sought.

Attempts to account for miracles through scientific or rational explanation were mocked even at the turn of the 19th–20th century. A belief in the authenticity of miracles was one of five tests established in 1910 by the Presbyterian Church in the United States of America to distinguish true believers from what they saw as false professors of faith such as "educated, 'liberal' Christians."

Contemporary liberal Christians may prefer to read Jesus' miracles as metaphorical narratives for understanding the power of the Lord. Not all theologians with liberal inclinations reject the possibility of miracles, but may reject the polemicism that denial or affirmation entails.

Nonreligious views

The Scottish philosopher David Hume published an influential essay on miracles in his *An Enquiry Concerning Human Understanding* (1748) in which he argued that any evidence for miracles was outweighed by the possibility that those who described them were deceiving themselves or others:

As the violations of truth are more common in the testimony concerning religious miracles, than in that concerning any other matter of fact; this must diminish very much the authority of the former testimony, and make us form a general resolution, never to lend any attention to it, with whatever specious pretence it may be covered.

Historian Will Durant attributes Jesus's miracles to "the natural result of suggestion—of the influence of a strong and confident spirit upon impressionable souls; similar phenomena may be observed an y week at Lourdes". Russian skeptic Kirill Eskov in his "Nature"-praised work The Gospel of Afranius argues that it was politically prudent for the local Roman administration to strengthen Jesus's influence by spreading rumours about his miracles via active measures and eventually even staging the resurrection itself.

Scholarly views

New Testament scholar Bart Ehrman argues that what makes science possible is the assumption of the uniformity of the laws of nature, but given that miracles are by definition events that go against the usual way nature works, historians are virtually unable to confirm or refute reports of Jesus's miracles. According to the Jesus Seminar, Jesus probably cured some sick people, but described Jesus's healings in modern terms, relating them to "psychosomatic maladies." They found six of the nineteen healings to be "probably reliable". Most participants in the Jesus Seminar believe Jesus practiced exorcisms, as Josephus, Philostratus and others wrote about other contemporary exorcists, but do not believe the gospel accounts were accurate reports of specific events or that demons exist. They did not find any of the nature miracles to be historical events.

According to scholar Maurice Casey, it is fair to assume that Jesus was able to cure people affected with psychosomatic disorders, although he believes that the healings were likely due to naturalistic causes and placebo effects. John P. Meier believes that Jesus as healer is as well supported as almost anything about the historical Jesus. In the Gospels, the activity of Jesus as miracle worker looms large in attracting attention to himself and reinforces his eschatological message. Such activity, Meier suggests, might have added to the concern of authorities that culminated in Jesus's death. E.P. Sanders and Géza Vermes also agree that Jesus was indeed a healer and that this helped increase his following among the people of His.

Tim McConnell states that as we read throughout the Bible we run into common, ordinary people who pray. These people talked to the Lord in response to him speaking to them or because of some need. Prayer seems to me to be the glue that holds together the relationship between the Lord and his people. The Lord sometimes chooses to perform miracles because people pray. People are healed both physically and spiritually because of prayer.

We think it is an important part of our worship each Sunday, Wednesday night, and whenever we come together; so prayer becomes a focal point of our worship in many different ways. Not only the pastoral prayer, but our silent prayers, the hymns and songs, the affirmations of faith, the prayer of confession, and the call to worship, very necessary.

Every part of our worship can be considered a form of prayer; talking to the Lord, listening to what he has to say to us.

We also think prayer is a necessary part of our daily walk, so we pray during each day.

We know there is power in prayer, so we ask each other to pray for our particular needs and us. Prayer is a gift that we can give each other. We can give prayer when we can give nothing else.

We can ask the Father's blessings, his intervention, or his will to be done, even when we do not know the specific details of what or for whom we are praying. Prayer is reaching out to the Father in faith, not only asking for his help, but giving him praise and adoration.

As we read the book of Acts, we see the early church formed in the spirit of prayer. Jesus' disciples and the many followers, both men and women, devoted themselves to prayer. The church was founded on prayer.

Jesus slipped off many times during his ministry in order to pray. He felt that prayer was necessary in order to stay in touch with the Father 's will for his life and ministry. The disciples learned from Jesus asking him, "Lord, would you teach us how to pray?"

That is when Jesus gave them and us what we call the "Lord's Prayer."

If prayer was that important to Jesus and the disciples of the early church, maybe we should consider it important to us as well.

I know Jesus must have prayed a lot. He had much to pray about, and so do we. He wanted to be in conversation with His Father, and so should we.

We have a few of his prayers written down for us, but none are more beautiful than the one found in John 17. Jesus had gathered his disciples for one last meal together before his arrest and crucifixion. He had passed around the bread and wine—the first Holy Communion. He had washed their feet as a symbol of servanthood. And after he had taught them for the last time, Jesus said, "Let's close in prayer."

So John tells us that Jesus looked up toward heaven and prayed. In the first five verses Jesus prays that the Father will honour Jesus' mission as it comes to a physical end. Jesus gives the Father the credit, in advance, for the success of his earthly ministry.

Is it possible that we can give the Lord thanks, in advance, for the things we ask in our prayers? Is it possible for us to be thankful for the things we know the Lord will do in lives, even the things that we have never seen him do?

Then Jesus continues to pray from verses 6-19, but now is asking the Father to help his disciples remain true to what he has taught them after he has left them. The Father's church depends on the faithfulness of Jesus' disciples, then and today.

Do we ask the Father in our prayers to give us the willingness to be faithful to him at all cost? Do we ask the Father, as we begin each day, to keep us from the many forms of sin and temptation that would cause us to be unfaithful?

The remainder of the chapter Jesus prays for the future disciples—for you and me. He prays that we will have love for him and each other, unity with him and each other, and everlasting life in heaven with him.

It is an awesome thought that Jesus prayed for me then, and continues to pray even today. But are we willing to pray for love, unity and everlasting life for ourselves and for others? Are we willing to pray like Jesus?

Though not mentioned directly in the Bible, fasting is deeply engraved in the Holy Scriptures. In the realm of the Christian faith, fasting, and prayer hold much significance and transformative powers. These two, when combined create a powerful force that brings us closer to the Father.

Fasting, voluntary abstinence from food or certain activities, prayer, the communication with the Father, are powerful spiritual disciplines that open the door to supernatural breakthroughs. In this article, we will explore the importance of fasting, delve into the optimal times to fast, and discover the incredible power that fasting and prayer hold for every believer.

Importance of Fasting

Fasting is not merely a religious ritual that is carried out as a duty, it is devotion; it is a profound spiritual discipline with deep biblical roots. By denying ourselves and our physical needs, we are humbling ourselves before the Father.

During fasting, we are focusing only on Him. Our hearts and minds are devoted to Him. It is an act of surrender and dependency where we recognise that our life is dedicated to the Lord and our strength comes only from him. It is a powerful expression of devotion and a way to express our hunger for a deeper relationship with the Lord.

When To Fast?

There is no specific time to fast. It is a personal choice and individuals practice fasting to get closer to the Lord. However, there are certain seasons and circumstances that call for specific fasting periods. Below, we have listed a few significant moments where one can fast.

Seeking Spiritual Breakthrough

When we face challenges, hurdles, or situations that are beyond our capabilities and require divine intervention, fasting and prayer is the best way to find solutions. Like how apostles, disciples, and others sought the Lord's guidance and help through fasting in the Bible, we also can approach Him with fasting when we require help in our lives. Fasting demonstrates our desperation for His intervention and aligns our hearts with His will, positioning us to experience His power and provision.

Times of Repentance

Fasting has a purifying effect on our spiritual lives and rejuvenates them with light. When we recognise areas of sin, bondage, or lethargy in our lives, fasting can be a medium for repentance, revival, and renewal. By willingly sacrificing our physical nourishment, we show the Lord our sincerity and desire for transformation and guidance toward the right path. Fasting creates space for the Lord to reveal hidden sins, leading us to genuine repentance and restoring our passion and devotion for Him.

Discerning God's Will

The Lord is always at the front leading us on the right path. However, worldly affairs prevent us from hearing his voice of righteousness and divert our path. Fasting and prayer provide clarity and sensitivity to the Father's voice. When faced with important decisions, fasting helps quiet the noise of the world and our own desires, enabling us to discern the Father's leading more effectively. By abstaining from distractions through fasting, we position ourselves to hear His voice and receive guidance in accordance with His perfect will.

Times of Intense Intercession

When we are in dire need of others and unable to manage the burden, then fasting and prayers come to our rescue. It deepens our compassion, increases our spiritual authority, and aligns our hearts with the Lord's heart for those we are praying for. Fasting helps us prioritize intercession, recognizing that the battles we fight are not against flesh and blood but against spiritual forces. Hence, through fasting, one can strengthen their intercession.

The Power of Fasting and Prayer

Fasting and prayer hold extraordinary power in the spiritual realm. They have the capability to change the lives of people and guide them to the holy kingdom of Jesus. Fasting and prayer start with internal cleansing followed by the path toward the Lord. When we engage in this discipline with a humble and sincere heart, incredible things happen.

Overcome Obstacles

There are instances in life when we come across hurdles that challenge our willpower and make us question our beliefs. When we come across hardships, it is best to practice prayer and fasting. The combined power of fasting and prayer breaks through spiritual barriers that create a void in our hearts, thereby, releasing the Lord's power and enabling us to overcome obstacles that seemed unconquerable.

They dismantle barriers, and obstacles, break addictions, and bring deliverance. As we persist in fasting and prayer, we witness unimaginable growth and transformation of lives and circumstances by the mighty hand of the Father.

Spiritual Sensitivity

Fasting along with prayer makes us sensitive to the voice of the Lord. You can feel His presence and find Him guiding you in life. As we deny our physical appetites for a specific period of time, our spiritual senses become more attuned to His leading. This combined with Prayer during the fasting period further enhances spiritual sensitivity.

We experience heightened discernment, clarity, and revelation of our life and our purpose. Fasting and prayer enable us to walk in step with the Holy Spirit, perceiving the spiritual realm more clearly with a deeper understanding.

Deepened Relation With the Father

As Christians, we aim to build a deeper relationship with the Father. Everything we do and seek is to get closer to the Lord and join His holy kingdom of peace and righteousness. Fasting and prayer are effective ways to attain that through abstinence from worldly affairs and embarking on the divine journey. Fasting and prayer cultivate intimacy with the Lord.

As we set aside time to seek Him, we draw near to His heart. Fasting allows us to hunger for the Lord's presence, His Word, and His love. In return, He meets us with an outpouring of His grace, peace, and joy, satisfying the hunger of our souls.

Strengthened Faith

When we are facing hurdles in life, we are put through a test where we question our belief in the Lord. During these hardships, we may feel the pressure to question our beliefs and enclose ourselves in darkness. Fasting and prayer strengthen our faith in the Father and his decisions. It makes us realize that everything happens for a reason.

Fasting and prayer deepen our trust in the Lord and reinforce our dependence on Him. Through the act of fasting, we declare that He is our ultimate provider and sustainer. As we rely on Him for physical sustenance during the fast, our faith grows, and we become more confident in His unfailing love and care for every aspect of our lives.

The power of fasting and prayer is undeniable. When approached with humility, sincerity, and a heart completely surrendered to the Lord, fasting and prayer have the ability to bring about supernatural breakthroughs, revival, and deepen our relationship with the Father. May we never underestimate the significance of fasting and prayer as we seek to draw closer to the Lord, experience His power, and align our lives with His divine purposes.

Let us embark on this transformative journey of fasting and prayer, trusting that the Lord will meet us in an extraordinary way through Breath of the Spirit holy ministries.

Tim McConnell further states that, prayer seems to me to be the glue that holds together the relationship between Lord and his people. Lord sometimes chooses to perform miracles because people pray. People are healed both physically and spiritually because of prayer.

We think it is an important part of our worship each Sunday, Wednesday night, and whenever we come together; so prayer becomes a focal point of our worship in many different ways. It is not only the pastoral prayer, but our silent prayers, the hymns and songs, the affirmations of faith, the prayer of confession, and the call to worship.

Every part of our worship can be considered a form of prayer; talking to the Lord, listening to what he has to say to us.

We also think prayer is a necessary part of our daily walk, so we pray during each day.

We know there is power in prayer, so we ask each other to pray for our particular needs and us. Prayer is a gift that we can give each other. We can give prayer when we can give nothing else. We can ask the Father's blessings, his intervention, or his will to be done, even when we do not know the specific details of what or for whom we are praying. Prayer is reaching out to the Father in faith, not only asking for his help, but giving him praise and adoration.

As we read the book of Acts, we see the early church formed in the spirit of prayer. Jesus' disciples and the many followers, both men and women, devoted themselves to prayer. The church was founded on prayer.

Jesus slipped off many times during his ministry in order to pray. He felt that prayer was necessary in order to stay in touch with the Father 's will for his life and ministry. The disciples learned from Jesus asking him, "Lord, would you teach us how to pray?"

That is when Jesus gave them and us what we call the "Lord's Prayer."

If prayer was that important to Jesus and the disciples of the early church, maybe we should consider it important to us as well.

I know Jesus must have prayed a lot. He had much to pray about, and so do we. He wanted to be in conversation with the Lord, his Father, and so should we.

We have a few of his prayers written down for us, but none are more beautiful than the one found in John 17. Jesus had gathered his disciples for one last meal together before his arrest and crucifixion. He had passed around the bread and wine—the first Holy Communion. He had washed their feet as a symbol of servanthood. And after he had taught them for the last time, Jesus said, "Let's close in prayer."

So John tells us that Jesus looked up toward heaven and prayed. In the first five verses Jesus prays that the Father will honour Jesus' mission as it comes to a physical end. Jesus gives the Father the credit, in advance, for the success of his earthly ministry.

Is it possible that we can give the Lord thanks, in advance, for the things we ask in our prayers? Is it possible for us to be thankful for the things we know the Lord will do in lives, even the things that we have never seen him do?

Then Jesus continues to pray from verses 6-19, but now is asking the Lord to help his disciples remain true to what he has taught them after he has left them.

The Lord's church depends on the faithfulness of Jesus' disciples, then and today.

Do we ask the Lord in our prayers to give us the willingness to be faithful to him at all cost? Do we ask the Lord, as we begin each day, to keep us from the many forms of sin and temptation that would cause us to be unfaithful?

The remainder of the chapter Jesus prays for the future disciples—for you and me. He prays that we will have love for him and each other, unity with him and each other, and everlasting life in heaven with him.

It is an awesome thought that Jesus prayed for me then, and continues to pray even today. But are we willing to pray for love, unity and everlasting life for ourselves and for others? Are we willing to pray like Jesus?

Top of Form

Bottom of Form

Prayer in the life of Jesus

The journalist Ambrose Bierce once defined praying as asking "that the laws of the universe be annulled in behalf of a single petitioner confessedly unworthy"

Whatever you make of that, according to one poll, Americans as a whole today have more faith in prayer than that definition would indicate Bierce had. We are a prayerful people—well, that is, about three quarters of us believe that prayer has the power to actually help heal an injury or illness (even if most people who say that to pollsters don't really spend much time praying themselves). [2] People who were least likely to affirm that this is the case, the poll reported, were men, Democrats, white, under 35, making more than $50 000 a year, and those with college degrees. Lest you be encouraged by the faith of the nation, I should tell you that most Americans also believe that it doesn't matter who you pray to.

But in Christianity, prayer isn't quite that vague. Who you pray to is actually understood to make a difference, as is *why* you pray. Other matters, too, are significant, like where we pray, with whom we pray, and when we pray.

So where can we go to learn more about these things? I suggest that we turn to Mark, to two small, often ignored verses stuck in between the famous stories of the feeding of the 5000, and Jesus walking on the water.

> Immediately [Jesus] made his disciples get into the boat and go before him to the other side, to Bethsaida, while he dismissed the crowd. And after he had taken leave of them, he went up on the mountain to pray. (Mark 6:45-46)

I want us to consider what we may learn from these verses about prayer, and what we may learn about Jesus. You'll remember the context of these verses: Jesus had originally called his disciples away on a retreat earlier in the chapter (vv. 31-32). There's a cycle for Jesus and his disciples going on, a rhythm of spending and replenishing—so after the episode of feeding the 5000, Jesus made his disciples get into a boat bound for Bethsaida while he went off to pray.

Why would Jesus insist on his disciples going on ahead of him? Some have speculated that perhaps he was trying to separate them out from the crowd's move to make him king. As we know from John 6, Jesus had just gone through a moment of supreme peril in his mission. After the feeding of the 5000, the crowd attempted to make him king (John 6:15). But Jesus refused, and in Mark's account he successfully dispersed the crowd, perhaps preventing a messianic uprising in the desert. (As a side note, it's exactly this kind of refusal to encourage political action which kept Jesus off the screen of secular historians.)

Whatever the reason, Jesus moved both the disciples and the crowds, and takes time to pray. He takes control of the disciples ("he made his disciples get into the boat"), the crowd ("dismissed the crowd"), and himself ("he went up on the mountain"). These verses are clear about who is in authority! But the main thing I want us to notice is where, with whom, and when Jesus prayed.

1. Where Jesus prayed

After farewelling his disciples, Jesus went up on a mountainside to pray.

I won't make a major point of this, but do realise that place can be significant. A certain amount of detachment from your surroundings can be helpful, especially if you're busy. The more public you are in your ministry, the more there is showing above the water, the more you better take care to have great weight below the water, out of sight, in your private life, and most especially before the Lord.

So you can try to have quiet times of prayer during your morning commute on the way in to the office, but there is something to be said for—when you can—heading to the hills to pray. Or going to the park, or at least taking a walk, or sitting down with no glowing computer or TV screen in front of you or iPod feeding your ears. We can learn from Jesus' example here in realising that where we go in order to pray can be important.

But after looking at this, I wonder if the location of Jesus' prayer has more significance than simply encouraging us to take care where we pray.

SIGNIFICANCE FOR JESUS

This isn't the only time you see Jesus on the mountainside, you know. Jesus was on the mountain in Mark 3:13 when he called out the twelve. In the other Gospels, we see that Jesus both prayed and preached on mountainsides. Other accounts of calling his disciples take place on the mountain (Luke 6:12), he was transfigured on the mountain (Luke 9:28-36), and preached the Sermon on the Mount (Matt 5:1-8:1).

So, we're not surprised to find here Jesus going up to the mountainside to pray. Personally, I have always enjoyed praying from higher places, not so that the reception will be clearer, but so that I can look out and my own eyes can quite literally give me a larger perspective.

Is Jesus seeking a wider view? Think for a moment. More than simply the obvious symbolism of going up to the Lord, where had Moses received his revelation from the Father? On the mount (Exod 19:24; 33-34). And where was Elijah when the Lord would speak to him? He was up in the mountain (1 Kgs 19:8).

Mark's record here of Jesus on the mountain speaking with his Father shows us who he really is. So too later, in chapter 9:

And after six days Jesus took with him Peter and James and John, and led them up a high mountain by themselves. And he was transfigured before them, and his clothes became radiant, intensely white, as no one on earth could bleach them. And there appeared to them Elijah with Moses, and they were talking with Jesus. (Mark 9:2-4)

The Law and the Prophets bore witness to the identity of Jesus. The fact that Jesus here went up to the mountainside to pray may be instructive for us about *what we should do*, but it is even more instructive to us about *who Jesus is*.

2. With whom Jesus prayed

In Mark's Gospel Jesus always prays alone.

I don't mean that Mark thought that Jesus never prayed with others. In the preceding passage, Mark records Jesus looking up to heaven and thanking God for the food (Mark

<u>6:41</u>). What I mean is that every time Jesus is recorded as simply praying, he does it by himself.

Three passages in Mark narrate Jesus praying:

- At the beginning of Jesus' ministry (1:35): "And rising very early in the morning, while it was still dark, *he departed and went out to a desolate place*, and there he prayed".

- At the end of Jesus' ministry (14:32-35): "And they went to a place called Gethsemane. And he said to his disciples, 'Sit here while I pray.' And he took with him Peter and James and John, and began to be greatly distressed and troubled. And he said to them, 'My soul is very sorrowful, even to death. *Remain here* and watch.' And *going a little farther*, he fell on the ground and prayed..."

- In the middle of Jesus' ministry (6:45-46): "Immediately he *made his disciples get into the boat and go before him to the other side, to Bethsaida, while he dismissed the crowd*. And after he had taken leave of them, he went up on the mountain to pray."

SIGNIFICANCE FOR US

Now, I don't know exactly how each of you feels about prayer, but I hope you're paying attention. I don't think that these passages mean that Jesus is against us praying together.

You know, some people think of prayer as only something you do at church. They'd no sooner do it alone than they would sit in their living room all by themselves and break out singing the national anthem. Not that there's anything wrong with doing it, it's just something they're not used to doing by themselves.

Prayer alone is no less real than prayer with others. Certainly Jesus prayed in the synagogue on one day; but then he would also pray alone the day after. This, of course, was consistent with his own teaching:

"And when you pray, you must not be like the hypocrites. For they love to stand and pray in the synagogues and at the street corners, that they may be seen by others. Truly, I say to you, they have received their reward. But when you pray, go into your room and shut the door and pray to your Father who is in secret. And your Father who sees in secret will reward you." (Matt 6:5-6)

Private prayer in that sense saves us from insincerity and hypocrisy, because there's no human to impress. Sometimes people seem to feel that it is wrong to ever send others away, or to stop what you're doing simply to have time alone with the Father, but Jesus didn't seem to feel that way. We can learn from Jesus' example here.

But after looking at this, I wonder if Jesus' practice of praying alone has even greater significance than simply encouraging us to pray alone.

SIGNIFICANCE FOR JESUS

In the medieval period in Europe, when a serf would pledge fealty and loyalty to their liege lord, they would kneel before him and clasp their hands together. I've read that the way that Christians began to pray in this posture was when a medieval bishop of Rome, the Pope, prayed in front of his cardinals this way. While this may at first seem a show of humility, it was in fact a way of showing that he understood himself to derive his authority directly from the Father, and from no-one else.

Whether or not that was the case for that medieval bishop, it seems to me that Jesus' praying alone indicated his authority. His disciples (and perhaps others) knew that he did this, and that it was to demonstrate who Jesus was working for. He was directed by no-one but the Father.

Even as Moses' authority was underscored by him going by himself to talk with the Father, so this practice was meant as evidence that Jesus was taking his direction only from the Father.

3. When Jesus prayed

Sometimes, it was before the sun rose: "And rising very early in the morning, while it was still dark, he departed and went out to a desolate place, and there he prayed" (Mark 1:35). Two other recorded times of prayer are in the evening (6:45-46, 14:32-39). Mark implies that this occasion on the mountainside and the later events in the Garden of Gethsemane are at night; John tells us this explicitly (John 6:16). But it's much more instructive to notice when in his ministry Jesus prayed.

As I said above, the three times Mark records Jesus simply praying are at the beginning of his ministry (1:35), the middle (6:45-46), and the end of his ministry (14:32-39). Each of these times are decisive points in his ministry where he is faced with decisions and temptations regarding his messianic mission.

SIGNIFICANCE FOR US

Jesus is a model for us in this, too: we should pray at crucial times. Like Jesus, we should be defined by the Father's call.

Prayer reminds us of who we are—the Father's adopted children in Christ. It also reminds us of what we're about—doing the Father's will, as we serve him and serve others.

I don't think it's possible to emphasize enough the importance of being defined by your relationship with the Father more than by any other characteristic. Prayer reminds us of this relationship, and encourages us to keep defining ourselves by this relationship.

This kind of prayer—prayer about significant matters with submitted hearts—will grow your relationship with the father. This kind of prayer is what will grow the roots of your congregation and your ministries. For all that it may be helpful talking over a big decision with a friend or family member, who should you talk with more than God?

If you need some help on knowing how you should pray, and what the substance of your prayers should be, let me encourage you to get a copy of Don Carson's *A Call to Spiritual Reformation.*

We can learn from Jesus' example of giving himself to prayer at decisive moments in his life. But after looking at this, I wonder if when in his life Jesus prayed has even more significance than simply encouraging us to give ourselves to prayer at such times.

SIGNIFICANCE FOR JESUS

Some people may feel it's strange that Jesus would pray at all! Like the child who wrote, "Dear Father, who do *you* pray to?" Why would Jesus pray?

Simply, we know that Jesus prayed for others and for himself to be strengthened in doing the will of God. Here in Mark 6, Jesus had certainly had an eventful, draining day! You see, it's not helpful to think of Jesus as Superman. The Gospels are very clear that Jesus was dependent on his heavenly Father. He needed guidance. Prayer might help Jesus in discerning what he must teach, and how to teach it, and maybe even some lesson planning.

Perhaps he was troubled by the prospect of the popular response to his miracles overshadowing his message. Perhaps he was praying for his disciples to finally come to understand who he was, before time ran out? Because that's what he's doing in chapters 6-8—teaching his disciples who He is. So He prayed.

His praying was a symbol of his whole life being lived out in fellowship with and in submission to the Father. It was his Father, after all, who had sent him (John 8:42). And it would have to be his Father who would continue to direct him.

This time in prayer with the Father would only reinforce the certainty of Jesus, and clarify the source of his direction, that he had come to do his Father's will.

So, Jesus withdrew to pray at defining moments, so that his life could continue to be defined by the Father's will.

Conclusion

The testing in the wilderness at the beginning of Jesus' ministry wasn't the only place or time he faced temptation. The allure of caring primarily for the body, or to rule primarily over nations, or to throw away his physical body (or wrongly preserve it) were ongoing temptations.

In Mark 1:35 he is, perhaps, resolving not to be a Messiah who is primarily a physician-healer. In 6:45-46, at what is arguably the height of his earthly temptation, problems were piling up. Herod, Pharisees, nationalists—here perhaps he is resolving not to be a Messiah who is primarily a provider-king. Political answers are not the right way to analyse and pursue every question, or to solve every problem. And in chapter 14, he is resolving to be the one who has come to heal our diseases, give Himself as the bread of heaven, and be the suffering servant who bears our sins. He is resolving to therefore heal with his wounds and to rule from his cross.

By his choices of where to pray, with whom to pray, and when to pray, Jesus shows us something of the practice of prayer. But he also shows us something more about who he is. The choice of the mountainside demonstrates that he is the Messiah of Divine. Praying alone shows that he took his direction from the Father, and the Father alone. Praying at significant points in his life demonstrates that his life is defined by the Father's will.

And so, through his practice of prayer, we see something of who Jesus is: He is Divine Himself, come to establish a new covenant with a new people who would believe in Him.

PART FIVE

FAITH IN JESUS CHRIST FOR SALVATION

CHAPTER 5

DID JESUS CREATE EVERYTHING, INCLUDING THE WORLD?

The scriptures state that Jesus was involved in the creation of the world and the entire universe. This was possible because Jesus is then **Holy Spirit** and the **Spirit** is the **Word**. The overwhelming <u>message of the Scriptures teaches that **Jesus is the Holy Spirit**</u>. The reader is encouraged to listen or read the study series, "The Bible Teaches **Jesus Is the Holy Spirit** and discover this wonderful and vital truth. There are a number of passages that teach Jesus was not just involved in the creation, He was the One creating the universe and everything that is in it and in heaven.

DID JESUS CREATE EVERYTHING, INCLUDING THE WORLD?

All Things Came Into Being Through Him

John 1:1-3 is the first important passage that teaches "all things" were created by Christ.

In the beginning was the Word, and the Word was with the Holy Spirit, and the Word was the Holy Spirit. He was in the beginning as the Holy Spirit. All things came into being through Him, and apart from Him nothing came into being that has come into being. John 1:1-3 (NASB)

In the first verse we are told that the Word was the Holy Spirit. For an explanation of the meaning of John 1:1, you are encouraged to read, "In The Beginning Was The Word" and the Word Created the universe." The studies teach that the Word is Christ (John 1:14) He created everything. He created all that is in heaven and in the universe.

The next passage is 1 Corinthians 8:6.

. . . yet for us there is but one Father, the Father, from whom are all things and we exist for Him; and one

Lord, Jesus Christ, by whom are all things, and we exist through Him. 1 Corinthians 8:6 (NASB)

This verse is important since it reveals that Christ did the exact same things that the Father did. The Father created all things and we live because of the Father. The apostle Paul also states that Christ will maintain all things. This reveals Christ is also the Father and He created!

By Him Everything Visible and Invisible Were Created

Colossians 1:15-17 helps us understand that when He and the Father created, they created everything in heaven and earth.

He is the image of the invisible Father, the firstborn of all creation. For by Him all things were created, both in the heavens and on earth, visible and invisible, whether thrones or dominions or rulers or authorities — all things have been created through Him and for Him. He is before all things, and in Him all things hold together. Colossians 1:15-17 (NASB)

What did He create? Everything! Everything includes the visible and invisible. The descriptions of dominions or rulers or authorities includes the entire angelic realm. Notice the word "all" is repeated. Now the word all includes everything imaginable. Notice that Christ was before the beginning, that is, before everything, and He continues holding everything together.

But notice that we are told that everything was created by Christ. That means that Christ was not created. He is not a created being; He is the Holy Spirit!

The Father in Heaven Made All Things Through Christ

. . . in these last days has spoken to us in His Son, whom He appointed heir of all things, through whom also He made the world. Hebrews 1:2 (NASB)

Notice that Jesus Christ is the One referred to in this verse. We are told that the Father and Christ created the heavens and the earth together. The Trinity acted together.

Did Jesus create everything, including the world? **The answer is yes!** He created more than just the world. He created everything. He created everything in heaven and on earth. He made the angels, the stars, the universe and all that is on the earth. Christ is with the Father and the Spirit, who also created everything. They created everything together.

Christ with the Father Created All Things in Heaven and Earth

There are many people who wonder if Jesus always existed or if He was created, and it was Christ and the Father who created the World in John 1:3:

"For by Him all things were created that are in heaven and that are on earth, visible and invisible, whether thrones or dominions or principalities or powers. All things were created through Him and for Him. 17 And He is before all things, and in Him all things consist. 18 And He is the head of the body, the church, who is the beginning, the firstborn from the dead, that in all things He may have the preeminence. 19 For it pleased the Father that in Him all the fullness should dwell,

20 and by Him to reconcile all things to Himself, by Him, whether things on earth or things in heaven, having made

peace through the blood of His cross. 21 And you, who once were alienated and enemies in your mind by wicked works, yet now He has reconciled 22 in the body of His flesh through death, to present you holy, and blameless, and above reproach in His sight"

The words "He" and "Him" in the passage "All things were created through Him and for Him. 17 And He is before all things, and in Him all things consist. 18 And He is the head of the body, the church, who is the beginning, the firstborn from the dead, that in all things He may have the preeminence" refer to Jesus because He was chosen by the Father to be King over everything in heaven and on earth.

In the phrase "For it pleased the Father that in Him all the fullness should dwell,

20 and by Him to reconcile all things to Himself, by Him" the words "Him" are referring to Jesus and the word "Himself" is referring to the Father because Jesus is reconciling fallen man to the Father as explained in the following passage:

I believe in the Father Almighty,
Maker of heaven and earth,
and in Jesus Christ,
His only Son, our Lord:
Who was conceived by the Holy Spirit,
born of the Virgin Mary,
suffered under Pontius Pilate,
was crucified, died, and was buried.
He descended into hell.
On the third day He rose again from the dead.
He ascended into heaven
and sits at the right hand of the Father Almighty,
from there He shall come to judge the living and the dead.
I believe in the Holy Spirit,

the Holy Christian Church,
the communion of saints,
the forgiveness of sins,
the resurrection of the body,
and the life everlasting.
Amen.

This chapter is a reflection of in faith of Jesus highlighted by Melissa Henderson. According to Henderson, faith is not only the example for our faith, but he is also the object of our faith. We endure and persevere because we want to know him and join him and share the blessings of his Grace.

She adds that faith can be defined as complete trust or confidence in someone or something. Faith can also be a strong belief in the Lord. Where do you place your faith? Have you ever considered the strength of your faith? What does it mean to have faith in Jesus? Scripture shares how faith is the assurance of things hoped for, but not seen (Hebrews 11:1). Can you think of times when your faith helped during troubles or uncertainty? Placing our full trust in the Lord and having faith that His plan is best may bring comfort and peace to weary souls.

Praying in the name of Jesus helps us acknowledge the sovereignty and power of the Lord.

We don't physically see Jesus on this earth, yet, we have faith in His promises and love. We can trust He is with us and will guide us through every moment. Jesus died for our sins. Having faith in Jesus reminds us of the sacrifice He made for us, according to the plan of His Father.

THE UNIQUENESS OF JESUS CHRIST THE SAVIOUR

What Is Faith in Jesus?

Perhaps you have heard someone say, "I have faith in Jesus. I'll get through this ordeal." Or maybe, "Just have a little faith. That's all you need." Have you paused to consider what that means? Is the person saying they have faith in Jesus because they are a Christian? There may have been a situation when the outcome is unknown at present and worry invaded all thoughts. You may have been the person saying, "I have faith in Jesus."

the truth and the life. No-one comes to the Father except through me" (John 14:6). The apostles proclaimed: *"Salvation is found in no-one else, for there is no other name under heaven given to men by which we must be saved"* (Acts 4:12). The Old Testament prophets agree: *"All the prophets testify about Him that everyone who believes in Him receives forgiveness of sins through His name"* (Acts 10:43). The message of the Bible, then, is clear: *"Whoever believes in the Son has eternal life, but whoever rejects the Son will not see life, for the Father's wrath remains on him"* (John 3:36; compare 1 John 5:11-12).

What about other religions?

But, what about other religions? Why can't we be saved through philosophy and 'spiritual enlightenment', as Buddha taught? **Why can't we be** saved by our sincere prayers and good works, as Muhammad taught**? Why can't we** be saved by worshiping other gods, as Hinduism teaches? *The reason why <u>there is no salvation in these other religions</u> is because, whatever good things other religions might teach us, none of them deals with our deepest need: <u>a restored relationship with the Father.</u>*

185

Wrath and friendship

The salvation we need is two-sided: salvation FROM the Lord's wrath (Romans 1:18); and salvation FOR friendship with the Lord (James 2:23).

The Uniqueness of Jesus Christ

Only Jesus can help us here, because of what Jesus has uniquely DONE, and because of Who Jesus uniquely IS.

Only Jesus has done what nobody else has ever done

Jesus has done what nobody else has ever done. *Only Jesus lived a perfectly righteous life (John 8:46; 1 Peter 2:22),* for our sake (Romans 3:22; 5:17), that we may be credited righteous through faith (Philippians 3:9). Only Jesus died an atoning death (1 John 2:2; 4:10), for our sins (Isaiah 53:4-6; 1 Peter 3:18), to rescue us from the wrath of th Father (Romans 5:8-9). Only Jesus was resurrected from the dead (Acts 1:22), for our justification (Romans 4:25; 1 Corinthians 15:17), to raise us to spiritual life (Romans 6:5-11). Only Jesus washes us with the Holy Spirit (Matthew 3:11), for our regeneration (John 3:5-8; Titus 2:5-6), to fill our hearts with true love for the Father (Romans 5:5).

Jesus is unique

No other person or religion can do what Jesus has done, because Jesus Himself is unique (John 1:18). Other men and women may have lived comparatively good lives by human standards (e.g. Luke 1:28), but even they need a Saviour (Luke 2:47), for only the **fully human** (John 1:14; Hebrews 2:14), **fully Divine** (John 1:1; Hebrews 1:8) Son of the Father (John 3:16) offers to the Father, on our behalf (Romans 10:3-4), an acceptable righteousness (Galatians 2:21).

Other priests may have prayed for their people and <u>offered sacrifices for sins</u> (Hebrews 10:11), but only the eternal High Priest is able to pray for His people forever (Hebrews 7:25) and offer a sacrifice that is fully sufficient once for all (Hebrews 7:27; 10:12). Other men and women may have been raised from the dead (e.g. John 11:43-44), but only the One with life in Himself (John 5:26) has been raised with an immortal resurrection body (1 Corinthians 15:42-54) and authority to forgive sins (Mark 2:5-12) and grant life on judgment day (John 5:27-30). Finally, whatever earthly authority other religious leaders may have possessed, <u>only Jesus is now seated at the father's right hand</u> (Luke 22:69; Ephesians 1:20), with all authority in heaven and on earth (Ephesians 1:21-22), even to pour out the Holy Spirit (Acts 2:33).

The great commission

The Father's command to followers of non-Christian religions is gracious but uncompromising: turn *"to the Father from <u>**idols**</u> **to serve the living** and true Lord, and to wait for His Son from heaven, Whom He raised from the dead – Jesus, Who rescues us from the coming **wrath"** *(1 Thessalonians 1:9-10), *"for, 'Everyone who calls on the name of the Lord will be **saved.**' How, then, can they call on the One they have not believed in? And how can they believe in the One of Whom they have not heard? And how can they hear without someone preaching to them? And how can they preach unless they are sent?"* (Romans 10:14-15) Therefore, <u>Christians must obey the **Great Commission.**</u> *"Then Jesus came to them and said, 'All authority in heaven and on earth has been given to me. Therefore go and make disciples of all nations, baptizing them in the name of the Father and of the Son and of the Holy Spirit, and teaching them to obey everything I have commanded you. And surely*

I am with you always, to the very end of the age'" (Matthew 28:18-20).

Our physical eyes tell us. Through faith in Jesus Christ, we obtain "the victory that has overcome the world (1 John 5: 4-5)

Over the last several decades, a lively debate has been taking place over the meaning of the phrase *faith of Christ* or *faith of Jesus Christ* in Paul's writings. The recent debate was triggered by Richard Hays's dissertation on Galatians 3. He took the position that the phrase refers to Christ's own faith or faithfulness rather than to the believer's faith in Christ, which has been common in English translations (Hays 2002). However, we should notice that in subsequent debate Hays has taken a moderate position, resisting the now fashionable trend to see this meaning in many other formulations of Pauline faith.

The faith of Christ is the literal translation of the Greek *pistis tou christou*. The expression appears in Galatians in 2:16 (twice); 2:20 (*Son of the Lord*); and 3:22. It appears elsewhere in the undisputed letters of Paul in Romans 3:22, 26; and Philippians 3:9. The two principal ways this phrase is currently translated in the debate are *Jesus Christ's faith/ faithfulness*, or, *faith in Jesus Christ*. Thus, the person named can be either the doer (the subject) or the receiver (the object) of the action implied by the other noun—*faith*, in this case.

The expression *baptism of the Spirit*, for example, can mean either the baptism done by the Spirit or the baptism in which the Spirit is given. In Greek grammar these options are known respectively as the subjective genitive or the objective genitive. Consequently, if we take our phrase in the subjective sense, the meaning is the faith or faithfulness that Jesus Christ displays, while the objective sense is expressed as faith directed to Jesus Christ. The Greek phrase can be used either way. In fact, there are more than two ways to understand it. This kind of ambiguity is common in language, and we depend on something in the context or our experience to determine the correct meaning. For instance, when Paul says, "The love of Christ compels us" in 2 Corinthians 5:14 (NIV), does he mean *our* love for *Christ* (objective genitive), or *Christ's* love for *us* (subjective genitive)? Either possibility exists in both the Greek and the English.

Martin Luther's translation is the first known instance where our phrase was rendered in a German equivalent to *faith in Jesus Christ*. Before that, translations tended to preserve the ambiguity by translating word for word. The history of English translations is interesting in this regard. The King James Version translated our phrase in its usual literal way as *faith of Jesus Christ*. How the common reader understood this is unclear, but the overwhelming number of commentators before the late twentieth century interpreted it in the sense of the believer's faith in Jesus Christ. Presumably that was the popular understanding as well. Later the translation *faith* in *Jesus Christ* became nearly universal. Only recently have translations begun to footnote the possible alternate reading of the faith of Jesus Christ. For this reason, modern English readers remain largely unaware of the ambiguity in Paul's expression.

Adding to our difficulty is the fact that *pistis*, the biblical word for faith, has a range of meanings. It can mean "trust, faith or faithfulness, fidelity, or beliefs" in the sense of the thing believed. Particularly relevant to the present question is the choice between placing trust in something or someone and being faithful or trustworthy. Is Paul emphasizing the disposition with which one relates to the Lord (i.e., faith as trust), or with a behavior that displays fidelity toward the Lord (as with faithfulness), or a combination of the two? If Paul means Jesus Christ's faith (subjective genitive), did Christ himself exercise trust in the Lord (as do other believers), or did he demonstrate faithfulness to the Lord in his life and work, or both?

One can also see why major questions of theology soon surface in this discussion. What is Paul trying to do? Is he emphasizing Jesus Christ's work in redemption by grounding it in Christ's own faith or faithfulness? Or is he accenting the fact that the believer is redeemed through the believer's faith, based on Jesus Christ's work? Moreover, is Paul focusing more directly on salvation (by faith) or on ethics (in faithfulness)? Or does Paul focus equally on both? If *faith* means the thing believed, is the question of who does the action beside the point, since the emphasis is on the character of the gospel rather than on someone's action, whether Jesus Christ's or the believer's? Such fundamental theological issues make this debate lively and lasting!

Despite the preceding ambiguities, most interpreters agree that none of the options in this debate fundamentally changes Paul's theology. Adequate evidence for his views exists in other parts of his writing. Nevertheless, accurate assessments of Paul's meaning in each context can help us weigh nuances and accents in his theology.

Many students of Paul find, in the concept of Christ's faith or faithfulness, a fresh way to understand Paul that opens new options for old problems in interpretation or that can reinforce established confessional views. For example, understanding faith as faithfulness can open up new ways to relate the saving benefit of Christ's death and his life as a model or example for Christian living. Relating salvation and ethics more closely makes Paul more congenial to Christian traditions, such as the one represented in the present commentary series, for which discipleship and holiness of life are central (see Toews on the Romans texts). However, the traditions that emphasize the sovereignty of the Lord stress faith over faithfulness in the translation and are attracted to the strong accent on the divine action in faith: in Christ himself, the Lord supplies the faith that saves (see Martyn on the Galatians texts). This helps explain why the translation *Christ's faith* or *faithfulness* has become popular across a wide theological spectrum.

In light of the recent trend just identified, it seems appropriate to test the strength of the translation as Christ's own faith or faithfulness. Despite the potential of this translation to stimulate new insights in Paul's thought, there is no claim that it introduces a totally new dimension. It supports the highlighting of other topics in Paul that have not always been given their due. Principal here is the concept of Christ's obedience, which closely parallels the idea of faithfulness. And identification with Christ makes the life example of Jesus Christ essential. Thus a theology of Christ's own faith is compatible with Paul's thought. It also indicates that how we understand our expression does not determine how we understand Paul's theology overall.

Whatever the strengths of understanding *pistis tou christou* as referring to Christ's own faith or faithfulness, there are weaknesses in attributing this meaning to Paul.

First, Paul nowhere gives an extended exposition of such an understanding, using this specific vocabulary. If it actually had the importance that proponents find in the phrase, it would be surprising that this phrase appears only this way in Paul's writing. Paul never uses either the noun *faith*, or the verb *believe*, or the adjective *faithful* for

Christ apart from this expression. Paul never engages in an expanded discussion of such a concept. The fact that Paul never uses faith language unambiguously as an act of Jesus Christ himself, while he consistently uses the language of obedience in this sense (see Phil 2:1-11; Rom 5:19), makes it unlikely that our phrase refers to Jesus Christ's own faith.

Second, in both the Galatians and Romans contexts where our phrase appears, Paul uses Abraham as an example of faith in support of his argument. In Galatians 3, Paul shows that Abraham's faith exemplifies human response to the promise of God, or to the divine initiative of God. Note the large number of references in the chapter to *promise*, which has *faith* as its corollary. Attempts to make faithful Abraham a type of the faithful Christ (cf. Hays 2002; Gorman 2009) in support of the concept of Christ's faith or faithfulness in Galatians do not do justice to this context. Although Paul cites Christ as the seed of Abraham and thus shows that Christ stands in the tradition of the promises to Abraham (3:16), Paul's point is that God's *promise* is what endures to the present time and what characterizes the gospel of Christ—not the Law! Christ is not an exact parallel to Abraham; Christ is not said to have faith in divine promise in the way that Abraham did. To the contrary, in Galatians 3 Christ is presented as the fulfillment of promise, not as one who submits to promise. Furthermore, Paul's appeal to Abraham focuses on faith as trust and openness to the Lord's promise, not on faithfulness or obedience. The same is true in Romans 4. This applies also to the allegory in Galatians 4. Not that one should contrast or even separate these two meanings in Paul's thought! But close attention to Paul's arguments in this context suggests that Paul is emphasizing *faith* more than *faithfulness*. Faith in Galatians refers predominantly to human receptivity to Lord's gift of redemption and to the Lord's gift of the Spirit.

Third, Paul's view of faith was a matter of dispute in the earliest church. The letter of James reflects this debate. Interestingly, the debate in James centers on *faith* in relation to *works*—both of which are actions of the believer. Clearly the debate is not about faith as faithfulness; otherwise James would have had no reason to emphasise works. The idea of faithfulness does appear in Hebrews and Revelation, which refer to Christ as faithful. This fits the themes of those books, which call for the perseverance of believers under testing. But Galatians deals with a different issue.

Fourth, the earliest commentators of Paul, whose native Greek language was the same as Paul's, show no evidence of understanding the phrase as referring to Christ's own faith (Harrisville). This is a significant observation! Most of the occurrences of the expression in the Greek writers carry the same ambiguity as they do in Paul. But scholars generally agree that, in some instances, *faith* clearly refers to the response of the believer. No instance refers unambiguously to Christ's own faith or faithfulness.

Fifth, no interpretation of our phrase as Christ's own faith has been identified before the eighteenth century (Bird and Sprinkle: 15). It is rare until the twentieth century. Translations of the phrase into other languages from the early centuries to the King James Version use equivalents of *faith of Jesus Christ* without indicating how it was interpreted. Translators in premodern times translated as literally as possible out of reverence for the sacred text. How the expression was understood must be shown by commentaries, sermons, and explicit discussions of the interpretation. But so far, no case is known where the reference is to Christ's faith.

So although understanding *pistis tou christou* as a reference to Christ's own faith or faithfulness is grammatically and theologically possible and even attractive, no certain case exists of this sense, either in Paul, in his early interpreters who shared a common language, or in any interpreter before modern times.

Readers of the Toews volume on Romans in this same series will note that he understands the phrase to refer to Christ's faith. He gives four reasons for his view. The first two reasons are based on language usage. He states that the usage in Greek outside and inside the New Testament is overwhelmingly in support of his position. However, later study has not sustained this claim, and today the more typical view is that appeals to language usage cannot answer our question. Both subjective and objective meanings are possible in the Greek (for details, see Bird and Sprinkle: 16–26). Toews's third reason takes the earlier translations of our phrase as *faith of Jesus Christ* as evidence for his position. But this does not constitute solid evidence, as noted in point 5 above. The full evidence points in the opposite direction. His last reason is that taking the phrase in an objective sense would introduce a redundancy in many of the relevant Pauline texts, with the human act of believing being stated twice in immediate succession. Not everyone sees the redundancy, but the position defended below makes the question mute.

Traditional meaning of Faith compared with Faith in Christ

Now let us consider the traditional meaning of faith as that which the believer directs to Christ and the divine promises centred in him (the objective genitive)—*faith in Christ*. This reading assumes a more consistent meaning in the literary settings where the phrase appears. All agree that faith as an act of response to the gospel by the believer is prominent in these contexts. Without clear evidence to the contrary, it is better to assume that Paul is not mixing the meaning. As noted above, the trusting response of the believer fits best both the theme of Galatians and the example of Abraham that Paul invokes.

Two objections to this traditional understanding *appear* to carry serious weight. First, in Galatians and in Romans, the phrase *faith of Jesus Christ* is immediately followed by a statement that clearly refers to a human act of receiving (believing) the truth just affirmed in the phrase *faith of Jesus Christ*. This creates the appearance of redundancy when the latter phrase is translated *faith in Jesus Christ*. The objection has some justification, especially if our phrase is taken to emphasise the act of faith, or believing, as the English translation suggests. However, if the phrase stresses faith as the thing believed rather than the believing act itself, the redundancy disappears. This is the viewpoint that is defended below.

Second, some offer a *theological* argument against the traditional meaning. This has a negative and positive side. Negatively, some claim that it places too much emphasis on the human contribution to redemption. In Paul's discussion, it may seem more worthy to contrast the works of the Law, which imply human action and which Paul critiques, with the faith of Jesus Christ as a divine action. Some have even suggested that the objective meaning in effect makes faith a human work—the very thing Paul is combating. But this last point is irrelevant. In Paul's understanding, faith is not a work, as Romans 4:5 expressly states. Positively, the theological argument finds the idea of Christ's own faith (subjective genitive) useful and fruitful in rounding out Paul's view of the saving work of Christ (see the discussion above). We will address this objection in what follows.

One approach avoids focus on the word faith as a noun expressing action. *Faith* can refer to the thing believed. This is common today when we speak of the "Christian faith." This meaning is already present in Galatians. In 1:23 Paul is said to be *proclaiming the faith he once tried to destroy*, and in 6:10 the church is called the *household of faith* (KJV). Clearly these refer to the gospel message in its entirety, with one part of the message standing for the whole (called "metonymy"). In Galatians 3:23 and 25, Paul uses *faith* to refer to the historical event of Jesus' life: *faith came*. This means that a third option exists for understanding the expression *faith of Jesus Christ*. Here *Jesus Christ* refers neither to the one having faith nor the one receiving faith. Rather, the name specifies or defines which faith is meant. *Faith* is not just any faith; it is qualified or characterised in some way by the person of Jesus Christ. This is commonly called the qualifying genitive, though genitives of authorship, source, or possession all fit within this third option. In this case one may still ask who the "doer" of the faith is. However, such a question is not central to the phrase itself and is not the point Paul is making. The *substance* of faith is in view, not *who* exercises the faith.

It seems best to take our phrase primarily in this sense, recognising that different contexts may support differing nuances. Although this is not a new proposal, it has not figured prominently in the discussion until recently. Such English translations as *Christ-faith* or *Christic faith* have been suggested, but they are awkward. Retaining the literal *faith of Jesus Christ* seems preferable. Since we have found reason to reject a Pauline idea of Christ's own faith or faithfulness, we can assume that *faith* in our phrase originates in the idea of the faith of the believer, with that idea lying in the background. However, in the present phrase, *faith* names that message whose character is defined essentially by the person of Jesus Christ. Therefore the phrase reflects both Paul's Christ-centered theology and his conviction that faith is the single means for appropriating Father's provision in Christ.

The expression *faith of Jesus Christ* is thus Paul's shorthand way of defining the gospel he preaches in a form that evokes the fundamental concerns in his debates with believers who continue to observe the Law on circumcision and expect Gentile believers to do the same. This is exactly the way Paul uses our phrase in 2:16, where he contrasts it to the phrase *works of the Law*, a shorthand expression for the position he rejects. Both phrases express a larger theological perspective rather than a particular action.

This proposal has the strength not only of tersely capturing Paul's conviction that Christ is central to the gospel. It also has the advantage of overcoming the main objections to the traditional meaning as *faith in Christ*. It removes the appearance of redundancy in the Pauline contexts. Paul is not repeating a reference to the human response of believing. Rather, Paul is expressing the essence of the gospel. In what immediately follows, he refers to the act of the person who accepts that offer by believing. Another advantage of this proposal is that it reshapes the debate about whether the traditional translation places too much weight on the human side of salvation. In our solution, Paul defines the substance of the gospel exclusively in terms of the person of Jesus Christ. The expression does not draw attention to the human aspect of salvation, but rather to the divine provision that has come in and through the person and work of Jesus Christ.

In conclusion, this essay does not discount the legitimacy of Christ's personal faithfulness or its relevance for discipleship in Paul's theology. On the contrary, this emphasis is present in and crucial to Paul, but he makes this point with other language and concepts. That emphasis exists particularly in the theme of identification with Christ (2:20; 3:26-28; 4:19). Paul's language of faith makes a different point.

PART SIX

JESUS CHRIST AS SON OF MAN

CHAPTER 6

IS JESUS THE SON OF MAN?

T his is an expression in the sayings of Jesus in Christian writings, including the Gospels, the Acts of the Apostles and the Book of Revelation. The meaning of the expression is controversial. Interpretation of the use of "the Son of man" in the New Testament has remained challenging and after 150 years of debate no consensus on the issue has emerged among scholars.

The expression "the Son of man" occurs 81 times in the four canonical gospels (mainly quoting Jesus) and another four times in the rest of the New Testament. The equivalent Hebrew expression "son of man" appears in the Old Testament 103 times.

The use of the definite article in "the Son of man" in the Koine Greek of the Christian gospels is original, and before its use there, no records of its use in any of the surviving Greek documents of antiquity exist. Geza Vermes has stated that the use of "the Son of man" in the Christian gospels is unrelated to Hebrew Torah usages.

For centuries, the Christological perspective on Son of man ("man" referring to Adam) has been seen as a possible counterpart to that of Son of the Lord and just as Son of the Father affirms the divinity of Jesus, in a number of cases Son of man affirms his humanity. The profession of Jesus as the Son of the Father has been an essential element of Christian creeds since the Apostolic age, and while some do not think profession of Christ as Son of man was necessary for Christians, the proclamation of Jesus as the Son of man has been an article of faith in Christianity since at least the Nicene Creed which reads in the English as: "by the power of the Holy Spirit he became incarnate from the Virgin Mary, and was made man." Christ being a Man-Divine was so important that it was the major issue addressed at the Council of Chalcedon where the heresy of monophysitism was addressed. Monophysites regarded Christ as having a single nature that was a co-mingling of the two, Divine and Man, whereas the Orthodox Catholic position held that he was completely Divine, and completely man, simultaneously. These positions in the Creed of the Nicene council, and the primary subject of the Chalcedonian, shows the importance of early Christian belief in the nature of Jesus as both Divine and Man, so much so that believing the two could be reduced to a third, intermingled, nature was considered heresy.

In the Koine Greek of the New Testament, "the son of man". The Hebrew expression "son of man", also appears over a hundred times in the Hebrew Bible. In thirty-two cases, the phrase appears in intermediate plural form "sons of men", i.e. human beings.

The expression "the Son of man" appears 81 times in the Koine Greek of the four Gospels: 30 times in Matthew, 14 times in Mark, 25 times in Luke and 12 times in John. However, the use of the definite article in "the Son of man" is novel, and before its use in the canonical gospels, there are no records of its use in any of the surviving Greek documents of antiquity.

Geza Vermes has stated that "the son of man" in the New Testament is unrelated to Hebrew Bible usages. Vermes begins with the observation that there is no example of "the" son of man in Hebrew sources and suggests that the term originates in Aramaic. He concludes that in these sources "Son of man" is a regular expression for *man* in general and often serves as an indefinite pronoun and in none of the extant texts does "son of man" figure as a title.

However, other sources argue that the Son of Man is a title, claimed by Jesus as a way of asserting his own divine nature. Whitefield, for example, argues that within the biblical context, all humans are referred to as "Sons of Man", or more specifically, sons of Adam. Jesus' claiming this specific title was a direct claim to divine authority, alluding to that of Daniel, the one who is prophesied to "[come] with the clouds of heaven" and who is to be "given authority, glory and sovereign power" As such, though the title itself could refer to any human being, the title itself refers to a specific religious messianic figure.

The occurrences of Son of man in the Synoptic gospels are generally categorized into three groups: (i) those that refer to his "coming" (as an exaltation); (ii) those that refer to "suffering" and (iii) those that refer to "now at work" i.e. referring to the earthly life.

The presentation of Son of man in the Gospel of John is somewhat different from the Synoptics: in John 1:51 he is presented as contact with The Lord through "angelic instrumentality", in John 6:26 and 6:53 he provides life through his death, and in John 5:27 he holds the power to judge men.

Synoptic gospels

In Matthew 8:20 and Luke 9:58 Jesus states: "The foxes have holes, and the birds of the sky have nests, but the Son of man has nowhere to lay his head." This phrasing seems to tie in with the Old Testament prophetic expressions used by such prophets as Ezekiel, and it shows Jesus' understanding of himself as the "man" that God has singled out as a friend and representative.

Johannine literature

The first chapter of the Book of Revelation refers to "one like a Son of man" in Revelation 1:12-13 which radiantly stands in glory and speaks to the author. In the Gospel of John Jesus is not just a messianic figure, nor a just prophet like Moses, but the key emphasis is on his dual role as Son of the Father and Son of man.

Book of Moses

The title "Son of Man" is used nine times in the Book of Moses, a 19th-century work considered canonical scripture by the Church of Jesus Christ of Latter-day Saints and included in its publication The Pearl of Great Price. According to Nontrinitarianism, Moses 6:57 suggests that a name of God the Father is "Man of Holiness," and that the title "Son of Man" points to Jesus' divine Sonship.

Book of Daniel

The title "Son of Man" appears in the Book of Daniel, and most sources allude specifically to this particular verse. According to the Daniel 7, The Son of Man is seen "coming with the clouds of heaven. He approached the Ancient of Days and was led into his presence. He was given authority, glory and sovereign power; all nations and peoples of every language worshiped him. His dominion is an everlasting dominion that will not pass away, and his kingdom is one that will never be destroyed." (Daniel 7:13–14)

Scholarly views

The interpretation of the use of "the Son of man" in the New Testament has proven to be challenging, and James D. G. Dunn and separately Delbert Burkett state that it is a prime example of the limits of New Testament interpretation because after 150 years of debate no consensus on its meaning has emerged.

The earliest approaches, going back to the Fathers of the Church, relied on the Greek expression and interpreted "son" in a parental sense. This approach continued into the Middle Ages. By the time the Protestant Reformation was under way, three new approaches had emerged, one that saw it as an expression of the humanity of Jesus, another that viewed it as a messianic title derived from the Book of Daniel (7.13) and a third which considered it as a general idiom for self-reference. By the 17th century, the first approach (focusing on his humanity) had gained ground, yet by the 19th century the messianic view had increased in popularity.

In the last part of the 20th century, the messianic view was highly criticized and the concept of idiomatic use began to gain support among some scholars. In the 21st century, a simple approach has been made: "Adam means 'man.' So when Christ is called the Son of Man the entire generating line all the way from Adam down to Jesus is being recalled." However, no consensus has emerged among scholars on how the expression can be interpreted. Another view put forward by Bart D. Ehrman (1999) is that there are some passages (as such Mark 8:38, 13:26, 14:62; Matthew 19:28, 25:31–46; and Luke 12:8–9) in which Jesus mentions 'the Son of Man' and does not appear to be talking about himself, but about someone else, namely a cosmic judge who would come down from heaven to bring judgment. The identification of the Son of Man with Jesus might thus be a later, inauthentic tradition.

Ingolfsland (2001) argued that Ehrman's examples were not valid, or did not meet his own criteria.

Jewish views

In Judaism, "son of man" denotes mankind generally, in contrast to deity or godhead, with special reference to their weakness and frailty (Job 25:6; Psalms 8:4; Psalms 144:3; Psalms 146:3; Isaiah 51:12, etc.) or the term "ben Adam" is but a formal substitute for the personal pronoun.

Sixty-nine times in the Synoptic Gospels, Jesus calls himself (the) "Son of man", a Greek expression which in its Aramaic (and Hebrew) background could be an oblique way of indicating the speaker's own self (e.g., Matt 8:20), or else simply mean "someone" or "a human being" (as in Ps 8:4, where it is a poetic variant for "man"). In Daniel 7:13–14 the "Son of man" seems to symbolize the angels (perhaps the archangel Michael) and/or the righteous and persecuted Jews who will be vindicated and given authority by the Father (Dan 7:18,21–22,27; 10:13, 21; 12:1) rather than function as one individual, heavenly figure who represents the people. What is clear from the evidence is that "Son of man" did not function in pre-Christian messianic expectations as a title for a deliverer expected to come in the last times. But to the Israelites and other readers and followers of the Torah this phrase would have meaning and point to the Messiah. It was not even a sharply defined concept, with a specific content and reference. It could simply denote a member of the human race (Ps. 8:4) or be a way of pointing to a prophet's insignificance and finite dependence in the face of the Father's glory and infinite power. Therefore, the Lord addresses Ezekiel ninety-three times as "son of man".

Three contexts

According to the Synoptic Gospels, Jesus referred to himself as "Son of man" in three contexts, each with its own circle of fairly distinct meanings. He used this self-designation of **(1)** his earthly work and its (frequently) humble condition (e.g., Mark 2:10, 28 parr.; Matt 11:19 and Luke 7:34; Matt 8:20 and Luke 9:58); **(2)** his coming suffering, death, and resurrection (Mark 9:9,12; Mark 14:21 and, above all, Mark 8:31; 9:31; 10:33–34 parr.); **(3)** his future coming in heavenly glory to act with sovereign power at a final judgement (e.g., Mark 8:38; 13:26–27 parr.; Matt 24:27 and Luke 17:24; Matt 25:31–32; see John 5:27). These classifications show how the "Son of man" served as a way of indicating Jesus' importance and even universal relevance. This was especially true of the class (3) sayings. In other words, "Son of man" was used to say what Jesus did rather than what he was. It was not and did not become a title in the normal sense—at least not on the lips of Jesus himself.

At the same time, the evangelists (and/or their sources) do not always seem to distinguish "Son of man" sharply from "Christ/Messiah" or "Son of the Father". For Mark, the Davidic Messiah and Daniel's Son of man are one and same person, and their name is Jesus. In Mark 14:61-62, the reply that Jesus makes to the high priest's question ("Are you the Messiah, the Son of the Blessed One?") conveys some glorious connotations of "the Son of the Father" as a figure who will come in triumph on the clouds of heaven to judge his enemies: "I am; and you will see the Son of man seated at the right hand of the Power, and coming with the clouds of heaven". In John's Gospel, the expression gains a significant element not found in the Synoptic Gospels under any of the three meanings listed above: the "Son of man" is a personally pre-existent figure (e.g., John 3:13; John 6:62).

Regarding Jesus himself, much debate originated in deciding whether any or all of the three classes of self-referential sayings derived from what he said in his ministry. A few scholars have even attempted to prove that none of the "Son of man" sayings came from Jesus himself. However, there remain good and convergent reasons for maintaining that, while there was some editorial reworking, Jesus did speak of himself as "Son of man", filled the term with his own meanings, and was responsible for the three classes of "Son of man" sayings listed above. Along with the way he used the image of the kingdom of the Father and that of the Lord as Father, here a third classic example is supplied of Jesus taking an inherited expression and using it massively but in his own way.

First, one does not find others ever describing, addressing, or confessing Jesus as the Son of man apart from four marginal cases (Acts 7:56; Rev. 1:13; 14:14; Heb. 2:6). The last three cases deal with quotations from the Old Testament. In the Gospels, other people address and speak about Jesus in a variety of ways, but never directly as "Son of man". According to John 12:34, the audience of Jesus were puzzled when he referred to himself as "the Son of man". Now, if the early Church had freely created the Son of man sayings, it would be puzzling that this designation for Jesus is not found on the lips of others. The puzzle disappears once it is agreed that there is here a genuine historical recollection: only Jesus used the term, and the evangelists and their sources faithfully recorded that.

Second, the Son of man sayings in which Jesus refers to his (often humble and merciful) earthly activity are attested by both Mark (e.g., Mark 2:10, 28) and Q source (Matt 8:20 and Luke 9:58; Matt 11:19 and Luke 7:34). The sayings dealing with the coming or apocalyptic Son of man likewise turn up in Mark (Mark 8:38; 13:26; 14:62) and in Q (e.g., Matt 24:27and Luke 17:24. This double strand of tradition or multiple attestation can encourage one to attribute to Jesus at least class (1) and class (3) of the Son of man sayings.

Third, there was some Jewish background to Jesus' Son of man sayings, but there was scarcely any follow-up in the emerging Church. Later on, the Church Fathers would use the term as a way of referring to Christ's humanity as opposed to his divinity or to his being the son of the Divine. However, in the first century the designation does not seem to have been useful in preaching the good news. It does not appear in credal and liturgical formulas. It was too flexible and even vague: it ranges from the mysterious heavenly being of Daniel 7 to simply serving as a circumlocution for "I". Linguistically, it was a particularly odd expression for Greek-speaking people. The fact that the designation was strange and unsuitable for the early Church's life and ministry suggests that the Son of man sayings did not derive from groups in the Church, but from another source, which could only really be Jesus.

Fourth, the sayings about the coming Son of man sometimes imply a certain differentiation between this figure and Jesus. Therefore, Luke reports Jesus as declaring: "Everyone who acknowledges me before men, the Son of man also will acknowledge before the angels of the Lord" (Luke 12:8). Matthew modifies this saying to read: "Everyone who acknowledges me before men, I also will acknowledge before my Father who is in heaven" (Matt. 10:32). Apparently, Luke has preserved the original form of the saying, which indicates a certain unity of function between Jesus himself and the Son of man, but at the same time introduces some differentiation between the two figures. The differentiation makes sense once it is recognised that it recalls a turn of phrase actually used by Jesus to distinguish his present preaching from his future judging. The distinction had its point in the historical context of his ministry, but not later in the post-Easter situation where believers acknowledged the personal unity between the risen Jesus and the Son of man who would come in glory. Matthew's modification reflects precisely that shift.

Fifth, there are some unusual features about the preservation of the "Son of man" sayings. The three classes are not blended together. Thus (2) the passion predictions about the Son of man do not go beyond the death and resurrection to include (3) statements about the future coming of the Son of man. Furthermore, the sayings about the Father's kingdom (and, specifically, the parables) never introduce the Son of man. The absence of a clear and strong connection between the Son of man and the divine kingdom is puzzling. After all, Daniel 7 was relevant for the functions of the Son of man, and the Danielic imagery had included the Father's kingdom (Daniel 2:44; 4:3; 7:27). The independence of the three classes of Son of man sayings and the separation of the kingdom sayings from the Son of man can be explained if one sees the Gospels (and the traditions behind them) accurately preserving here distinctions that genuinely went back to Jesus' actual preaching and teaching.

Son of the Father

For centuries, the Christological perspective on Son of man has been seen as a possible counterpart to that of Son of the Father and just as Son of Divinity affirms the humanity of Jesus, the title Son of Man affirms his divinity. Though many sources claimed that the title referred to his human nature, these sources may stem from a cursory and shallow understanding of the title. It must be noted that in other parts of Scripture, the title "Son of the Lord" is bestowed on other historical figures like Jacob and Solomon; but the Son of Father title is claimed only by Jesus. Thus, paradoxically, the title Son of Man actually refers to Christ's Divine nature, alluding to the One mentioned in Daniel 7, while the title Son of the Man refers to his humanity, as seen in the Old Testament.

While of all the Christological titles used in the New Testament, Son of the Father has had one of the most lasting impacts in Christian history and has become part of the profession of faith by many Christians, the proclamation of Son of man has never been an article of faith in Christianity. Thus in the mainstream popular context it is the Son of the Father title which implies the full divinity of Jesus as part of the Holy Trinity of Father, Son and the Spirit.

In the 5th century, Saint Augustine wrote at length on the Son of the Father and its relationship with the Son of man, positioning the two issues in terms of the dual nature of Jesus as both divine and human in terms of the hypostatic union. He wrote:

Christ Jesus, the Son of the Father, is Divine and Man: Divine before all worlds, man in our world... But since he is the only Son of Divine, by nature and not by grace, he became also the Son of Man that he might be full of grace as well.

Although Son of man is a distinct concept from Son of Divine, some gospel passages may seem to equate them in some cases, e.g. in Mark 14:61, during the Sanhedrin trial of Jesus when the high priest asked Jesus: "Are you the Messiah, the Son of the Blessed one?" Jesus responded "I am: and you shall see the Son of man sitting at the right hand of Power, and coming with the clouds of heaven." This seems to build on the statement in Mark 9:31 that "The Son of man is delivered up into the hands of men, and they shall kill him; and when he is killed, after three days he shall rise again." In the parable of the Sheep and the Goats, the returning Son of man has the power to judge, by separating men from "all the nations" into distinct groups, in Matthew 25:31–46. However, James Dunn has pointed out that there is no overall scholarly agreement on these issues, and the Christological debates have continued for well over a century without the emergence of consensus.

Bible Question:

When Jesus refers to Himself as the Son of Man, what does that mean? Why does He say Son of Man and Son of Divine?

Bible Answer:

The phrases **"Son of man"** and **"Son of the Father"** are used for Jesus Christ to refer to His humanity and deity. The message of Scripture was that Jesus Christ was both Divine and Man. What follows below is a fuller explanation of both terms.

Son of Man – Old Testament

The phrase "Son of Man" occurs 195 times in the Old and New Testaments. It occurs 107 times in the Old Testament, but 93 times in the book of Ezekiel. Each time the phrase refers to a human. Here are a few examples. Our first clue regarding the meaning of "son of man" occurs in Numbers 23:19.

Divine is not a man, that He should lie, nor a son of man, that He should repent; has He said, and will He not do it? Or has He spoken, and will He not make it good? Numbers 23:19 (NASB)

Here it refers to humans – men or women. The verse simply says that the Lord is not like us. He is not a man. Men and women lie and the Lord does not lie. "Son of man" also refers to the offspring or descendants of mankind (Psalm 144:3; Isaiah 51:12; Jeremiah 49:18; Jeremiah 51:43; Ezekiel 2:1, 3, 6, 8; Daniel 8:17). Another excellent example of this phrase occurs when the Lord speaks to the prophet Ezekiel and calls him a "son of man." Then He said to me, "Son of man, stand on your feet that I may speak with you!" Ezekiel 2:1 (NASB)

But the most important usage of this phrase occurs when it is used in reference to Jesus Christ. The important example occurs in the book of Daniel when it refers to the second coming or the return of Jesus Christ in the future. Jesus referred to Himself as the "Son of Man" on numerous occasions (Matthew 8:20; 9:6; 11:19; 16:27; 19:28; 26:64).

I kept looking in the night visions, And behold, with the clouds of heaven. One like a Son of Man was coming. And He came up to the Ancient of Days

And was presented before Him. Daniel 7:13 (NASB)

In this verse "Son of Man" has messianic overtones and refers to a person of human descendent. It refers to the Messiah who would be born of a virgin (Genesis 3:15; Isaiah 7:14; 9:6; Micah 5:2). Son of man normally just means human, but also when it is used as a title of the Messiah, who is Jesus Christ.

Son of Man – New Testament

The phrase "Son of Man" occurs 88 times in the New Testament and only four times outside of the gospels. In the New Testament, the term has additional meaning. It still refers to a human, but it is also a title for Jesus Christ. Jesus was the ultimate human. He was Divine in human flesh.

But in order that you may know that the Son of Man has authority on earth to forgive sins" –then He said to the paralytic–"Rise, take up your bed, and go home." Matthew 9:6 (NASB)

For the Son of Man is Lord of the Sabbath. Matthew 12:8 (NASB)

. . . for just as JONAH WAS THREE DAYS AND THREE NIGHTS IN THE BELLY OF THE SEA MONSTER, so shall the Son of Man be three days and three nights in the heart of the earth. Matthew 12:40 (NASB)

In Luke 24:7 Jesus refers to Himself as the "Son of Man" and says that He must be delivered up to be crucified. Men in human flesh die a physical death and not an eternal Divine. "Son of Man" refers to the humanity of Jesus Christ, the Messiah (John 4:25; 9:35-36).

Son of Man

The phrase "Son of Man" only occurs 43 times in the New Testament and it always refers to Jesus. It means that Jesus is Divine. It does *not* mean that He was born of Divine. It does not mean that He was the offspring of Divine. This truth is clearly explained in John 10:30-35. In the passage it is obvious that the Jews understood Jesus claimed to be Divine. In John 10:30 Jesus declared that He was one with the Father.

I and the Father are one. John 10:30 (NASB)

The Greek word that Jesus used for "one" is *eis*. It is a cardinal number such as 1, 2, 3 and so forth. That is Jesus said that He was the Father and the Father was Himself. He referred to the concept of the trinity. Both the Old and New Testament teach that the Divine is one (Deuteronomy 6:4; 1 Timothy 2:5; James 2:19). Now notice the response of the religious leaders. They understood that He claimed to be Divine.

The Jews answered Him, "For a good work we do not stone You, but for blasphemy; and because You, being a man, make Yourself out to be Divine." (NASB) John 10:33

So Jesus responded to the Jews with this comment,

. . . do you say of Him, whom the Father sanctified and sent into the world, "You are blaspheming," because I said, "I am the Son of the Father"? (NASB) John 10:36

Jesus apparently had said He was the "Son of Man." The Jews understood this term to be a claim of deity. They understood that Jesus had declared He was Divine. Therefore, they accused Jesus of blasphemy. They knew Jesus was claiming to be Divine. That is the meaning of the "Son of Divine." The phrase "Son of the Father" means Divine.

In summary, when "Son of Man" is used as a title it refers to the humanity of Jesus Christ and "Son of the Father" refers to the deity of Christ. Both terms were used of Christ because He was man and He was Divine. "Son of Man" also referred to the Messiah. The Jews understood the meaning of these terms. Today, we focus in on the word "son" and sometimes are not aware that both expressions had special meanings.

Romans 1:2-4 is an important passage in the Bible since it tells us that Jesus Christ is both a man and Divine.

He promised beforehand through His prophets in the holy Scriptures, concerning His Son, who was born of a descendant of David according to the flesh, who was declared the Son of Man with power by the resurrection from the dead, according to the Spirit of holiness, Jesus Christ our Lord . . . Romans 1:2-4 (NASB)

"Son of Man" reminds us that Jesus became a man so that He could die. "Son of the Father" reminds us that Jesus is Divine so that He could live a sinless life or be the perfect Lamb of the Father. Only as the Dvine-man could He die a sinless, holy sacrifice for our sins. All that is left for us to do is to believe that He is the only way. He is the only Saviour of our sins, if we will believe that.

. . . that Christ died for our sins according to the Scriptures, and that He was buried, and that He was raised on the third day according to the Scriptures . . . 1 Corinthians 15:3-4 (NASB)

Together, they mean that Jesus was completely man and He was completely Divine. He was the Divine-man. He was the eternal, holy Divine who came in human flesh. Without being a man, He could not have died. If He was not a Divine, He would have been a sinner. But as the Divine-man, He was the sinless man – the perfect sacrifice – a sinless sacrifice for our sins. He returned to life and ascended back to heaven. Praise the Lord

Top of Form

Son of man (Christianity)

This article is about the Christian teachings. For an overview, see Son of man. For other usage, see Son of man (disambiguation).

The Son of man with a sword among the seven lampstands, in John's vision. From the Bamberg Apocalypse, 11th century.

Son of man is an expression in the sayings of Jesus in Christian writings, including the Gospels, the Acts of the Apostles and the Book of Revelation. The meaning of the expression is controversial. Interpretation of the use of "the Son of man" in the New Testament has remained challenging and after 150 years of debate no consensus on the issue has emerged among scholars.

The expression *"the Son of man" occurs 81 times in the four canonical gospels (mainly quoting Jesus)* and another four times in the rest of the New Testament. The equivalent Hebrew expression "son of man" appears in the Old Testament 103 times.

The use of the definite article in "the Son of man" in the Koine Greek of the Christian gospels is original, and before its use there, no records of its use in any of the surviving

Greek documents of antiquity exist. Geza Vermes has stated that the use of "the Son of man" in the Christian gospels is unrelated to Hebrew Torah usages.

For centuries, the Christological perspective on Son of man ("man" referring to Adam) has been seen as a possible counterpart to that of Son of the Father and just as Son of the Father affirms the divinity of Jesus, in a number of cases Son of man affirms his humanity. The profession of Jesus as the Son of the Father has been an essential element of Christian creeds since the Apostolic age, and while some do not think profession of Christ as Son of man was necessary for Christians, the proclamation of Jesus as the Son of man has been an article of faith in Christianity since at least the Nicene Creed which reads in the English as: "by the power of the Holy Spirit he became incarnate from the Virgin Mary, and was made Man." Christ being a Man-Divine was so important that it was the major issue addressed at the Council of Chalcedon where the heresy of monophysitism was addressed. Monophysites regarded Christ as having a single nature that was a co-mingling of the two, Divine and Man, whereas the Orthodox Catholic position held that he was completely God, and completely man, simultaneously. These positions in the Creed of the Nicene council, and the primary subject of the Chalcedonian, shows the importance of early Christian belief in the nature of Jesus as both Divine and Man, so much so that believing the two could be reduced to a third, intermingled, nature was considered heresy.

Etymology and usage.

In the Koine Greek of the New Testament, "the son of man". The Hebrew expression "son of man" also appears over a hundred times in the Hebrew Bible. In thirty-two cases, the phrase appears in intermediate plural form "sons of men", i.e. human beings.

The expression "the Son of man" appears 81 times in the Koine Greek of the four Gospels: 30 times in Matthew, 14 times in Mark, 25 times in Luke and 12 times in John. However, the use of the definite article in "the Son of man" is novel, and before its use in the canonical gospels, there are no records of its use in any of the surviving Greek documents of antiquity.

Geza Vermes has stated that "the son of man" in the New Testament is unrelated to Hebrew Bible usages. Vermes begins with the observation that there is no example of "the" son of man in Hebrew sources and suggests that the term originates in <u>Aramaic</u>. He concludes that in these sources "Son of man" is a regular expression for *man* in general and often serves as an indefinite pronoun and in none of the extant texts does "son of man" figure as a title.

However, other sources argue that the Son of Man is a title, claimed by Jesus as a way of asserting his own divine nature. Whitefield, for example, argues that within the biblical context, all humans are referred to as "Sons of Man", or more specifically, sons of Adam. Jesus' claiming this specific title was a direct claim to divine authority, alluding to that of Daniel, the one who is prophesied to "[come] with the clouds of heaven" and who is to be "given authority, glory and sovereign power". As such, though the title itself could refer to any human being, the title itself refers to a specific religious messianic figure.

The occurrences of Son of man in the Synoptic gospels are generally categorized into three groups: (i) those that refer to his "coming" (as an exaltation); (ii) those that refer to "suffering" and (iii) those that refer to "now at work" i.e. referring to the earthly life.

The presentation of Son of man in the Gospel of John is somewhat different from the Synoptics: in John 1:51 he is presented as contact with the Lord through "angelic instrumentality", in John 6:26 and 6:53 he provides life through his death, and in John 5:27 he holds the power to judge men.

Synoptic gospels

In Matthew 8:20 and Luke 9:58 Jesus states: "The foxes have holes, and the birds of the sky have nests, but the Son of man has nowhere to lay his head." This phrasing seems to tie in with the Old Testament prophetic expressions used by such prophets as Ezekiel, and it shows Jesus' understanding of himself as the "man" that the Father has singled out as a friend and representative.

Johannine literature.

The first chapter of the Book of Revelation refers to "one like a Son of man" in Revelation 1:12-13 which radiantly stands in glory and speaks to the author. In the Gospel of John Jesus is not just a messianic figure, nor a just prophet like Moses, but the key emphasis is on his dual role as Son of Divine and Son of man.

Book of Moses.

The title "Son of Man" is used nine times in the Book of Moses, a 19th-century work considered canonical scripture by the Church of Jesus Christ of Latter-day Saints and included in its publication The Pearl of Great Price. According to Nontrinitarianism, Moses 6:57 suggests that a name of the Father is "Man of Holiness," and that the title "Son of Man" points to Jesus' divine sonship.

Book of Daniel

The title "Son of Man" appears in the Book of Daniel, and most sources allude specifically to this particular verse. According to the Daniel 7, The Son of Man is seen "coming with the clouds of heaven. He approached the Ancient of Days and was led into his presence. He was given authority, glory and sovereign power; all nations and peoples of every language worshiped him. His dominion is an everlasting dominion that will not pass away, and his kingdom is one that will never be destroyed." (Daniel 7:13–14)

Scholarly views.

The interpretation of the use of "the Son of man" in the New Testament has proven to be challenging, and James D. G. Dunn and separately Delbert Burkett state that it is a prime example of the limits of New Testament interpretation because after 150 years of debate no consensus on its meaning has emerged.

The earliest approaches, going back to the Fathers of the Church, relied on the Greek expression and interpreted "son" in a parental sense. This approach continued into the Middle Ages. By the time the Protestant Reformation was under way, three new approaches had emerged, one that saw it as an expression of the humanity of Jesus, another that viewed it as a messianic title derived from the Book of Daniel (7.13) and a third which considered it as a general idiom for self-reference. By the 17th century, the first approach (focusing on his humanity) had gained ground, yet by the 19th century the messianic view had increased in popularity.

In the last part of the 20th century, the messianic view was highly criticized and the concept of idiomatic use began to gain support among some scholars. In the 21st century, a simple approach has been made: "Adam means 'man.' So when Christ is called the Son of Man the entire generating line all the way from Adam down to Jesus is being recalled." However, no consensus has emerged among scholars on how the expression can be interpreted. Another view put forward by Bart D. Ehrman (1999) is that there are some passages (as such Mark 8:38, 13:26, 14:62; Matthew 19:28, 25:31–46; and Luke 12:8–9) in which Jesus mentions 'the Son of Man' and does not appear to be talking about himself, but about someone else, namely a cosmic judge who would come down from heaven to bring judgment. The identification of the Son of Man with Jesus might thus be a later, inauthentic tradition. Ingolfsland (2001) argued that Ehrman's examples were not valid, or did not meet his own criteria.

Jewish views.

In Judaism, "son of man" denotes mankind generally, in contrast to deity or godhead, with special reference to their weakness and frailty (Job 25:6; Psalms 8:4; Psalms 144:3; Psalms 146:3; Isaiah 51:12, etc.) or the term "ben adam" is but a formal substitute for the personal pronoun. *Christ*, by Titian – (detail) 1553, oil on canvas, 68x62cm, Prado Museum Madrid.

Sixty-nine times in the Synoptic Gospels, Jesus calls himself (the) "Son of man", a Greek expression which in its Aramaic (and Hebrew) background could be an oblique way of indicating the speaker's own self (e.g., Matt 8:20), or else simply mean "someone" or "a human being" (as in Ps 8:4, where it is a poetic variant for "man"). In Daniel 7:13–

14 the "Son of man" seems to symbolise the angels (perhaps the archangel Michael) and/or the righteous and persecuted Jews who will be vindicated and given authority by the Lord (Dan 7:18,21–22,27; 10:13, 21; 12:1) rather than function as one individual, heavenly figure who represents the people. What is clear from the evidence is that "Son of man" did not function in pre-Christian messianic expectations as a title for a deliverer expected to come in the last times. But to the Israelites and other readers and followers of the Torah this phrase would have meaning and point to the Messiah. It was not even a sharply defined concept, with a specific content and reference. It could simply denote a member of the human race (Ps. 8:4) or be a way of pointing to a prophet's insignificance and finite dependence in the face of the Lord's glory and infinite power. Therefore, the Lord addresses <u>Ezekiel</u> ninety-three times as "son of man".

Three contexts

According to the Synoptic Gospels, Jesus referred to himself as "Son of man" in three contexts, each with its own circle of fairly distinct meanings. He used this self-designation of **(1)** his earthly work and its (frequently) humble condition (e.g., Mark 2:10, 28 parr.; Matt 11:19 and Luke 7:34; Matt 8:20 and Luke 9:58); **(2)** his coming suffering, death, and resurrection (Mark 9:9,12; Mark 14:21 and, above all, Mark 8:31; 9:31; 10:33–34 parr.); **(3)** his future coming in heavenly glory to act with sovereign power at a final judgement (e.g., Mark 8:38; 13:26–27 parr.; Matt 24:27 and Luke 17:24; Matt 25:31–32; see John 5:27). These classifications show how the "Son of man" served as a way of indicating Jesus' importance and even universal relevance. This was especially true of the class (3) sayings. In other words, "Son of man" was used to say what Jesus did rather than what he was. It was not and did not become a title in the normal sense—at least not on the lips of Jesus Himself.

At the same time, the evangelists (and/or their sources) do not always seem to distinguish "Son of man" sharply from "Christ/Messiah" or "Son of the Father". For Mark, the Davidic Messiah and Daniel's Son of man are one and same person, and their name is Jesus. In Mark 14:61-62, the reply that Jesus makes to the high priest's question ("Are you the Messiah, the Son of the Blessed One?") conveys some glorious connotations of "the Son of the Father" as a figure who will come in triumph on the clouds of heaven to judge his enemies: "I am; and you will see the Son of man seated at the right hand of the Power, and coming with the clouds of heaven". In John's Gospel, the expression gains a significant element not found in the Synoptic Gospels under any of the three meanings listed above: the "Son of man" is a personally pre-existent figure (e.g., John 3:13; John 6:62).

Jesus' ministry

Regarding Jesus himself, much debate originated in deciding whether any or all of the three classes of self-referential sayings derived from what he said in his ministry. A few scholars have even attempted to prove that none of the "Son of man" sayings came from Jesus himself. However, there remain good and convergent reasons for maintaining that, while there was some editorial reworking, Jesus did speak of himself as "Son of man", filled the term with his own meanings, and was responsible for the three classes of "Son of man" sayings listed above. Along with the way he used the image of the kingdom of the Father and the of Father, here a third classic example is supplied of Jesus taking an inherited expression and using it massively but in his own way. First, one does not find others ever describing, addressing, or confessing Jesus as the Son of man apart from four marginal cases (Acts 7:56; Rev. 1:13; 14:14; Heb. 2:6). The last three cases deal with quotations from the Old Testament. In the Gospels, other people address and speak about Jesus in a variety of ways, but never directly as "Son of man". According to John 12:34, the audience of Jesus were puzzled when he referred to himself as "the Son of man". Now, if the early Church had freely created the Son of man sayings, it would be puzzling that this designation for Jesus is not found on the lips of others. The puzzle disappears once it is agreed that there is here a genuine historical recollection: only Jesus used the term, and the evangelists and their sources faithfully recorded that.

Second, the Son of man sayings in which Jesus refers to his (often humble and merciful) earthly activity are attested by both Mark (e.g., Mark 2:10, 28) and Q source (Matt 8:20 and Luke 9:58; Matt 11:19 and Luke 7:34). The sayings dealing with the coming or apocalyptic Son of man likewise turn up in Mark (Mark 8:38; 13:26; 14:62) and in Q (e.g., Matt 24:27 and Luke 17:24. This double strand of tradition or multiple attestation can encourage one to attribute to Jesus at least class (1) and class (3) of the Son of man sayings.

Third, there was some Jewish background to Jesus' Son of man sayings, but there was scarcely any follow-up in the emerging Church. Later on, the Church Fathers would use the term as a way of referring to Christ's humanity as opposed to his divinity or to his being the Son of Man. However, in the first century the designation does not seem to have been useful in preaching the good news. It does not appear in credal and liturgical formulas. It was too flexible and even vague: it ranges from the mysterious heavenly being of Daniel 7 to simply serving as a circumlocution for "I". Linguistically, it was a particularly odd expression for Greek-speaking people. The fact that the designation was strange and unsuitable for the early Church's life and ministry suggests that the Son of man sayings did not derive from groups in the Church, but from another source, which could only really be Jesus.

Fourth, the sayings about the coming Son of man sometimes imply a certain differentiation between this figure and Jesus. Therefore, Luke reports Jesus as declaring: "Every one who acknowledges me before men, the Son of man also will acknowledge before the angels of the Lord" (Luke 12:8). Matthew modifies this Q saying to read: "Every one who acknowledges me before men, I also will acknowledge before my Father who is in heaven" (Matt. 10:32). Apparently, Luke has preserved the original form of the saying, which indicates a certain unity of function between Jesus himself and the Son of man, but at the same time introduces some differentiation between the two figures. The differentiation makes sense once it is recognised that it recalls a turn of phrase actually used by Jesus to distinguish his present preaching from his future judging. The distinction had its point in the historical context of his ministry, but not later in the post-Easter situation where believers acknowledged the personal unity between the risen Jesus and the Son of man who would come in glory. Matthew's modification reflects precisely that shift.

Fifth, there are some unusual features about the preservation of the "Son of man" sayings. The three classes are not blended together. Thus (2) the passion predictions about the Son of man do not go beyond the death and resurrection to include (3) statements about the future coming of the Son of man. Furthermore, the sayings about the Father's kingdom (and, specifically, the parables) never introduce the Son of man. The absence of a clear and strong connection between the Son of man and the divine kingdom is puzzling. After all, Daniel 7 was relevant for the functions of the Son of man, and the Danielic imagery had included the Father's kingdom (Daniel 2:44; 4:3; 7:27). The independence of the three classes of Son of man sayings and the separation of the kingdom sayings from the Son of man can be explained if one sees the Gospels (and the traditions behind them) accurately preserving here distinctions that genuinely went back to Jesus' actual preaching and teaching.

Comparison to *Son of Man*

For centuries, the Christological perspective on Son of man has been seen as a possible counterpart to that of Son of Man and just as Son of affirms the humanity of Jesus, the title Son of Man affirms his divinity. Though many sources claimed that the title referred to his human nature, these sources may stem from a cursory and shallow understanding of the title. It must be noted that in other parts of Scripture, the title "Son of the Father" is bestowed on other historical figures like Jacob and Solomon; but the Son of Man title is claimed only by Jesus. Thus, paradoxically, the title Son of Man actually refers to Christ's Godly nature, alluding to the One mentioned in Daniel 7, while the title Son of the Father refers to his humanity, as seen in the Old Testament.

While of all the Christological titles used in the New Testament, Son of Father has had one of the most lasting impacts in Christian history and has become part of the profession of faith by many Christians, the proclamation of Son of man has never been an article of faith in Christianity. Thus in the mainstream popular context it is the Son of the Father title which implies the full divinity of Jesus as part of the Holy Trinity of Father, Son and the Spirit.

In the 5th century, Saint Augustine wrote at length on the Son of the Father and its relationship with the Son of man, positioning the two issues in terms of the dual nature of Jesus as both divine and human in terms of the hypostatic union.[31] He wrote:

Christ Jesus, the Son of the Father, is Divine and Man: the Father before all worlds, man in our world... But since he is the only Son of the Father, by nature and not by grace, he became also the Son of Man that He might be full of grace as well.

Top of Form

Son of man (Christianity)

- *This article is about the Christian teachings. For an overview, see Son of man. For other usage, see Son of man (disambiguation).*

The Son of man with a sword among the seven lampstands, in John's vision. From the Bamberg Apocalypse, 11th century.

Son of man is an expression in the sayings of Jesus in Christian writings, including the Gospels, the Acts of the Apostles and the Book of Revelation. The meaning of the expression is controversial. Interpretation of the use of "the Son of man" in the New Testament has remained challenging and after 150 years of debate no consensus on the issue has emerged among scholars.

The expression "the Son of man" occurs 81 times in the four canonical gospels (mainly quoting Jesus) and another four times in the rest of the New Testament. The equivalent

Hebrew expression "son of man" appears in the Old Testament 103 times.

The use of the definite article in "the Son of man" in the Koine Greek of the Christian gospels is original, and before its use there, no records of its use in any of the surviving Greek documents of antiquity exist. Geza Vermes has stated that the use of "the Son of man" in the Christian gospels is unrelated to Hebrew Torah usages. For centuries, the Christological perspective on Son of man ("man" referring to Adam) has been seen as a possible counterpart to that of Son of Man and just as Son of Man affirms the divinity of Jesus, in a number of cases Son of man affirms his humanity.

The profession of Jesus as the Son of Man has been an essential element of Christian creeds since the Apostolic age, and while some do not think profession of Christ as Son of man was necessary for Christians, the proclamation of Jesus as the Son of man has been an article of faith in Christianity since at least the Nicene Creed which reads in the English as: "by the power of the Holy Spirit he became incarnate from the Virgin Mary, and was made man." Christ being a man-Divine was so important that it was the major issue addressed at the Council of Chalcedon where the heresy of monophysitism was addressed.

Monophysites regarded Christ as having a single nature that was a co-mingling of the two, Divine and Man, whereas the Orthodox Catholic position held that he was completely Divine, and completely man, simultaneously. These positions in the Creed of the Nicene council, and the primary subject of the Chalcedonian, shows the importance of early Christian belief in the nature of Jesus as both Divine and Man, so much so that believing the two could be reduced to a third, intermingled, nature was considered heresy. The production of these prayers by the Catholic Church shows why and their position to **replace Mithra with Jesus as their sun-god:**

The Apostles' Creed

I believe in God, the Father almighty, creator of heaven and earth.

I believe in Jesus Christ, his only Son, Our Lord, who was conceived by the Holy Spirit, born of the Virgin Mary, suffered under Pontius Pilate, was crucified, died, and was buried; he descended to the dead. On the third day he rose again; he ascended into heaven, he is seated at the right hand of the Father, and he will come to judge the living and the dead.

I believe in the Holy Spirit, the holy Catholic Church, the communion of saints, the forgiveness of sins, the resurrection of the body, and the life everlasting. Amen.

Nicene Creed

We believe in one God, the Father the Almighty, maker of heaven and earth, of all that is seen and unseen.

We believe in one Lord, Jesus Christ, the only Son of God, eternally begotten of the Father, God from God, Light from Light, true God from true God, begotten, not made, consubstantial to the father. Through him all things were made. For us and for our salvation he came down from heaven: by the power of the Holy Spirit he became incarnate from the Virgin Mary, and was made man. For our sake he was crucified under Pontius Pilate; he suffered death and was buried. On the third day he rose again in accordance with the Scriptures; he ascended into heaven and is seated at the right hand of the Father. He will come again in glory to judge the living and the dead, and his kingdom will have no end.

We believe in the Holy Spirit, the Lord, the giver of life, who proceeds from the Father and the Son. With the Father and the Son he is worshiped and glorified. He has spoken through the Prophets. We believe in one holy catholic and apostolic Church. We acknowledge one baptism for the forgiveness of sins. We look for the resurrection of the dead, and the life of the world to come. Amen.

- ### *Jesus and Mithra:* the sun-gods of the Romans

According to Siamak Adhami, Ph.D, December 25 was the: Birthday of Mithra and Jesus as the Roman Gods. And Romans had replaced Mithra, (who was worshipped by Constantine), with Jesus Christ and now worshipping Him as their **sun-god.**

December 25: The Birthday of the Iranian God, Mithra and Jesus of Nazareth.

"Grass-land magnate Mithra is worshipped, whose words are correct, who is challenging, has a thousand ears, is well built, has ten thousand eyes, is tall, has a wide outlook, is strong, sleepless, (ever-)waking, whom the warriors worship. Mithra, who is the first supernatural god to approach across the Har, in front of the immortal swift-horsed sun; who is the first to seize the beautiful gold-painted mountain top; from there the most mighty surveys the whole land inhabited by Iranians, where gallant rulers organize many attacks, where high, sheltering mountains with ample pasture provide solicitous for cattle; where deep lakes stand with surging waves; where navigable rivers rush wide with a swell towards Parutian Iškata, Haraivian Margu, Sogdian Gava, and Chorasmia."

This essay begins with one of the most beautiful passages from the Avestan hymn in praise of Mithra as translated by the eminent Iranist Ilya Gershevitch. Mithra was a deity common to at least two branches of Indo-European people, namely Iranians and Indo-Aryans. In addition to the hymn in the Avesta, we are also aware of the presence of the **god Mithra or Mithras** (Vedic "Mitra", Middle Persian "Mihr," and Persian "Mehr") in the ancient Indian scriptures known as the Rig-Veda (1400 BC). For the ancient Iranians, the god Mithra had two significant functions: he was first and foremost the sun-god whose thousands of eyes spied on every deed and nothing, particularly evil deeds, could escape from his gaze. Secondly, he was the god of contracts. For example, even in late Pahlavi/Middle Persian texts which are concerned with legal and religious matters, there exists a severe crime and sin which is related to the functions of Mithra, which signifies "breaking promise or contract," and by extension, "perfidy." Perfidy was classified as one of the most heinous crimes with severe punishment prescribed for the offender. During late antiquity, **the worship of Mithra became popular, particularly among Roman soldiers and merchants.** The reasons for the popularity of the cult of Mithra among these two groups are easily understood: the martial nature of the hymn can explain the popularity of Mithra among soldiers. Similarly, his reverence by the merchant class is equally clear as he was the god of contracts. It is not unreasonable to think that merchants traversing across ancient commercial highways such as the famed Silk Road in antiquity preferred to conduct business with those whom they trusted and the affiliation with this mysterious fraternity only served to cement the bond between them. The adherents of the Mithraic cult, similar to those of **other**

religions such as Judaism, Christianity and Islam, also held festivals celebrating different aspects of their religion. It appears that **the annual celebration held on December 25, the winter solstice, was the most important celebration of the cult; it was believed that Mithra was born on this day, hence "the birthday of the _unconquered sun" (Latin: natalis solis invicti)._** Later, the practices of the cult seem to have gained much in popularity. With the advent of Christianity, a number of pagan practices which could not be abandoned found their way into this new religion. **The most significant of these was the identification of the birthday of Jesus, commonly known as <u>Christmas</u> <u>(Old English Cristes maesse: Christ's mass)</u>, with that of the undying _Mithra._**

Much has been written on pagan cults in the Roman empire and particular attention has been paid to the cult of Mithra. In fact Ernest Renan went as far as stating that "if the growth of Christianity had been halted by some mortal illness, the world would have become Mithraic." As Walter Burkert points out, Renan may have exaggerated the case as the worship of Mithra belonged to a rather elitist segment of the society. However according to Werner Jaeger, there is no doubt that Mithraism and Manichaeism, two religions with well-established Iranian connections, posed a serious threat to **the spread of the new faith which became known as Christianity.**

The followings are for further readings on Mithraism: Adhami, Siamak, PAITIMĀNA, Essays in Iranian, Indo-European, and Indian Studies in Honour of HANNS-PETER SCHMIDT. (2003) Mazda Publishers, Costa Mesa, CA. Burkert, Walter, Ancient Mystery Cults. (1987). Early Christianity and Greek Paideia. Cambridge, MA. Merkelbach, R. (1982).

List of Gods Born By A Virgin On 25th December by music writer.

ALTHOUGH THE BIBLICAL STORY OF JESUS CONTRADICTS THIS.

FOR INSTANCE IN Luke 2:7-8 SAYS THAT SHEPHERD WERE WATCHING THEIR FLOCK IN THE FIELDS WHEN HE WAS BORN. SHEPHERD DON'T WATCH THEIR FLOCK IN THE FIELDS IN DECEMBER!

JESUS' PARENTS CAME TO BETHLEHEM TO REGISTER IN A ROMAN CENSUS (Luke 2:1-4). SUCH CENSUSES WERE NOT TAKEN IN WINTER, WHEN TEMPERATURES OFTEN DROPPED BELOW FREEZING AND ROADS WERE IN POOR CONDITION. TAKING A CENSUS UNDER SUCH CONDITIONS WOULD HAVE BEEN SELF-DEFEATNG.

Some of the names might be the inventions of early man. However, a **Yeshua or Yehoshua existed, from where Jesus was supposedly plagiarized by Rome** since they didn't believe him.

Also, list Of Gods Born By A Virgin On 25th December provided by Oga Sir Ade

Here are names of Gods throughout history that were said to have been born by a virgin on 25th December.

HORUS

An Egypt or Ethiopian-Sudanese God, born 25th December, by a Virgin around 3,000 YEARS before Jesus.

BUDDHA

A Nepal God, born 25th December, by a Virgin around 563 YEARS before Jesus.

KRISHNA

An Indian God, born 25th December, by a Virgin around 900 YEARS before Jesus.

ZARATHUSTRA

An Indian God, born 25th December, by a Virgin around 1,000 YEARS before Jesus.

HERCULES

A Greek God, born 25th December, by a Virgin around 800 YEARS before Jesus.

MITHRA

A Persian God, born 25th December, by a Virgin- 600 YEARS before Jesus.

DIONYSUS

A Greek God, born 25th December, by a Virgin around 500 YEARS before Jesus.

THAMMUZ

A Babylonian God, born 25th December, by a Virgin around 400 YEARS before Jesus.

HERMES

A Greek God, born 25th December, by a Virgin around 200 YEARS before Jesus.

ADONIS

A Phoenician God, born 25th December, by a Virgin around 200 YEARS before Jesus.

JESUS CHRIST

A Roman God, born 25th December, by a Virgin around 300 AD

Pagan gods born December 25th, thus this date is celebrated every year by all pagan gods.

According to the ancient Babylonian traditions... Tammuz was supposedly born on December 25th around 2600 BC. And also some false pagan gods were supposedly born December 25th.

<u>Jesus was not born on December 25th</u>

Altering Jesus' character in any way, including His birthdate, a false Christ is created. And following a false Jesus is just as dangerous and damning as no Jesus! Be wise, pray for discernment, don't follow the world blindly, research all things you entertain and encourage, come away from the pagan Christmas lies, have nothing to do with any of the ways of the pagans... light and the darkness can never co-exist! May Jesus bless you and open your eyes, help you shed your Christmas blinders, so you can better see, grow, and be a faithful follower of Christ. His coming is near!

In the Koine Greek of the New Testament, "the son of man". The Hebrew expression "son of man" also appears over a hundred times in the Hebrew Bible. In thirty-two cases, the phrase appears in intermediate plural form "sons of men", i.e. human beings.

The expression "the Son of man" appears 81 times in the Koine Greek of the four Gospels: 30 times in Matthew, 14 times in Mark, 25 times in Luke and 12 times in John. However, the use of the definite article in "the Son of man" is novel, and before its use in the canonical gospels, there are no records of its use in any of the surviving Greek documents of antiquity.

Geza Vermes has stated that "the son of man" in the New Testament is unrelated to Hebrew Bible usages. Vermes begins with the observation that there is no example of "the" son of man in Hebrew sources and suggests that the term originates in Aramaic – *bar nash/bar nasha*. He concludes that in these sources "Son of man" is a regular expression for *man* in general and often serves as an indefinite pronoun and in none of the extant texts does "son of man" figure as a title.

However, other sources argue that the Son of Man is a title, claimed by Jesus as a way of asserting his own divine nature. Whitefield, for example, argues that within the biblical context, all humans are referred to as "Sons of Man", or more specifically, sons of <u>Adam</u>. Jesus' claiming this specific title was a direct claim to divine authority, alluding to that of <u>Daniel</u>, the one who is prophesied to "[come] with the clouds of heaven" and who is to be "given authority, glory and sovereign power". As such, though the title itself could refer to any human being, the title itself refers to a specific religious messianic figure.

The occurrences of Son of man in the <u>Synoptic gospels</u> are generally categorized into three groups: (i) those that refer to his "coming" (as an exaltation); (ii) those that refer to "suffering" and (iii) those that refer to "now at work" i.e. referring to the earthly life.

The presentation of Son of man in the <u>Gospel of John</u> is somewhat different from the Synoptics: in John 1:51 he is presented as contact with God through "angelic instrumentality", in John 6:26 and 6:53 he provides life through his death, and in John 5:27 he holds the power to judge men.

Synoptic gospel.

In Matthew 8:20 and Luke 9:58 Jesus states: "The foxes have holes, and the birds of the sky have nests, but the Son of man has nowhere to lay his head." This phrasing seems to tie in with the Old Testament prophetic expressions used by such prophets as Ezekiel, and it shows Jesus' understanding of himself as the "man" that the Lord has singled out as a friend and representative.

Johannine literature

The first chapter of the Book of Revelation refers to "one like a Son of man" in Revelation 1:12-13 which radiantly stands in glory and speaks to the author. In the Gospel of John Jesus is not just a messianic figure, nor a just prophet like Moses, but the key emphasis is on his dual role as Son of the Father and Son of man.

Book of Moses

The title "Son of Man" is used nine times in the Book of Moses, a 19th-century work considered canonical scripture by the Church of Jesus Christ of Latter-day Saints and included in its publication The Pearl of Great Price. According to Nontrinitarianism, Moses 6:57 suggests that a name of God the Father is "Man of Holiness," and that the title "Son of Man" points to Jesus' divine sonship.

Book of Daniel

The title "Son of Man" appears in the Book of Daniel, and most sources allude specifically to this particular verse. According to the Daniel 7, The Son of Man is seen "coming with the clouds of heaven. He approached the Ancient of Days and was led into his presence. He was given authority, glory and sovereign power; all nations and peoples of every language worshiped him. His dominion is an everlasting dominion that will not pass away, and his kingdom is one that will never be destroyed." (Daniel 7:13–14)

Scholarly views

The interpretation of the use of "the Son of man" in the New Testament has proven to be challenging, and James D. G. Dunn and separately Delbert Burkett state that it is a prime example of the limits of New Testament interpretation because after 150 years of debate no consensus on its meaning has emerged.

The earliest approaches, going back to the Fathers of the Church, relied on the Greek expression and interpreted "son" in a parental sense. This approach continued into the Middle Ages. By the time the Protestant Reformation was under way, three new approaches had emerged, one that saw it as an expression of the humanity of Jesus, another that viewed it as a messianic title derived from the Book of Daniel (7.13) and a third which considered it as a general idiom for self-reference. By the 17th century, the first approach (focusing on his humanity) had gained ground, yet by the 19th century the messianic view had increased in popularity.

In the last part of the 20th century, the messianic view was highly criticized and the concept of idiomatic use began to gain support among some scholars. In the 21st century, a simple approach has been made: "Adam means 'man.' So when Christ is called the Son of Man the entire generating line all the way from Adam down to Jesus is being recalled." However, no consensus has emerged among scholars on how the expression can be interpreted. Another view put forward by <u>Bart D. Ehrman</u> (1999) is that there are some passages (as such Mark 8:38, 13:26, 14:62; Matthew 19:28, 25:31–46; and Luke 12:8–9) in which Jesus mentions 'the Son of Man' and does not appear to be talking about himself, but about someone else, namely a cosmic judge who would come down from heaven to bring judgment. The identification of the Son of Man with Jesus might thus be a later, inauthentic tradition. Ingolfsland (2001) argued that Ehrman's examples were not valid, or did not meet his own criteria.

Jewish views

In Judaism, "son of man" denotes mankind generally, in contrast to deity or godhead, with special reference to their weakness and frailty (Job 25:6; Psalms 8:4; Psalms 144:3; Psalms 146:3; Isaiah 51:12, etc.) or the term "ben Adam" is but a formal substitute for the personal pronoun.

Sixty-nine times in the Synoptic Gospels, Jesus calls himself (the) "Son of man", a Greek expression which in its Aramaic (and Hebrew) background could be an oblique way of indicating the speaker's own self (e.g., Matt 8:20), or else simply mean "someone" or "a human being" (as in Ps 8:4, where it is a poetic variant for "man"). In Daniel 7:13–14 the "Son of man" seems to symbolize the angels (perhaps the archangel Michael) and/or the righteous and persecuted Jews who will be vindicated and given authority by the Lord (Dan 7:18,21–22,27; 10:13, 21; 12:1) rather than function as one individual, heavenly figure who represents the people. What is clear from the evidence is that "Son of man" did not function in pre-Christian messianic expectations as a title for a deliverer expected to come in the last times. But to the Israelites and other readers and followers of the Torah this phrase would have meaning and point to the Messiah. It was not even a sharply defined concept, with a specific content and reference. It could simply denote a member of the human race (Ps. 8:4) or be a way of pointing to a prophet's insignificance and finite dependence in the face of Lord's glory and infinite power. Therefore, the Lord addresses Ezekiel ninety-three times as "son of man".

Three contexts

According to the Synoptic Gospels, Jesus referred to himself as "Son of man" in three contexts, each with its own circle of fairly distinct meanings. He used this self-designation of **(1)** his earthly work and its (frequently) humble condition (e.g., Mark 2:10, 28 parr.; Matt 11:19, Luke 7:34; Matt 8:20, Luke 9:58); **(2)** his coming suffering, death, and resurrection (Mark 9:9,12; Mark 14:21 and, above all, Mark 8:31; 9:31; 10:33–34 parr.); **(3)** his future coming in heavenly glory to act with sovereign power at a final judgement (e.g., Mark 8:38; 13:26–27 parr.; Matt 24:27, Luke 17:24; Matt 25:31–32; see John 5:27). These classifications show how the "Son of man" served as a way of indicating Jesus' importance and even universal relevance. This was especially true of the class (3) sayings. In other words, "Son of man" was used to say what Jesus did rather than what he was. It was not and did not become a title in the normal sense—at least not on the lips of Jesus himself.

At the same time, the evangelists (and/or their sources) do not always seem to distinguish "Son of man" sharply from "Christ/Messiah" or "Son of the Father". For Mark, the Davidic Messiah and Daniel's Son of man are one and same person, and their name is Jesus. In Mark 14:61-62, the reply that Jesus makes to the high priest's question ("Are you the Messiah, the Son of the Blessed One?") conveys some glorious connotations of "the Son of the Father" as a figure who will come in triumph on the clouds of heaven to judge his enemies: "I am; and you will see the Son of man seated at the right hand of the Power, and coming with the clouds of heaven". In John's Gospel, the expression gains a significant element not found in the Synoptic Gospels under any of the three meanings listed above: the" Son of man" is a personally pre-existent figure (e.g., John 3:13; John 6:62).

Jesus' ministry

Jesus himself, much debate originated in deciding whether any or all of the three classes of self-referential sayings derived from what he said in his ministry. A few scholars have even attempted to prove that none of the "Son of man" sayings came from Jesus himself. However, there remain good and convergent reasons for maintaining that, while there was some editorial reworking, Jesus did speak of himself as "Son of man", filled the term with his own meanings, and was responsible for the three classes of "Son of man" sayings listed above. Along with the way he used the image of the kingdom of the Father and that of the Father as Father, here a third classic example is supplied of Jesus taking an inherited expression and using it massively but in his own way.

First, one does not find others ever describing, addressing, or confessing Jesus as the Son of man apart from four marginal cases (Acts 7:56; Rev. 1:13; 14:14; Heb. 2:6). The last three cases deal with quotations from the Old

Testament. In the Gospels, other people address and speak about Jesus in a variety of ways, but never directly as "Son of man". According to John 12:34, the audience of Jesus were puzzled when he referred to himself as "the Son of man". Now, if the early Church had freely created the Son of man sayings, it would be puzzling that this designation for Jesus is not found on the lips of others. The puzzle disappears once it is agreed that there is here a genuine historical recollection: only Jesus used the term, and the evangelists and their sources faithfully recorded that.

Second, the Son of man sayings in which Jesus refers to his (often humble and merciful) earthly activity are attested by both Mark (e.g., Mark 2:10, 28) and (Matt 8:20, Luke 9:58; Matt 11:19, Luke 7:34). The sayings dealing with the coming or apocalyptic Son of man likewise turn up in Mark (Mark 8:38; 13:26; 14:62) and in (e.g., Matt 24:27, Luke 17:24. This double strand of tradition or multiple attestation can encourage one to attribute to Jesus at least class (1) and class (3) of the Son of man sayings.

Third, there was some Jewish background to Jesus' Son of man sayings, but there was scarcely any follow-up in the emerging Church. Later on, the Church Fathers would use the term as a way of referring to Christ's humanity as opposed to his divinity or to his being the Son of the Father. However, in the first century the designation does not seem to have been useful in preaching the good news. It does not appear in credal and liturgical formulas. It was too flexible and even vague: it ranges from the mysterious heavenly being of Daniel 7 to simply serving as a circumlocution for "I". Linguistically, it was a particularly odd expression for Greek-speaking people. The fact that the designation was strange and unsuitable for the early Church's life and ministry suggests that the Son of man sayings did not derive from groups in the Church, but from another source, which could only really be Jesus.

Fourth, the sayings about the coming Son of man sometimes imply a certain differentiation between this figure and Jesus. Therefore, Luke reports Jesus as declaring: "Every one who acknowledges me before men, the Son of man also will acknowledge before the angels of the Father" (Luke 12:8). Matthew modifies this Q saying to read: "Every one who acknowledges me before men, I also will acknowledge before my Father who is in heaven" (Matt. 10:32). Apparently, Luke has preserved the original form of the saying, which indicates a certain unity of function between Jesus himself and the Son of man, but at the same time introduces some differentiation between the two figures. The differentiation makes sense once it is recognised that it recalls a turn of phrase actually used by Jesus to distinguish his present preaching from his future judging. The distinction had its point in the historical context of his ministry, but not later in the post-Easter situation where believers acknowledged the personal unity between the risen Jesus and the Son of man who would come in glory. Matthew's modification reflects precisely that shift.

Fifth, there are some unusual features about the preservation of the "Son of man" sayings. The three classes are not blended together. Thus (2) the passion predictions about the Son of man do not go beyond the death and resurrection to include (3) statements about the future coming of the Son of man. Furthermore, the sayings about Father's kingdom (and, specifically, the parables) never introduce the Son of man.[27] The absence of a clear and strong connection between the Son of man and the divine kingdom is puzzling. After all, Daniel 7 was relevant for the functions of the Son of man, and the Danielic imagery had included Father's kingdom (Daniel 2:44; 4:3; 7:27). The independence of the three classes of Son of man sayings and the separation of the kingdom sayings from the Son of man can be explained if one sees the Gospels (and the traditions behind them) accurately preserving here distinctions that genuinely went back to Jesus' actual preaching and teaching.

For centuries, the Christological perspective on Son of man has been seen as a possible counterpart to that of Son of Man and just as Son of Man affirms the humanity of Jesus, the title Son of Man affirms his divinity. Though many sources claimed that the title referred to his human nature, these sources may stem from a cursory and shallow understanding of the title. It must be noted that in other parts of Scripture, the title "Son of the Father" is bestowed on other historical figures like Jacob and Solomon; but the Son of Man title is claimed only by Jesus. Thus, paradoxically, the title Son of Man actually refers to Christ's Divine nature, alluding to the One mentioned in Daniel 7, while the title Son of the Father refers to his humanity, as seen in the Old Testament.

While of all the Christological titles used in the New Testament, Son of the Father has had one of the most lasting impacts in Christian history and has become part of the profession of faith by many Christians, the proclamation of Son of man has never been an article of faith in Christianity. Thus in the mainstream popular context it is the Son of the Father title which implies the full divinity of Jesus as part of the Holy Trinity of Father, Son and the Spirit.

In the 5th century, Saint Augustine wrote at length on the Son of the Father and its relationship with the Son of man, positioning the two issues in terms of the dual nature of Jesus as both divine and human in terms of the hypostatic union. He wrote:

Christ Jesus, the Son of the Father is and Man: the Lord before all worlds, man in our world... But since he is the only Son of the Father, by nature and not by grace, he became also the Son of Man that he might be full of grace as well.

THE SECOND COMING OF JESUS CHRIST THE SAVIOUR

CHAPTER 7

JESUS WAS MISUNDERSTOOD

H ence his rejection by His own people. In this conclusion chapter will be devoted to exploring the important verses relating to the Gospel of John 6:41-71 explaining the verse by Verse. For instance from verses 41-42 reveals thus: So the Jews grumbled about him, because He said, "I am the bread that came down from heaven." They said, "Is not this Jesus, the son of Joseph, whose father and mother we know? How does he now say, 'I have come down from heaven'?" The people would not accept Jesus' claim to Deity, nor that He had come down from Heaven. They were saying, "We've known Him all his life, and even his parents. How can He say that He came down from heaven?"

They had a point in saying they had known Jesus and His family all His life. Except, they were not there when the angel, "Gabriel" came to Mary, and they were not there when Mary, expecting Jesus, visited Elizabeth who at the time was expecting "John the Baptist."

Nor when the Spirit in John the Baptist, still in Elizabeth's womb had leaped when He recognized Jesus in the womb of Mary. (John the Baptist was filled with the Spirit from birth).

"And you will have joy and gladness, and many will rejoice at his birth, **15** for he will be great before the Lord. And he must not drink wine or strong drink, and he will be filled with the Holy Spirit, even from his mother's womb." (Luke 1:14-15). And where were they when the angels appeared to the shepherds? Saying unto you is born to you in the city of David a Saviour.

Where were they when at the age of twelve Jesus, speaking of the Lord His Father, told His parents "Know ye not that I must be about my Father's business." And when the Voice from Heaven said, "This is my Son in whom I am well pleased?" There are other references, but the point is that these people did not know Jesus. Rather than explain, Jesus simply rebuked their grumbling.

Verses 43-44: "Jesus answered them, "Do not grumble among yourselves. No one can come to me unless the Father who sent me draws him. And I will raise him up on the last day."

The Lord does not want His People to complain. If you remember, He threatened to destroy the people who had grumbled to Moses.

Jesus said that if they were in the right relationship with the Father, they would have recognized Him. Those who do not recognize Him, do not know the Father.

Verse 45: "It is written in the Prophets, 'And they will all be taught by the Lord.' Everyone who has heard and learned from the Father comes to me—"

Jesus was quoting from Isaiah 54:13, "All your children shall be taught by the LORD,…"

And these were the children. Their walk with the Father should have been such that they could have received the Spiritual revelation necessary to understand His Words.

The Father had sent John the Baptist to prepare the way for Jesus because the people were not spiritually ready to accept Jesus.

Verse 46-47: "not that anyone has seen the Father except he who is from the Father; he has seen the Father."

Only Jesus has seen the Father!

Verse 48-49: "I am the bread of life. Your fathers ate the manna in the wilderness, and they died."

Again, Jesus takes up the theme of the bread. He tells them the "Heavenly Bread" He offers is superior, because it gives eternal life.

Verses 50-51: "This is the bread that comes down from heaven, so that one may eat of it and not die. I am the living bread that came down from heaven. If anyone eats of this bread, he will live forever. And the bread that I will give for the life of the world is my flesh."

Some believe that when we lay this body down, we become, "nothingness." However, the Bible teaches that the unsaved will die two deaths:

1: The death of the body at the end of life on earth, (the death we are all aware of).

2: The Spiritual death at Judgment Day, (where they are totally and eternally separated from the Father).

According to this Scripture, those born again, or as Jesus said, "Eats of this bread," only suffer the death of the body, and then spend the rest of eternity with Christ.

Our life does not disappear, we do not die and then come back to life zillions of years later. In this Scripture, Jesus is saying that, those who believe in Him do not die but "Will live forever."

When this body wears out we go to where He is, and, in His timing, we will receive a new body like His Glorified Body.

Jesus has been drawing a sharp contrast between Himself and the manna in the desert throughout this study, by referring to Himself as, the "living bread."

The word "flesh," a reference to the human life of Jesus was misunderstood by the people.

Perhaps in our day, He would say, I have come from Heaven to bring you the gift of Eternal Life. I am going to pay for it with my own body, my flesh.

Verse 52: "The Jews then disputed among themselves, saying, "How can this man give us his flesh to eat?"

They were interpreting His Words literally.

According to Bible Background of this period:

The Romans considered themselves to be intellectuals, a civilised nation that abhorred cannibalism, which was occasionally practiced by various cults and barbarians.

They had heard of the "Lord's Supper," but did not understand that the eating of the blood of the Lord was a symbolic figure of speech, and had assumed the Christians were just another cult which practiced cannibalism. Which helps explain why the Christians were so hated by the Romans.

According to history, a first-century Roman Emperor, "Nero," had the martyred Christian bodies burned in His courtyard for entertainment

Back to the Jewish people:

It is difficult to understand how they could not have associated a metaphorical meaning with what Jesus was saying.

Reminds us of what the author of the book of Hebrews said: "About this, we have much to say, and it is hard to explain, since you have become dull of hearing," (Heb:5:11).

They were definitely dull of hearing

The Jews thought that since they were the Lord's Chosen People, they were the only ones He was interested in; However, John 3:16 tells us that the Father sent Jesus because He "so loved the World."

Time and again the Jewish Nation had refused to listen to the Lord, and at one point, when they had made a golden calf idol, He had called them a "Stiff-Necked People," and, if not for Moses, would have destroyed them all:

"And the LORD said unto Moses, I have seen this people, and behold, it is a stiffnecked people: Now therefore let me alone, that my wrath may wax hot against them, and that I may consume them; and I will make of thee a great nation" (Deut 9:13-14).

Much later, the Lord said:

"... Go and tell this people, hear indeed but understand not; and see but perceive not. Make the heart of this people fat and make their eyes heavy ... lest they see with their eyes and hear with their ears and convert and be healed." (Isaiah 6:9-10)

And this Scripture:

"In them is fulfilled the prophecy of Isaiah which says: By hearing you shall hear and not understand; and seeing you shall see but not perceive. For this people's heart is waxed gross and their ears are dull of hearing and their eyes they have closed lest at any time they should see with their eyes and hear with their ears and should understand with their hearts and should be converted and I should heal them." (Matt 13:14)

Apparently these Scriptures written hundreds of years earlier were still in effect.

Verse 53: "So Jesus said to them, "Truly, truly, I say to you, unless you eat the flesh of the Son of Man and drink his blood, you have no life in you."

The Jews saw this as a powerful and most unusual statement. They could not understand that the new "Passover Lamb of the Father," was speaking symbolically.

They could not grasp, or accept that these words were coming from the Son of the Father, the One whom John had said in John 1, was, "The Word."

"In the beginning was the Word and the Word was with the Word who" the Father sent to the "Word," ("His Son") to earth.

The One who had been, "Spirit" had come to earth to live in the restraints and limitations of a human body.

The "One" whose ways are higher than our ways, and thoughts higher than our thoughts, was trying to reach these people with His Message. The message was, "without Him they could have no eternal life."

Verse 54: "Whoever feeds on my flesh and drinks my blood has eternal life, and I will raise him up on the last day."

In Exod 12:8, eating of the Passover Lamb was required.

Soon Jesus would give his body and spill His blood on the cross. All who believe would be welcomed into the New Covenant of Christ, and receive the gift of eternal life.

Verse 55-56: "For my flesh is true food, and my blood is true drink. Whoever feeds on my flesh and drinks my blood abides in me, and I in him."

Jesus repeatedly spoke about the sacrifice of His body, and the spilling of His blood.

Faith in whom Jesus is and what He was soon to do on the cross, is vividly described in terms of eating and drinking.

Jesus repeatedly spoke about the sacrifice of His body and the spilling of His blood.

Summary of the "Communion

The "Last Supper" and "Communion," are recorded in the synoptic Gospels, but not in this Gospel. This summary is intended to help understand the communion as much as possible.

Under the Old Covenant, the Israelites fed upon the "Passover Lamb," and drank the "blood of the grape" as a symbol of its blood.

Under the New Covenant, Jesus, the "Lamb of the Father," is now the "Sacrificial Lamb."

In Luke 22:19 Jesus and His disciples celebrated the Passover meal, the last supper they would have before His death. At this supper, Jesus inaugurated the "New Covenant," and commanded His Followers to partake of the "Communion," in remembrance of Him.

At the "communion," a small cracker, or unleavened bread is eaten, symbolizing Jesus' body; then the fruit of the grape is taken, symbolizing the blood of Jesus. This is to confirm total faith and commitment to Jesus' New Covenant.

The Old Covenant is no longer in effect. It has been replaced with the "New Covenant" of Jesus.

Verse 57: "As the living Father sent me, and I live because of the Father, so whoever feeds on me, he also will live because of me."

The Father sent Jesus, and He lives because of the Father, and whoever feeds on Jesus will live, (have eternal life).

Verse 58: "This is the bread that came down from heaven, not like the bread the fathers ate and died. Whoever feeds on this bread will live forever."

The bread that came down from heaven is the Lamb of the Father that takes away the sin of the world. Not the kind of bread the Israelites ate in the desert and later died.

This "Bread from Heaven" is the "Son of the Father" who extends the offer of eternal life. Who could turn that down?

Verse 59: "Jesus said these things in the synagogue, as he taught at Capernaum."

Jesus is teaching from the Synagogue in Capernaum; (thought to be next door to Peter's house).

In this part of the study, Jesus extends the "Words of Eternal Life."

Verse 60: "When many of his disciples heard it, they said, "This is a hard saying; who can listen to it?"

According to the above Scripture, many of the people, including His disciples, found Jesus' statements, incomprehensible, and impossible to accept.

Verse 61: "But Jesus, knowing in himself that his disciples were grumbling about this, said to them, "Do you take offence at this?"

He might have said, even after all the miracles you have seen, is this going to become a stumbling block to you?

Knowing in himself: Reflects Jesus' supernatural ability to know what is on the mind of man.

Offence: Does this upset, displease, shock and scandalise you? Jesus was asking, are you going to be so offended that this becomes a stumbling block?

Verse 62: "Then what if you were to see the Son of Man ascending to where He was before?"

What they had seen to this point could hardly compare to what was to come; soon He would be crucified, die, rise from the grave, and ascend to Heaven, where He had previously been for longer than they could imagine.

Verse 63 "It is the Spirit who gives life; the flesh is no help at all. The words that I have spoken to you are spirit and life."

He was speaking of the gift of the Holy Spirit.

By saying, "The Words I have spoken to you are Spirit and Life," He was making a distinction between the Spirit and the flesh.

The flesh, or natural man, is worthless, no help at all. The answer is in the Spirit. The Spirit is what gives everlasting life. Many of the Jewish interpreters were masters of figurative interpretation. Incredibly, they miss the message when He said, "The Words I have spoken to you are Spirit and Life?"

Verse 64: "But there are some of you who do not believe." (For Jesus knew from the beginning who those were who did not believe, and who it was who would betray him.)"

Some in that day were like our modern day mind readers, who were called "miracle workers." They were thought to know the mind or heart of some people.

Only the Father was the "Searcher of Hearts," the One who knows the hearts of all people. Jesus knew in advance that Judas Iscariot, one of the disciples He had personally hand-picked, would be the one to betray Him.

Verse 65: "And he said, This is why I told you that no one can come to me unless it is granted him by the Father."

Here again, Jesus knows their faith is missing and stresses the initiative of the Father. Salvation is a gift granted through belief/faith in Jesus, and no one can come to Him unless the Father grants it.

Verse 66: "After this many of his disciples turned back and no longer walked with him."

The unbelievers were now separated from the genuine Believers. Some Bible references refer to the departure of these disciples as apostasy, "abandoning what one has believed, (as in a faith)."

We are not given a specific number, but there were likely hundreds and possibly thousands who rejected Jesus and would no longer walk with Him. Earlier in this study, He had fed thousands of these same people, and they had become Followers.

This is said to be the only recorded incidence in the New Testament where the Believers stop believing in Jesus. They rejected Him because of His Doctrine. Jesus did not run after, or beg them to come back. He just let them go. I am not aware of anywhere in Scripture where Jesus ran after, pleaded, or demanded people to follow and believe in Him?

A part of me says, "I am glad they rejected Him, because they didn't deserve Him;" and yet, I too am undeserving.

Next, a sharp contrast between the faith of the twelve, and those who left.

Verse 67: "So Jesus said to the Twelve, "Do you want to go away as well?"

The original hand-picked twelve were not among those who rejected Him. Speaking to His disciples as a group, He questions their faith, and asks if they also are going to leave?

Verse 68: "Simon Peter answered him, "Lord, to whom shall we go? You have the words of eternal life,"

With Simon Peter as the spokesperson, the twelve affirm their complete faith in Jesus.

Verse 69: "and we have believed, and have come to know, that you are the Holy One of the Father."

"Holy One of the Father" Positively identifies Jesus as the Father, Demons, knowing who Jesus was, once used this same phrase when speaking to Jesus, (Mark 1:24 and Luke 4:34).

Peter says, "We have believed, and we know! That you are the Messiah."

Verses 70-71: "Jesus answered them, "Did I not choose you, the Twelve? And yet one of you is a devil." He spoke of Judas the son of Simon Iscariot, for he, one of the Twelve, was going to betray him."

Earlier Jesus had said, "there are some of you who do not believe." Here He qualifies Peter's use of the word, "we," by saying, "yet one of you is a devil." "Judas," who rejected and betrayed Jesus, was one of the original Twelve, and was personally chosen by Him.

The twelve disciples had seen and heard enough to convince them that Jesus was who He claimed to be. They were saying, "Where else could we possibly go? You are the "Deliverer" there is no one else. We may not fully understand all you are saying, but we know that you are the Messiah, and we're not leaving."

And to give relief to the afflicted as well as to us, when the Lord Jesus is revealed from heaven with His mighty angels in flaming fire, inflicting vengeance on those who do not know the Lord and on those who do not obey the gospel of our Lord Jesus. These will suffer the punishment of eternal destruction, separated from the presence of the Lord and from the glory of His might (2 Thessalonians 1:7-9).

The Second Coming of Christ will be a time of relief for believers and vengeance for unbelievers.

Who Will Be Judged?

The following people will be judged when Christ returns.

The church, the body of Christ, will have already been judged and rewarded before Christ returns.

When Christ returns, He will judge those from the nation Israel, who have survived the Great Tribulation. This judgment is described in Ezekiel 20:34-38. Jesus also illustrates this judgment in Matthew 25:1-30 in the parables of the ten maidens and the ten talents.

These survivors of the Great Tribulation will be regathered from all over the world to the land of Israel. This will follow the victory of Christ over His enemies at Armageddon.

The purpose is to determine which individuals will enter the Father's kingdom on the earth-the Millennium. The righteous from Israel, those who have put their trust in Christ, will enter the father's kingdom. They will experience the long-promised blessings that the Father has given to that nation.

Unrighteous Sent Away

The unrighteous will be purged from the righteous and sent away. Jesus illustrated this truth in the parable of the talents.

As for this worthless slave, throw him into the outer darkness, where there will be weeping and gnashing of teeth (Matthew 25:30).

Awaiting Final Judgment

Although the Scripture does not say, they will probably be put to death. Their final judgment does not take place at this time. It will occur after the Millennium, the thousand reign of Christ upon the earth.

2. The Living Gentile Nations

Jesus spoke of judging the living Gentile (non-Jewish) nations at His Second Coming.

When the Son of Man comes in His glory, and all the angels with Him, then He will sit on the throne of his glory All the nations will be gathered before Him, and He will separate people one from another as a shepherd separates the sheep from the goats (Matthew 25:31,32).

Those Surviving Tribulation

These Gentiles are people who are still upon the earth during the Great Tribulation. They are the living, not the dead. The dead will be raised to judgment in the future. The prophet Isaiah wrote of these.

Even the nations are like a drop from a bucket, and are accounted as dust on the scales; see, He takes up the isles like fine dust. All the nations are as nothing before

Him; they are accounted by him as less than nothing and emptiness (Isaiah 40:15,17).

They will be brought to the city of Jerusalem and judged in the valley of Jehoshaphat.

For then, in those days and at that time, when I restore the fortunes of Judah and Jerusalem, I will gather all the nations and bring them down to the valley of Jehoshaphat, and I will enter into judgment with them there, on account of My people and My heritage Israel, because they have scattered them among the nations. They have divided My land, and cast lots for My people, and traded boys for prostitutes, and sold girls for wine, and drunk it down (Joel 3:1-3).

The righteous will enter into the Father's Millennial kingdom while the unrighteous will be taken to judgment. Like the unbelievers from the nation Israel, they will probably be killed at this time. Their final judgment is still future.

3. The Tribulation Saints

When Christ returns, those who were killed during the Great Tribulation will also be judged. They will be raised from the dead in a glorified body, receive rewards, and will enter into the kingdom of the Father. In the Book of Revelation we read.

I saw thrones on which were seated those who had been given authority to judge. And I saw the souls of those who had been beheaded because of their testimony for Jesus and because of the Word of the Lord. They had not worshiped the beast or his image and had not received his mark on their foreheads or their hands. They came to life and reigned with Christ a thousand years. (The rest of the dead did not come to life until the thousand years were ended.) This is the first resurrection. Blessed and holy are those who have part in the first resurrection. The second death has no power over them, but they will be priests of the Father and of Christ and will reign with Him for a thousand years (Revelation 20:4-6).

4. Old Testament Saints

There will also be a judgment of the Old Testament saints. They will be raised from the dead and judged. Daniel wrote.

Multitudes who sleep in the dust of the earth will awake: some to everlasting life, others to shame and everlasting contempt (Daniel 12:2).

Jesus said.

For the Son of Man is to come with His angels in the glory of His Father, and then He will repay everyone for what has been done (Matthew 16:27).

Not Everyone Agrees

Not everyone believes in these different judgments. There are many Christians who do not believe in a literal Millennium, or thousand year reign of Christ on the earth after He comes. They see only one general resurrection at the end of time. All people who have ever been born, both the righteous and unrighteous, will be judged at this final judgment. The resurrection and the judgment of the nations are part of one great judgment.

All Will Be Judged

All Christians agree that everyone, both the righteous and unrighteous, will be judged of the Lord. The righteous will go away into eternal life while the unrighteous will be eternally separated from the Lord. The only difference among believers is the timing of these judgments, not the fact of these judgments.

When Christ comes back, He will judge the nation Israel, the living nations, the tribulation saints, and the Old Testament saints. He will separate them as a shepherd separates sheep from the goats. The sheep, the believers, will enter into His kingdom, while the goats, the unbelievers, will be sent to judgment

Jesus Christ's second coming

Looking forward to the Saviour's Second Coming

Forty days after His Resurrection, Jesus and His Apostles were gathered together on the Mount of Olives. The time had come for Jesus to leave the earth. He had completed all the work that He had to do at that time. He was to return to our Heavenly Father until the time of His Second Coming.

After He had instructed His Apostles, Jesus ascended into heaven. While the Apostles looked up into the heavens, two angels stood beside them and said, "Ye men of Galilee, why stand ye gazing up into heaven? this same Jesus, which is taken up from you into heaven, shall so come in like manner as ye have seen him go" (Acts 1:11).

From that time until the present day, the followers of Jesus Christ have looked forward to the Second Coming.

What Will Jesus Do When He Comes Again?

For teachers: Consider assigning each class member or family member one of the five numbered items in this chapter. Ask each person to work individually, studying his or her assigned item, including the scripture passages. Then invite everyone to discuss what they have learned.

When Jesus Christ comes again to the earth, He will do the following things:

1. *He will cleanse the earth.* When Jesus comes again, He will come in power and great glory. At that time the wicked will be destroyed. All things that are corrupt will be burned, and the earth will be cleansed by fire (see D&C 101:24–25).

2. *He will judge His people.* When Jesus comes again, He will judge the nations and will divide the righteous from the wicked (see Matthew 25:31–46; see also chapter 46 in this book). John the Revelater wrote about this judgment: "I saw thrones, and they sat upon them, and judgment was given unto them: and I saw the souls of them that were beheaded for the witness of Jesus, and for the word of the Father, … and they lived and reigned with Christ a thousand years." The wicked he saw "lived not again until the thousand years were finished" (Revelation 20:4–5.

3. *He will usher in the Millennium.* The Millennium is the thousand-year period when Jesus will reign on the earth. The righteous will be caught up to meet Jesus at His coming (see D&C 88:96). His coming will begin the millennial reign. (See chapter 45 in this book.)

President Brigham Young said:

"In the Millennium, when the Kingdom of the Father is established on the earth in power, glory and perfection, and the reign of wickedness that has so long prevailed is subdued, the Saints of thee Lord will have the privilege of building their temples, and of entering into them, becoming, as it were, pillars in the temples of the Lord [see Revelation 3:12], and they will officiate for their dead. Then we will see our friends come up, and perhaps some that we have been acquainted with here. ... And we will have revelations to know our forefathers clear back to Father Adam and Mother Eve, and we will enter into the temples of the Lord and officiate for them. Then [children] will be sealed to [parents] until the chain is made perfect back to Adam, so that there will be a perfect chain of Priesthood from Adam to the winding-up scene" (*Teachings of Presidents of the Church: Brigham Young* [1997], 333–34).

4. *He will complete the First Resurrection.* Those who have obtained the privilege of coming forth in the resurrection of the just will rise from their graves. They will be caught up to meet the Saviour as He comes down from heaven. (See D&C 88:97–98.)

After Jesus Christ rose from the dead, other righteous people who had died were also resurrected. They appeared in Jerusalem and also on the American continent. (See Matthew 27:52–53; 3 Nephi 23:9–10.) This was the beginning of the First Resurrection. Some people have been resurrected since then. Those who already have been resurrected and those who will be resurrected at the time of His coming will all inherit the glory of the celestial kingdom (see D&C 76:50–70).

After the resurrection of those who will inherit celestial glory, another group will be resurrected: those who will receive a terrestrial glory. When all these people have been resurrected, the First Resurrection will be completed.

The wicked who are living at the time of the Second Coming of the Lord will be destroyed in the flesh. They, along with the wicked who are already dead, will have to wait until the last resurrection. All of the remaining dead will rise to meet the Lord. They will either inherit the telestial kingdom or be cast into outer darkness with Satan (see <u>D&C 76:32–33, 81–112</u>).

5. *He will take His rightful place as King of heaven and earth.* When Jesus comes, He will establish His government on the earth. The Church will become part of that kingdom. He will rule all the people of the earth in peace for 1,000 years.

When Jesus Christ first came to the earth, He did not come in glory. He was born in a lowly stable and laid in a manger of hay. He did not come with great armies as the Jews had expected of their Saviour. Instead, He came saying, "Love your enemies, ... do good to them that hate you, and pray for them which despitefully use you" (<u>Matthew 5:44</u>). He was rejected and crucified. But He will not be rejected at His Second Coming, "for every ear shall hear it, and every knee shall bow, and every tongue shall confess" that Jesus is the Christ (<u>D&C 88:104</u>). He will be greeted as "Lord of lords, and King of kings" (<u>Revelation 17:14</u>). He will be called "Wonderful, Counsellor, The mighty Father, The everlasting Father, The Prince of Peace" (<u>Isaiah 9:6</u>).

- What are your thoughts and feelings as you contemplate the events of the
- **Second Coming of Jesus Christ to Judge?**

How Will We Know When the Saviour's Coming Is Near?

When Jesus Christ was born, very few people knew that the Savior of the world had come. When He comes again, there will be no doubt who He is. No one knows the exact time that the Saviour will come again. "Of that day and hour knoweth no man, no, not the angels of heaven, but my Father only" (Matthew 24:36; see also D&C 49:7).

The Lord used a parable to give us an idea of the time of His coming:

"Now learn a parable of the fig tree; When her branch is yet tender, and putteth forth leaves, ye know that summer is near:

"So ye in like manner, when ye shall see these things come to pass, know that it is nigh, even at the doors" (Mark 13:28–29).

The Lord has also given us some signs to let us know when His coming is near. After revealing the signs, He cautioned:

"Watch therefore: for ye know not what hour your Lord doth come. …

"… Be ye also ready: for in such an hour as ye think not the Son of man cometh" (Matthew 24:42, 44).

For more information about how we will know when Jesus's Second Coming is near, see chapter 43 in this book.

How Can We Be Ready When the Saviour Comes?

The best way we can prepare for the Savior's coming is to accept the teachings of the gospel and make them part of our lives. We should live each day the best we can, just as Jesus taught when He was on the earth. We can look to the prophet for guidance and follow his counsel. We can live worthy to have the Holy Ghost guide us. Then we will look forward to the Saviour's coming with happiness and not with fear. The Lord said: "Fear not, little flock, the kingdom is yours until I come. Behold, I come quickly. Even so. Amen" (D&C 35:27).

- Why should we be concerned about our preparedness rather than the exact timing of the Second Coming.

Is Jesus the Son of Man or the Son of the Father? This sounds like some kind of contradiction at first glance, but in fact there is no contradiction. An examination of Scripture reveals that the phrase "<u>Son of Man</u>" carries broad significance.

First of all, even if the phrase "Son of Man" is a reference to Jesus' <u>humanity</u>, it is not a denial of His deity. By becoming a man, Jesus did not cease being Divine. The <u>incarnation</u> of Christ did not involve the subtraction of deity, but the addition of humanity. Jesus clearly claimed to be Lord on many occasions (<u>Matthew 16:16,17</u>; <u>John 8:58</u>; <u>10:30</u>). But in addition to being divine, He was also human (see <u>Philippians 2:6-8</u>). He had two natures (divine and human) conjoined in one person.

Further, Scripture indicates that Jesus was not denying His deity by referring to Himself as the Son of Man. In fact, it is highly revealing that the term "Son of Man" is used in Scripture in contexts of Christ's deity. For example, the Bible says that only the Father can <u>forgive</u> sins (<u>Isaiah 43:25</u>; <u>Mark 2:7</u>). But as the "Son of Man," Jesus had the power to forgive sins (<u>Mark 2:10</u>). Likewise, Christ will return to Earth as the "Son of Man" in clouds of glory to reign on Earth (<u>Matthew 26:63-64</u>). In this passage, Jesus is citing <u>Daniel 7:13</u> where the <u>Messiah</u> is described as the "<u>Ancient of Days</u>," a phrase used to indicate His deity (cf. <u>Daniel 7:9</u>).

Further, when Jesus was asked by the <u>high priest</u> whether He was the "Son of the Father" (<u>Matthew 26:63</u>), He responded affirmatively, declaring that He was the "Son of Man" who would come in power and great glory (verse <u>64</u>).

This indicated that Jesus Himself used the phrase "Son of Man" to indicate His deity as the Son of the Father.

Finally, the phrase "Son of Man" also emphasizes who Jesus is in relation to His incarnation and His work of salvation. In the Old Testament (Leviticus 25:25-26, 48-49; Ruth 2:20), the next of kin (one related by blood) always functioned as the "kinsman-redeemer" of a family member who needed redemption from jail. Jesus became related to us "by blood" (that is, He became a man) so He could function as our Kinsman-Redeemer and rescue us from sin.

In October 2017 general conference, Elder Christofferson gave a talk entitled "The Living Bread Which Came Down from Heaven" where he discusses how Jesus's disciples were perplexed when He taught. "Verily, verily, I say unto you, Except ye eat the flesh of the Son of man, and drink his blood, ye have no life in you. Whoso eateth my flesh, and drinketh my blood, hath eternal life; and I will raise him up at the last day" (John 6:53-54).

The disciples were confused, wondering if they had to literarily consume the body and blood of Jesus. We understand that Jesus was speaking symbolically, that those who wish to be like Him must live like Him. The sacrament (where His blood and flesh are symbolically present) provides a weekly opportunity to recommit to follow in His ways.

The purpose of this article is not to explain the symbolism of the sacrament but to provide clarity around two phrases in the Bible. Why did Jesus use the phrase "Son of man" in John 6 and what does it mean?

The phrases "Son of man" and "Son of the Father" actually mean the opposite of what we think they mean.

Son of the Lord is a human person, that is, the king who has been adopted by the Lord who grants authority to rule. The king demonstrates authority through power and miracles what kingdom is like. Son of the Father often refers to Jesus' first earthly rule.

Son of man is a heavenly person, who has divinely granted power to overthrow wickedness and to establish peace. The Son of man often refers to Jesus's divine qualities to save us or the phrase can refer to the conditions of His millennial reign.

When Jesus is referred to as the Son of the Father, we should think about His earthly and kingly traits. When Jesus is referred to as the Son of man, we should think about His heavenly, divine qualities.

Let's look at a few examples in scripture where this understanding could prove enlightening.

Son of Man

Old Testament scripture teaches that the Son of the Father is a kingly figure who has been chosen, established, ordained, and begotten, as seen in Psalm 2:6-7: "I set my king upon my holy hill of Zion. I will declare the decree: the LORD hath said unto me, Thou art my Son; this day have I begotten thee."

Since the Father is the true King of heaven and earth, then the Son of the Father is the prince regent, or the King acting in His stead.

We see this principle taught in the story of King David who desired to build a house (i.e., a temple) Instead, Yahweh promised David an everlasting house (i.e., a dynasty). Listen to the simple, yet beautiful father and son language that the

Lord used in making promises to David, designating the earthly King David (and his rightful heirs) as Father's son: "I will be his father, and he shall be my son. And thine house and thy kingdom shall be established for ever before thee: thy throne shall be established for ever" (1 Samuel 7:14, 16).

Because the king, as Father's son, represents Father's kingdom on earth, the king has unusual powers and abilities to demonstrate what the Father's kingdom is like. Peace and justice reign, sorrow is removed, sin is purged, and people are made whole physically and spiritually. That is why when Jesus came as the Son of the Father—the true king on earth and Lord's divine representative—He could demonstrate such mighty acts of miracles and healing. His healing acts and miracles demonstrated what the Kingdom of the Father is like.

With this in mind, let's consider some familiar New Testament scriptures.

In Matthew 14, Jesus miraculously calms the winds on the raging Sea of Galilee. Immediately His disciples fall down to worship Him and say, "Of a truth thou art the Son of the Father" (vs. 33). Why would the disciples say to Jesus, after such a tremendous display of miraculous power, "thou art the Son of the father"? Why not say, "Truly, thou art powerful" or "Of a truth, thou art a wonder worker"? Why use this specific phrase that, upon reflection, seems like a rather plain and generic phrase to describe any child of the Father? Because this phrase, "Son of Father," was a designation specifically for Lord's divinely appointed Heir and King upon the earth, the one who had the power to demonstrate what the Kingdom of the Father is like, effect cures, wonders, powers, and miracles to testify of Lord's reality.

In another instance in the Gospel According to Matthew, the devil tempts Jesus to throw Himself off the pinnacle of the temple and thereby demonstrate to the gawking onlookers that He is powerful enough to command the angels to catch Him:

"If thou be the Son of the Father, cast thyself down: for it is written, He shall give his angels charge concerning thee: and in their hands they shall bear thee up, lest at any time thou dash thy foot against a stone" (Matthew 4:6).

Notice how the devil challenges Jesus, the true King of the earth, who reigns not with blood and horror but with life-giving light, love, and peace. The devil says, "*IF* thou be the Son of the Father" (emphasis added). In other words, the devil says to Jesus, "Look, if you really are the King of the earth, representing the divine Father who has entrusted you with awesome and mighty power, well then, you have to convince us all by showing off your power as the King. The angels who are court ministers will do any and all your bidding, including saving you from a death fall. Come on! Prove to us that you are the divinely empowered king."

Of course, Jesus with serene power speaks truth when He replies, "Thou shalt not tempt [try, test, require proof of] the Lord" (Matthew 4:7).

Son of man

We've seen examples that the phrase "Son of the Father" refers to a human person chosen by the Lord as king and entrusted with powers to demonstrate the reality of the kingdom of Heaven.

What does the phrase "Son of man" mean?

A cursory reading of the phrase "Son of man" would lead us to think that this phrase refers to any regular human being. The lower-case version of this phrase "son of man" does mean a human (see for example Psalm 8:4; 144:3).

However, the real meaning of "Son of man" (with "Son" capitalised and "man" lowercase") is a heavenly character that comes down from on high to rid the world of wickedness, bringing peace and justice.

The first time "Son of man" appears in scriptures is when the wise Daniel saw "in the night visions, and, behold, one like the Son of man came with the clouds of heaven, and came to the Ancient of days, and they brought him near him. And there was given him dominion, and glory, and a kingdom, that all people, nations, and languages, should serve him: his dominion is an everlasting dominion, which shall not pass away, and his kingdom that which shall not be destroyed" (Daniel 7:13-14).

We learn from this scripture that the Son of man comes from down from the heavens and brings with Him the power of everlasting dominion.

This key scripture lays the groundwork for understanding many passages in the New Testament where Jesus refers to himself as the "Son of man."

For instance, when Jesus discourses with His disciples about His identity at Caesarea Philippi, He asks, "Whom do men say that I the Son of man am?" (Matthew 16:13). Jesus concludes the instructive conversation by explaining His heavenly attributes that are represented by the title "Son of man."

"For the Son of man shall come in the glory of his Father with his angels; and then he shall reward every man according to his works. Verily I say unto you, There be some standing here, which shall not taste of death, till they see the Son of man coming in his kingdom" (Matthew 16:27-29).

In this scripture, Jesus refers to Himself in His future, glorified, empowered, Second Coming state.

Many Jews understood that the Son of man would be a conquering hero from heaven, as we see these scriptures describe. However, the Jews, including some of Jesus' disciples, couldn't comprehend how such an unassailable hero could simultaneously be so humble and meek. Wasn't the Son of man come to destroy the sinners? This thinking led James and John to confusion. When they saw a village reject Jesus, they urged Jesus to call down fire from heaven to consume the people (Luke 9:51-54).

"But [Jesus] turned, and rebuked them, and said, ye know not what manner of spirit ye are of. For the Son of man is not come to destroy men's lives, but to save them" (Luke 9:55-56).

Yes, the Son of man is a heavenly figure who comes to earth to bring peace by ridding the world of wickedness. However, the Son of man is not simply a violent, conquering hero. He is also the humble Son of the Father who can heal.

Returning to Elder Christofferson's referral to the words of Jesus in John 6, let's take another look. We now understand that the Son of man represents Jesus's heavenly characteristics. So when Jesus says, "Except ye eat the flesh of the Son of man, and drink his blood, ye have no life in you. Whoso eateth my flesh, and drinketh my blood, hath eternal life; and I will raise him up at the last day" (John 6:53-54), Jesus is referring to His divine characteristics, not His earthly characteristics, to save, heal, atone, and resurrect.

Summary

When Jesus speaks of Himself as "Son of the Father," He is referring to His *heavenly* and *divine* attributes and that He has come to earth to establish justice and peace by abolishing wickedness. When Jesus is called the "Son of Man," He is referring to His *earthly human* attributes as a King who has been empowered by the Heavenly King (the Father Himself) to demonstrate the realities of the kingdom of heaven through power, healing, miracles, and glory.

The Final Summary.

The production of these prayers by the Catholic Church shows why and their position to **replace So; Invinctus-Mithra with Jesus as their sun-god:**

The two most important Prayers are: The Apostles' Creed for Individual Prayer, whilst the Nicene Creed for group Prayer as shown below.

The Apostles' Creed

I believe in God, the Father almighty,
creator of heaven and earth.

I believe in Jesus Christ, his only Son, our Lord, who was conceived by the Holy Spirit, born of the Virgin Mary, suffered under Pontius Pilate, was crucified, died, and was buried; he descended to the dead. On the third day he rose again; he ascended into heaven, he is seated at the right hand of the Father, and he will come to judge the living and the dead.

I believe in the Holy Spirit, the holy Catholic Church, the communion of saints, the forgiveness of sins, the resurrection of the body, and the life everlasting. Amen.

Nicene Creed

We believe in one God, the Father, the Almighty, maker of heaven and earth, of all that is seen and unseen.

We believe in one Lord, Jesus Christ, the only Son of God, eternally begotten of the Father, God from God, Light from Light, true God from true God, begotten, not made, consubstantial to the father. Through him all things were made. For us and for our salvation he came down from heaven: by the power of the Holy Spirit he became incarnate from the Virgin Mary, and was made man. For our sake he was crucified under Pontius Pilate; he suffered death and was buried. On the third day he rose again in accordance with the Scriptures; he ascended into heaven and is seated at the right hand of the Father. He will come again in glory to judge the living and the dead, and his kingdom will have no end.

We believe in the Holy Spirit, the Lord, the giver of life, who proceeds from the Father and the Son. With the Father and the Son he is worshiped and glorified. He has spoken through the Prophets. We believe in one holy catholic and apostolic Church. We acknowledge one baptism for the forgiveness of sins. We look for the resurrection of the dead, and the life of the world to come. Amen.

Jesus and Mithra: the sun-gods of the Romans

According to Siamak Adhami, Ph.D, December 25 was the: Birthday of Mithra and Jesus as the Roman Gods. And Romans had replaced Mithra, (who was worshipped by Constantine), with Jesus Christ and now worshipping Him as their **sun-god.**

December 25: The Birthday of the Iranian God, Mithra and Jesus of Nazareth.

"Grass-land magnate Mithra is worshipped, whose words are correct, who is challenging, has a thousand ears, is well built, has ten thousand eyes, is tall, has a wide outlook, is strong, sleepless, (ever-)waking, whom the warriors worship. Mithra, who is the first supernatural god to approach across the Har, in front of the immortal swift-horsed sun; who is the first to seize the beautiful gold-painted mountain top; from there the most mighty surveys the whole land inhabited by Iranians, where gallant rulers organize many attacks, where high, sheltering mountains with ample pasture provide solicitous for cattle; where deep lakes stand with surging waves; where navigable rivers rush wide with a swell towards Parutian Iškata, Haraivian Margu, Sogdian Gava, and Chorasmia."

This essay begins with one of the most beautiful passages from the Avestan hymn in praise of Mithra as translated by the eminent Iranist Ilya Gershevitch. Mithra was a deity common to at least two branches of Indo-European people, namely Iranians and Indo-Aryans. In addition to the hymn in the Avesta, we are also aware of the presence of the **god Mithra or Mithras** (Vedic "Mitra", Middle Persian "Mihr," and Persian "Mehr") in the ancient Indian scriptures known as the Rig-Veda (1400 BC). For the ancient Iranians, the god Mithra had two significant functions: he was first and foremost the sun-god whose thousands of eyes spied on every deed and nothing, particularly evil deeds, could escape from his gaze. Secondly, he was the god of contracts. For example, even in late Pahlavi/Middle Persian texts which are concerned with legal and religious matters, there exists a severe crime and sin which is related to the functions of Mithra, which signifies "breaking promise or contract," and by extension, "perfidy." Perfidy was classified as one of the most heinous crimes with severe punishment prescribed for the offender. During late antiquity, **the worship of Mithra became popular, particularly among Roman soldiers and merchants.** The reasons for the popularity of the cult of Mithra among these two groups are easily understood: the martial nature of the hymn can explain the popularity of Mithra among soldiers. Similarly, his reverence by the merchant class is equally clear as he was the god of contracts. It is not unreasonable to think that merchants traversing across ancient commercial highways such as the famed Silk Road in antiquity preferred to conduct business with those whom they trusted and the affiliation with this mysterious fraternity only served to cement the bond between them. The adherents of the Mithraic cult, similar to those of **other religions such as Judaism, Christianity and Islam,** also held festivals celebrating different aspects of their religion. It appears that **the annual celebration held on December 25, the winter solstice, was the most important celebration of the cult; it was believed that Mithra was born on this day, hence "the birthday of the _unconquered sun" (Latin: natalis solis invicti)._** Later, the practices of the cult seem to have gained much in popularity. With the advent of Christianity, a number of pagan practices which could not be abandoned found their way into this new religion. **The most significant of these was the identification of the birthday of Jesus, commonly known as Christmas (Old English Cristes maesse: Christ's mass), with that of the undying _Mithra._**

Much has been written on pagan cults in the Roman empire and particular attention has been paid to the cult of Mithra. In fact Ernest Renan went as far as stating that "if the growth of Christianity had been halted by some mortal illness, the world would have become Mithraic." As Walter

Burkert points out, Renan may have exaggerated the case as the worship of Mithra belonged to a rather elitist segment of the society. However according to Werner Jaeger, there is no doubt that Mithraism and Manichaeism, two religions with well-established Iranian connections, posed a serious threat to **the spread of the new faith which became known as Christianity.**

The followings are for further readings on Mithraism: Adhami, Siamak, PAITIMĀNA, Essays in Iranian, Indo-European, and Indian Studies in Honour of HANNS-PETER SCHMIDT. (2003) Mazda Publishers, Costa Mesa, CA. Burkert, Walter. Ancient Mystery Cults. (1987). Early Christianity and Greek Paideia. Cambridge, MA. Merkelbach, R. (1982).

The list Of Gods Born By A Virgin On 25th December by music writer.

ALTHOUGH THE BIBLICAL STORY OF JESUS CONTRADICTS THIS.

FOR INSTANCE IN Luke 2:7-8 SAYS THAT SHEPHERD WERE WATCHING THEIR FLOCK IN THE FIELDS WHEN HE WAS BORN. SHEPHERD DON'T WATCH THEIR FLOCK IN THE FIELDS IN DECEMBER!

JESUS' PARENTS CAME TO BETHLEHEM TO REGISTER IN A ROMAN CENSUS (Luke 2:1-4). SUCH CENSUSES WERE NOT TAKEN IN WINTER, WHEN TEMPERATURES OFTEN DROPPED BELOW FREEZING AND ROADS WERE IN POOR CONDITION. TAKING A CENSUS UNDER SUCH CONDITIONS WOULD HAVE BEEN SELF-DEFEATNG.

Some of the names might be the inventions of early man. However, a **Yeshua or Yehoshua existed, from where Jesus was supposedly plagiarized by Rome** since they didn't believe him.

Also, the following list Of Gods Born By A Virgin On 25th December provided by Oga Sir Ade:

Here are names of Gods throughout history that were said to have been born by a virgin on 25th December.

HORUS
An Egypt or Ethiopian-Sudanese God, born 25th December, by a Virgin around 3,000 YEARS before Jesus.

BUDDHA
A Nepal God, born 25th December, by a Virgin around 563 YEARS before Jesus.

KRISHNA
An Indian God, born 25th December, by a Virgin around 900 YEARS before Jesus.

ZARATHUSTRA
An Indian God, born 25th December, by a Virgin around 1,000 YEARS before Jesus.

HERCULES
A Greek God, born 25th December, by a Virgin around 800 YEARS before Jesus.

MITHRA
A Persian God, born 25th December, by a Virgin- 600 YEARS before Jesus.

DIONYSUS
A Greek God, born 25th December, by a Virgin around 500 YEARS before Jesus.

THAMMUZ
A Babylonian God, born 25th December, by a Virgin around 400 YEARS before Jesus.

HERMES
A Greek God, born 25th December, by a Virgin around 200 YEARS before Jesus.

ADONIS
A Phoenician God, born 25th December, by a Virgin around 200 YEARS before Jesus.

JESUS CHRIST
A Roman God, born 25th December, by a Virgin around 300 AD

Pagan gods born December 25th, hence this date is celebrated every year.

According to the ancient Babylonian traditions... **Tammuz** *was supposedly born on December 25tharound 2600 BC and has traditionally been worshipped ever since. This is the origin of yearly celebration of 25th December. And also some pagan gods were supposedly have been born on December 25th.*

Jesus was not born on December 25th

Altering Jesus' character in any way, including His birthdate, a false Christ is created. And following a false Jesus is just as dangerous and damning as no Jesus! Be wise, pray for discernment, don't follow the world blindly, research all things you entertain and encourage, come away from the pagan Christmas lies, have nothing to do with any of the ways of the pagans… light and the darkness can never co-exist! May Jesus bless you and open your eyes, help you shed your Christmas blinders, so you can better see, grow, and be a faithful follower of Christ. His coming is near!

Catholicism Influence

The book further explores the uniqueness of Jesus Christ the Saviour, who is both the Perfect Divine and Perfect man. He is Perfect Divine because He is the True and the Perfect Holy Spirit. He is Perfect Man because He was born without the cursed and tainted seed of a human being, thus without sin. The idea that Jesus is called god/God or the Son of God was introduced and promoted by Roman Catholic Church throughout the world in the year about 336-7 BC. Pope Julius I decided on the birth of Jesus Christ as December 25th in the year 336 BC which fitted in perfectly well with the yearly pagan-gods' celebration of the December 25th. The celebration is known in India as BADA DIN meaning, BIG DAY in English.

It was the Catholicism that introduced Christ Mass-Christmas in order to join in the **yearly** pagan-gods celebration of the **December 25th** in paying homage to their chief god Tammuz who is said to have been born on 25th December in Babylon in the year 2600 BC. Catholicism replaced their sun-god Sol Invictus-Mithra with Jesus and has been worshipping Jesus on Sun-days as their sun-god. And yet Jesus Christ is definitely NOT born on 25th December and therefore, He is NOT to be called a god/ God. In this respct, to be calling Jesus Christ a God/god is a **blasphemy** because He is NOT to be reduced to the level of the demonic lesser spirit as a god/God. He is the Mighty Holy Spirit and a Saviour, and will **save** everyone who will accept Him as the True and the Supreme Creator of the world. And because of His uniqueness, **salvation** is assured and found in Him alone. Jesus Christ is the Alpha and the Omega the Beginning and the End.

APPRECIATION TO CATHOLICISM

Whether wrongly or rightly, selfishly or otherwise, crucifixion or not, if Catholicism had not introduced and promoted Jesus Christ into the world as occurred, the mission and the wonderful work of our Lord Jesus Christ would have been left in the desert without recognition which have enabled Him to carry out His mission for salvation. This is because His own people the Jews rejected Him and His teachings of the truth for the benefits of human beings. The issue here is salvation would not depend on which denomination one belongs to as the Saviour Jesus Christ has made it clear that salvation belongs to anyone who will do His Father's will. Our Lord Jesus Christ the Saviour Himself revealed in **Matthew 7:21-23 thus**, on the **judgement Day**: ".... Not everyone that saith unto me Lord, Lord, shall enter into the kingdom of heaven; but he that doeth the **"WILL"** of my Father who is in heaven."

BIBLIOGRAPHY

Alexander, D. and P. (eds) (1973). A Lion Handbook to the Bible. Lion Publishing. UK

Anan, G. J. (2011). The Organic Church: A practical approach to managing change. LANTERN TOWER – An Imprint of Melrose Press Limited Cambridgeshire. UK

Anan, G. J. (2015). The Illusive World of Love, Demystifying the Mindset of True Love in theological Perspectives. Author House; UK, Bloomington. IN USA

Anan, G. J. (2015). The Truth About Material Wealth, Is it God's Blessing in Disguise? Author House; UK. Bloomington. IN USA

Anan. G. J. (2016). Discerning The Prophetic Message: Knowing the Truth. New Generation Publishing. UK

Avis, P. D. L. (2nded) (2002). Anglicanism and The Christian Church: Theological Resources in Historical Perspective. T and T Clark Publishers. Edinburgh UK

Backhouse, R. (edt) (1993). Spiritual Life: The Life of St. Augustine. Hodder & Stoughton Publishers. UK

Baker, L. M. (1976-77). PEARS: Cyclopaedia, Pelham London UK

Ballard, P. & Pritchard J. (1996). Practical Theology in Action SPCK. London UK

Baldick, J (1997) Black God: The Afroasiatic Roots of the Jewish, Christian, and Muslim Religions. New York: Syracuse University Press.

Bleicher, J. (1990). Contemporary Hermeneutics as Method, Philosophy and Critique. Routledge. UK

Bonner, G. (1986). St Augustine of Hippo: Life and Controversies. Canterbury Press. UK

Briggs, J. (1990). Early English Baptists in, A Lion Hand Book The History of Christianity. Lion Publishing. UK

Brown, P. (2000). Augustine of Hippo. Faber and Faber. UK.

Bruce, F. F. (1989). Romans. Inter-varsity Press. UK

Bullock, A., Stallybrass, O., and Trombley, S. (eds.) (1977). Modern Thought. The Fontana Dictionary. Fontana Press.

Calvocoressi, P. (1987). Who's Who in the Bible? Viking Publishers. UK

Cole, Herbert Mbari. Art and Life among the Owerri Igbo (Bloomington: Indiana University press, 1982).

Comfort, P. W. (990). Early Manuscripts and Modern Translations of the New Testament Tyndale House Publishers, Inc. WHEATON, ILLINOIS. USA

Crofton, I. (1990) (1st edt.) The Guinness Encyclopaedia. The Guinness Publishing. UK

Davison, L. (1969) Sender and Sent. Epworth Press London UK

Doumbia, A. & Doumbia, N (2004) The Way of the Elders: West African Spirituality & Tradition. Saint Paul, MN: Llewellyn Publications.

Dowley, T. (ed.) (1990). A Lion Hand Book The History of Christianity. The Lion Publishing UK

Ehret, Christopher, (2002) The Civilizations of Africa: a History to 1800. Charlottesville: University Press of Virginia.

Ehret, Christopher, An African Classical Age: Eastern and Southern Africa in World History, 1000 B.C. to A.D. 400, page 159, University of Virginia Press, ISBN 0-8139-2057-4

Einstein, Carl. African Legends, First English Edition, Pandavia, Berlin 2021.

Erickson, M. J. (ed.) (1972). Readings in Christian Theology: the Living God. Barker and Baker. UK Hall, F. (3rd Ed. – 1967), The Fasting Prayer. Publisher: Frank Hall, Phoenix AZ. USA

Herbermann, C. G. (ed.) (2014). The Catholic Encyclopaedia: An International work of Reference on the Constitution, Doctrine, Discipline, History. ... Catholic Way Publishing (Kindle Edition). USA

Hermon, N. B. (ed.) (1974). The Encyclopaedia of World Methodism. Abington Press UK

Hill, G. E (1973) Who Jesus Is. Publishers: International Correspondence Institute. Belgium. Europe.

Horton, S. M. (1989). What the Bible Says About the Holy Spirit. Gospel Publishing House USA

Hunnex, M.D. (1968) Chronological and Thematic Charts of Philosophies and Phil osophers. Zondervan Publishing House, Grand Rapids, Michigan USA.

Mbiti, John African Religions and Philosophy (1969) African Writers Series, Heinemann

McKim, D.K. (ed.) (1998). Historical Handbook of Major Biblical Interpreters. Inter Varsity Press UK

Oates, W. J. (ed.) (1976). Basic Writings of SAINT Augustine: the city of God and On the Trinity. Baker Book House Grand Rapids, Michigan USA

Oates, W. J. (ed.) (1992). Basic Writings of SAINT Augustine: Confession & Twelve Treaties. Baker Book House, Grand Rapids, Michigan USA

Olson, R. E. (1999). The Story of Christian Theology: Twenty Centuries of Tradition and Reform. APOLO Inter-Varsity Press USA

Pitt-Rivers, G. (1966). The Riddle of 'Labarum' and the Origin of Christian

Rotelle, J. E. (1986). Augustine Day By Day. Catholic Book Publishing Co. New York. USA

Soyinka, Wole:, Myth, Literature and the African World (Cambridge University Press, 1976).

Stokes, P. (2004) Philosophy 100 Essential Thinkers. Index Books Ltd

Swinburne, R. (1999) Is There A God? Oxford University Press UK

Vardy, P. (1995). The Puzzle of God. Fount Paperbacks, an imprint of Harper Collins Religious Publishers. Great Britain

Vardy, P. (1992). The Puzzle of Evil. Fount Paperbacks, an imprint of Harper Collins Religious Publishers. Great Britain. UK

Weatherhead, L. D. (1936). It Happened in Palestine. Hodder & Stoughton Publishers. UK

Wilke, R. B. (1989) Sigs and Wonders: The Mighty Work of God in the Church. Abingdon Press NASHVILLE.

Wilson, I. (2001). Before The Flood: Dramatic New Evidence That the Biblical Flood was a Real-Life Event. Orion Books Ltd. UK

A NOTE ON THE AUTHOR

The Revd Dr Gabriel J Anan was born and raised in Ghana where he received his primary and secondary education in the most challenging situation. He worked for the Ministry of Interior in Ghana for five years before leaving for Great Britain to study law, shipping and transport. His management training earned him the corporate membership of the professional bodies including Chartered Institute of Shipbrokers, Chartered Institute of Transport and the Institute of Export. He later worked as a manager and director for five years before engaging further in academic studies at the Greenwich University for his youth work qualification. He achieved a Master of Science **(MSc)** degree in Maritime Studies at the University of Somerset and a Master of Arts **(MA)** in Voluntary Sector Studies before gaining a Doctor of Philosophy **(PhD)** in the area of church leadership and management of change at the University of East London. Armed with authoritative knowledge of **"MANAGING CHANGE"**, has provided him the desire for seeking new ideas in **any field** of education for exploration.

After completing a programme for ministerial training course with a BA in Contextual Theology at the Middlesex University, he qualified as a Church of England clergy with

Roman Catholic background. In addition he studied for a BA Evangelical degree at Elim Bible College – now Regents Theological College. He had by then been appointed the **Honorary Professor of Contemporary Theology by the University of Europe**. His knowledge in Evangelism enables him to discern the theology of Paedobaptist and Credobaptist and many issues especially with regards to 'Born Again' Christian and infants Baptism.

The author has had several contacts with other traditional and African Praying Churches including Charismatic, Apostolic, Evangelical and Pentecostal and heir members, in the UK. These contacts gave him a firm grounding and insights for his understanding the gravity of the situation regarding prevailing issues affecting the followers in their churches.

He has vast practical experience in voluntary and charity organisations as he served as a chairman of Canning Town outlook, on the Board of Directors for Newham Credit Union and Vice Chair for Drew Primary School Governors for four years. He also worked as Youth Adviser for the London Borough of Newham for over ten years. Currently, he is a retired Associate Minister at the Church of England parish church of St George and St Ethelbert in East Ham London; but pursuing the direction of the Holy Spirit for the discernment of true Biblical **Sabbath**. He lives in Romford, Essex, UK with his family.

Catholicism Influence

The book further explores the uniqueness of Jesus Christ the Saviour, who is both the Perfect Divine and Perfect man. He is Perfect Divine because He is the True and the Perfect Holy Spirit. He is Perfect Man because He was born without the cursed and tainted seed of a human being, thus without sin. The idea that Jesus is called god/God or the Son of God was introduced and promoted by Roman Catholic Church throughout the world in the year between 336-7 BC. Pope Julius I decided on the birth of Jesus Christ as December 25th in the year 336 BC which served perfectly well with the yearly pagan-gods' celebration of the December 25th. This pagan-gods yearly celebration is known in India as BADA DIN meaning, BIG DAY in English, whilst in the Western world and other places it is known as Christmas.

It was the Catholicism that introduced Christ Mass-Christmas in order to join in the **yearly** pagan-gods celebration of the **December 25th** for paying homage to their chief god Tammuz who is said to have been born on 25th December in Babylon in the year 2600 BC. This is the origin of the Christmas that we celebrate yearly on 25th December. Catholicism replaced their sun-god Sol Invictus-Mithra with Jesus and has been worshipping Jesus on Sundays as their sun-god. And the truth of the matter is that Jesus Christ was definitely NOT born on 25th December and therefore, He is NOT to be called a god/God. In this respct, to be calling Jesus Christ a God/god is a **blasphemy** because He is NOT to be reduced to the level of the lesser, demon spirit as a god/God. He is the Mighty Holy Spirit and a Saviour and will **save** everyone who will accept Him as the True and the Supreme Creator of the world. And because of His uniqueness, **salvation** is assured and definitely found in Him alone. Jesus Christ is the Alpha and the Omega the Beginning and the End.

APPRECIATION TO CATHOLICISM

Whether wrongly or rightly, selfishly or otherwise, Crucifixion of Jesus Christ or not, if Catholicism had not introduced and promoted Jesus Christ into the

world as occurred, His mission and His other wonderful work would have ended up in the desert or left in the desert without recognition. This is because His own people the Jews rejected Him and His teachings of the truth for the benefits of human beings. The important thing to note here is that, salvation does not depend on which denomination one belongs to and as such the Saviour Jesus Christ has made it unequivocally clear that salvation belongs to anyone who will do His Father's will. For instance the 3 wise noble men from the East visited baby Christ and worshipped Him and called Him Isa meaning Lord. They presented Him with gold, frankincense and merryh these gifts are mostly reserved for kings. According to the Hadith of Abu Hirariah (Sahih Bukhari 4:55:657) says that Isa Al-Masih, Jesus, son of Mary will descend among you and will judge mankind and not Muhammad. Our Lord Jesus Christ the Saviour Himself revealed in Matthew 7:21-23 thus, on the judgement Day: "…. Not everyone that saith unto me Lord, Lord, shall enter into the kingdom of heaven; but he that doeth the "WILL" of my Father who is in heaven."